GLOBALIZATION IN THE 21ST CENTURY
HOW INTERCONNECTED IS THE WORLD?

GLOBALIZATION IN THE 21ST CENTURY
HOW INTERCONNECTED IS THE WORLD?

THE EMIRATES CENTER FOR STRATEGIC
STUDIES AND RESEARCH

THE EMIRATES CENTER FOR STRATEGIC STUDIES AND RESEARCH

The Emirates Center for Strategic Studies and Research (ECSSR) is an independent research institution dedicated to the promotion of professional studies and educational excellence in the UAE, the Gulf and the Arab world. Since its establishment in Abu Dhabi in 1994, the ECSSR has served as a focal point for scholarship on political, economic and social matters. Indeed, the ECSSR is at the forefront of analysis and commentary on Arab affairs.

The Center seeks to provide a forum for the scholarly exchange of ideas by hosting conferences and symposia, organizing workshops, sponsoring a lecture series and publishing original and translated books and research papers. The ECSSR also has an active fellowship and grant program for the writing of scholarly books and for the translation into Arabic of work relevant to the Center's mission. Moreover, the ECSSR has a large library including rare and specialized holdings, and a state-of-the-art technology center, which has developed an award-winning website that is a unique and comprehensive source of information on the Gulf.

Through these and other activities, the ECSSR aspires to engage in mutually beneficial professional endeavors with comparable institutions worldwide, and to contribute to the general educational and academic development of the UAE.

The views expressed in this book do not necessarily reflect those of the ECSSR.

First published in 2008 by
The Emirates Center for Strategic Studies and Research
PO Box 4567, Abu Dhabi, United Arab Emirates

E-mail: pubdis@ecssr.ae
Website: http://www.ecssr.ae

ISBN: 978-9948-00-958-0 hardback edition
ISBN: 978-9948-00-959-7 paperback edition

CONTENTS

FIGURES AND TABLES

ABBREVIATIONS AND ACRONYMS

ABM	Anti-Ballistic Missile
AEI	American Enterprise Institute
AG	Australia Group
ARAG	Advanced Research and Assessment Group
BRIC	Brazil, Russia, India and China
BWC	Biological Weapons Convention
CACM	Central American Common Market
CFE	Conventional Armed Forces in Europe
CFIUS	Committee on Foreign Investment in the United States
CARIFTA	Caribbean Free Trade Agreement
CIA	Central Intelligence Agency
CSR	corporate social responsibility
CTBT	Comprehensive Test Ban Treaty
CTR	Cooperative Threat Reduction
CWC	Chemical Weapons Convention
DFI	direct foreign investment
EC	European Community
ECM	European Common Market
EFTA	European Free Trade Association
EIA	economic integration agreement
EPA	Environmental Protection Agency
ETA	Euskadi Ta Askatasuna (Basque Homeland and Freedom)
EU	European Union
FARC	Revolutionary Armed Forces of Columbia
FBIS	Foreign Broadcast Information Service
FDI	Foreign Direct Investment
FMCT	Fissile Material Cut-off Treaty
FTA	Free Trade Agreement

GATT	General Agreement on Tariffs and Trade
GCC	Gulf Cooperation Council
GDP	gross domestic product
GM	General Motors Corporation
GTAP	Global Trade Analysis Project
HEU	Highly Enriched Uranium
IAEA	International Atomic Energy Agency
IDF	Israeli Defense Force
IISD	International Institute for Sustainable Development
IISS	International Institute for Strategic Studies
IPFM	International Panel on Fissile Materials
IRA	Irish Republican Army
ISG	Iraq Study Group
KRL	Khan Research Laboratories
LEU	Low-Enriched Uranium
MAD	mutually assured destruction
MENA	Middle East and North Africa
MNC	multinational corporation
MoD	Ministry of Defence (UK)
MPC&A	Material Protection Control and Accounting
NAC	North Atlantic Council
NAFTA	North America Free Trade Area
NASCAR	National Association for Stock Car Auto Racing
NATO	North Atlantic Treaty Organization
NMD	National Missile Defense
NPT	(Nuclear) Non-Proliferation Treaty
NSA	National Security Agency
NSC	National Security Council
NSG	Nuclear Suppliers Group
OECD	Organization for Economic Cooperation and Development

OPCW	Organization for the Prohibition of Chemical Weapons
P&O	Peninsular and Oriental Steam Navigation Company
PLO	Palestine Liberation Organization
PRC	Peoples' Republic of China
PwC	PricewaterhouseCoopers
SALT	Strategic Arms Limitation Talks
START	Strategic Arms Reduction Talks
UNSCOM	UN Special Commission
WMD	Weapons of Mass Destruction
WP	Warsaw Pact
WTO	World Trade Organization

The term 'globalization' describes an ongoing and pervasive phenomenon which is redefining the economic, social and cultural dynamics of contemporary societies. Increased communication and interconnection between countries through expanding political ties, greater economic integration and wider cultural reach, combined with augmented global wealth creation has resulted in greater interaction between diverse countries across the globe. However, although the process of globalization is generally considered a beneficial one, it is also viewed in some quarters as a threat to national sovereignty and indigenous culture.

Being an inevitable process, it is important to ensure that we benefit from globalization. There are a number of factors which drive globalization, all of which interact with and strengthen each other. Among the most important of these are the increased ease of communication and trade, scientific progress and technological advances, greater global wealth and higher standards of living. All of these factors have facilitated as well as necessitated increased interaction between populations.

However, there are obstacles to the progress of globalization and its attendant benefits. For example, although globalization has largely arisen as a result of a more stable and secure world, the very factors that have contributed to its rise also assist factions that are interested in destabilizing the world. Without global integration, terrorist groups, for example, would find it much more difficult to unobtrusively communicate, travel, and transfer money and materials. Another security concern is burgeoning illegal trade, be it in materials, people or money.

In order to contribute to the ever-expanding discussion regarding the impact of globalization on world development, the ECSSR hosted a specialized conference under the title *Globalization in the 21st Century:*

How Interconnected is the World? in Abu Dhabi from April 23–25, 2007. At the conference visiting experts were invited to share their views on globalization and to examine the phenomenon from a variety of different angles, so as to introduce as many perspectives as possible. The conference speakers hail from diverse academic, professional and decision-making backgrounds and represent a broad range of opinions and a high level of expertise.

This volume is a valuable collection of these expert views, covering: globalization and its economic foundations and manifestations; migration and freedom of mobility; the social implications of globalization; politics in a globalized international system; new security threats resulting from globalization; and evolving global responsibilities.

ECSSR would like to take this opportunity to thank the authors for their valuable contributions. A word of thanks is also due to ECSSR Editor Francis Field for coordinating the publication of this book.

Jamal S. Al-Suwaidi, Ph.D.
Director General
ECSSR

INTRODUCTION

Globalization in the 21st Century

Globalization is an economic and social phenomenon that has an impact on all our lives. Across the world, populations of differing national, ethnic and religious heritage are being drawn ever closer together. Globalization of the supply chain has linked our production and output like never before, and the phenomenon has also led to the abolition of numerous barriers and produced new and exciting opportunities for interaction. This is a process that will hopefully be of benefit to all, but it also presents a number of challenges, not only in terms of the simple manifestations of globalization, but also in the way that new modes of communication and certain aspects of greater interaction and openness can be exploited for nefarious purposes.

It is important that we are able to enjoy the obvious benefits of globalization while ensuring, as much as is possible, that its detrimental effects are avoided. The forces driving globalization are human development and progress, and as such the process is inevitable. Among the most important developments associated with globalization are increased ease of communication and trade, scientific progress and the advance of technology, greater global wealth and rising standards of living, and more integrated mechanisms for resolving disputes without resorting to conflict, all of which have facilitated as well as necessitated increased interaction between populations.

As William Cohen explains in his Keynote Address, by its very nature, globalization creates a competitive struggle, forcing countries and societies to constantly adjust their policies and principles in order to remain competitive and innovative in the global market place. He points out that the recent revolution in information technology has made the knowledge industry the common currency of our new global world. An innovative idea developed anywhere in the world can now be immediately added to, improved upon and implemented virtually anywhere else on the planet.

However, there are significant obstacles to the progress of globalization and its attendant benefits. The perceived and often all too tangible threats posed by globalization, usually seen at the political, economic and cultural levels, are often used as justification to reject the process entirely.

Hassan Abu Nimah, in his chapter "Globalization and the International Order," claims that some, especially in less developed states, have been caught unawares by the effects of globalization, since the phenomenon has not developed in a controllable manner that states and citizens are able to adapt to and comprehend. This has served to suddenly unveil the realities of global imbalance, stressing the critical differences between those who have advanced and those who have been left behind. He points to this as the reason behind the initial, sober reactions to globalization, with many leaning towards rejection, fear, caution and the perception that globalization is nothing more than an effort by the prosperous countries of the West – in particular the United States – to impose an all-encompassing cultural, economic and political system on the rest of the world.

Advocates of globalization, who try to counter such views, are let down by the actions of the governments of many affluent countries, which espouse globalization in the form of free trade and fair development, but prove unwilling to expose themselves to the risk of domestic repercussions. The negative impacts of globalization, some argue, lead countries to abandon norms that protect the rights of their peoples. Many in the United States, for example, feel threatened by this process and fear that they

[4]

will lose jobs to workers in less developed countries. An example of the manifestation of such fears includes the furor raised in the United States over the Dubai Ports World fiasco in early 2006. The overwhelming influence of large nations in various multinational organizations such as the World Trade Organization (WTO) has led to the perception that economic integration is only meant for their benefit, not for that of mid-sized and smaller countries. Indeed, this perception led directly to the creation of the G-20 bloc of developing nations in August 2003.

Who Benefits from Globalization?

Identifying who benefits from globalization is far from straightforward. While real per capita income should rise with trade, this does not guarantee the distribution of benefits on an even basis. Moreover, those who lose out or are left behind as a result of globalization are likely to be concentrated in certain, specific areas of the world.

Duane Windsor, in his chapter entitled "Free Trade and Open Market Policies: Who Benefits?" points out that the proponents of economic globalization tend to conclude that dissent and criticism is the result of ignorance or vested interest.

He explains that the deceptively simple retort to this debate is that over some abstract "long run" time period, aggregate world real welfare should increase as a result of the operation of the principle of comparative advantage. According to this principle, the world as a whole cannot ever lose from free trade and open markets.

However, he also reminds us that despite the well-established theory and empirical evidence favoring free trade and open market policies, there is both considerable popular unease over the immediate effects of globalization and open expression of important reservations by some prominent economists. The practical difficulties in the deceptively simple answer of comparative advantage, and the unequal distribution of gains and losses shift controversy over free trade and open markets from the economics textbook to the real world of political economy—where economics and politics meet over distribution of real welfare within and between countries. Benefits and losses will be unevenly distributed. There is no guarantee of continuing advantage for advanced economies. Thus, markets may help the poor at the bottom of the pyramid but arguably not what Windsor refers to as "globalization's missing middle."

John Rapley draws our attention to the fact that with the spread of globalization, inequality has become an important object of study in the social sciences. In particular, there has been great debate involving two propositions; first, that inequality has worsened as a result of free-market reform programs and, second, that this inequality is leading to rising social instability throughout the world. He argues that the significant question is not what is happening to income distribution *within* societies, but rather *between* them; and in particular, how this distribution is affected by an increasingly globalized world economy.

Globalization and Trade Agreements

Jeffrey Bergstrand, Scott Baier and Patrick McLaughlin, in their chapter entitled "Regional and Inter-Regional Trade Agreements: Examining their Role for the Middle East," explore the role of trade agreements in facilitating globalization and providing potential opportunities for countries to develop further and raise their standards of living, especially in the Middle East.

They state that the growth in the number of parties to the WTO and the more modest declines in countries' barriers to international trade have lowered the relative economic and political costs of forming bilateral and regional trade agreements.

They argue that the worldwide "market" for FTAs is now a fact and this market will likely continue to grow in step with globalization. Regions of the world that do not form economically rationalized FTAs and participate in this market will likely lose in relative economic terms, continuing to suffer from falls in relative per capita income and increased economic and political instability.

[6]

The Effects of Globalization on Security

Although globalization has largely arisen as a result of a more stable and secure world, the very factors that have contributed to its expansion also assist elements that aim to destabilize the world. Without global integration, terrorist groups, for example, would find it much more difficult to unobtrusively communicate, transfer money, travel and transport materials.

The spread of weapons of mass destruction (WMD), their delivery systems and related materials and technologies represents a fundamental threat to global security and peace. As Mohamed Kadry Said points out in his chapter "Pathways to Proliferation and Containing the Spread of WMD," the increasing ease of air travel, financial transactions and trade may play a key role in enabling the emergence of complicated, global proliferation networks. Increased privatization of trade, financial and information flows have widened the "non-governed" spaces in the international system, he states, and this has provided space and resources for non-state actors to exploit, thus leaving states devoid of control over such activities. Countering the proliferation threat in the globalization age therefore requires a comprehensive approach to prevent such weapons falling into the hands of certain states and groups. It also calls for a new globalized security system which reflects the growing economic, political and social interconnectedness of the world today.

Religion in a Globalized World

Many feel that globalization also poses a threat to religion, in that a process of greater interaction and integration will ultimately dilute religious beliefs within communities. In his chapter "Globalization and Religion," Bahman Baktiari highlights the fact that millions of people today, regardless of their nationality, perceive global conflicts in terms of competing revelations, dogmatic purity and divine duty. For many scholars of globalization and international relations, it is assumed that greater economic and political interdependence will ultimately weaken the hold of traditional religions, he claims, and that human beings have learned to separate religious issues from political ones. This assumption has shaped the way scholars of globalization view religion—often either as a force that succumbs to the pressures of globalization and becomes pluralistic or one which remains an atavistic ideology requiring sociological analysis but not serious intellectual engagement.

Baktiari reminds us that a standard assertion about globalization's impact on religion and cultural values claims that globalization leads to cultural homogeneity, increases integration and diminishes difference, and inculcates global norms, ideas or practices that overtake local mores. In other words, globalization itself is a form of religion with universalistic objectives. However, a counter-argument maintains that increased interaction is leading to new mixtures of cultures and that integration is provoking a defense of tradition, while yet another claims that globalization has increased religious fundamentalism because it has led not only to uneven economic growth and greater disparity between rich and poor, but also to increased secularization.

Concentrating on the Benefits of Globalization

While it is undeniably the case that some aspects of this phenomenon harm certain interests in selected countries, societies have always needed to adapt to changing patterns of human behavior and interaction. This inevitable process is taking place on a global scale and thus its benefits should be harnessed, not thwarted. The benefits gained from embracing the positive aspects of globalization and adapting to its influences are evident. Countries that have shirked globalization, usually for political reasons (such as Iran and North Korea) or for security reasons (such as Somalia), have not gained from global integration, and have thus been unable to provide a better future for their populations. Among the larger global economies, China and India have shown the greatest enthusiasm for absorbing the economic benefits of globalization. In both cases, their economies and "presence" have boomed since their respective governments began in the 1990s to encourage a more globalized and liberalized approach to macro-economic management. Small countries in particular must accept and adapt to the process of globalization in order to prosper and develop in an increasingly competitive environment.

This does not mean that absorbing all foreign influences is the key to national development, as there will always be inherent challenges and threats. There will still be conflict, hot and cold wars, and strategic maneuvering among nations. Governments will continue to give priority to their own national interests above all else, especially during times of apparent short-term gain. Countries, governments, companies and individuals will adapt to and face the challenges of globalization in differing degrees and at various levels. Globalization does pose certain challenges to societies, but these should be confronted by means of an holistic approach that balances political, economic, security and social concerns. The greatest conceptual challenges for a country are the risks stemming from undermining the nation state through reduced sovereignty and control over security affairs, the perceived suppression of national culture and identity, and the eroding of national economic independence.

We witness various effects of globalization in our everyday lives, from the meals we eat to the cars we drive and the people we meet, and we all have our own perception of how we are affected by it. This collection of papers aims to assess the current and future nature of the phenomenon that we call globalization and its impact both today and in the coming years.

KEYNOTE ADDRESS

Globalization Today:
How Interconnected is the World?

William S. Cohen

This is my fourth trip to the Middle East in the last year. All of these trips have included visits to the United Arab Emirates (UAE), thus underscoring the importance of the UAE and what is happening here in Abu Dhabi and Dubai in conjunction with the greater Middle East and the wider world.

In addition to visiting the UAE, I had the pleasure of attending the International Institute for Strategic Studies (IISS) Conference in Bahrain in December where I met with the foreign ministers and senior defense officials of all the Gulf countries. I have also conducted numerous visits to Saudi Arabia, Qatar, Bahrain, Oman and Kuwait, where I have had the chance to hear first hand the hopes and concerns of the leadership and the people in these countries.

Following this visit to the UAE, I plan to meet with King Abdullah in Jordan and will stop in Israel for meetings with Prime Minister Olmert and other senior Israeli officials. My frequent recent visits to the Gulf and the wider region have provided me with an excellent appreciation of the great opportunities, as well as the risks that await this region as it becomes more interconnected with the world.

This topic is one that has been very much at the center of world discussion and debate in recent years, and particularly in recent months. The theme of "How Interconnected is the World?" evokes important questions about how the forces of globalization today are reshaping our economic, political and cultural landscape, presenting us with both new opportunities and challenges.

By its very nature, globalization creates a competitive struggle, forcing countries and societies to constantly adjust their policies and principles in order to remain competitive and innovative – and indeed, survive – in the global market place. The recent revolution in information technology has made the knowledge industry the common currency of our new global world. An innovative idea developed anywhere in the world can now be immediately added to, improved upon and implemented virtually anywhere else on the planet. Similarly, the globalization of the supply chain has linked our output and production as never before.

Today, very few products are produced completely in one place, and the concept of "just-in-time delivery" means that the production and manufacture of parts, supplies and services must utilize efficiencies of scale, labor and knowledge from disparate corners of the globe to remain competitive. Globalization has enabled individuals, corporations and nation-states to influence actions and events around the world faster, cheaper and more significantly than ever before. It has led to the breaking down of many barriers, and has the potential for further innovation as well as social and cultural exchanges, while offering outstanding opportunities for dialogue and understanding.

The leadership of the UAE recognized a decade ago the need to diversify its economy beyond the oil sector, and has made the UAE a world-renowned tourist destination with buildings that are spectacular both in terms of their beauty and ambition. Today, the UAE is harnessing that same bold vision to transform the country into a cultural center of the region and is in the process of developing a financial sector that will rival those the world over.

However, globalization has a dark side to match the glitter of its promise and possibilities: the demand for energy resources; the deterioration of the environment; the spread of pandemics (AIDS, bird flu); the growing interdependence of economies and financial markets; the ensuing complexity of analyses and forecasts, the predictability of profits and the movement of money; and the desperate migratory shifts provoked by insecurity, poverty, famine or political instability. It is fair to say that in some instances, globalization has simply reinforced strong economies and weakened those that were already anemic.

Some writers – although a minority – claim that globalization is a cyclical phenomenon; that we have seen periods of globalization very similar to ours before and that we might view this as a passing phase, followed by a cycle that spins out in the opposite direction—nationalism, protectionism and anti-growth.

I remain convinced, however, that the current wave of globalization involves a permanent structural change in many of the world's institutions. Nations and companies alike have been forced to adjust and to manage the global challenges we face today in a very different way. Today, countries such as the UAE, Brazil, Turkey, China and India are much more a part of the world economy than they were even a decade ago, and are continuing to grow in importance and in terms of their impact on world trade. Indeed, consider that China could surpass the United States to become the world's largest exporter by 2010.[1] It is also thought that China is on the cusp of overtaking the United States in terms of its CO_2 emissions.[2] For its part, India has continued to meet impressive growth targets of 8–9 percent annually, largely as a result of reform and opening up to the outside world.

The impact of these processes is plain for all to see, whether in increased world demand for energy, or in the flood of imports that will arrive on our shores. Consider, for instance, these facts:

- Since 1987 exports have jumped from 16 to 27 percent of the world economy.
- Foreign Direct Investment (FDI) has tripled since 1990 and cross-border portfolio investment has risen five times as a percentage of world output.

- Today, any one product contains parts or inputs from 15 to 20 different countries. We see a world production system which is highly integrated in many sectors—in the sense that global corporations plan, design and organize production on a global scale.

- In 2005 the American retail store Wal-Mart imported US$18 billion worth of goods from its 5,000 Chinese suppliers. So far this year Indian firms have announced 34 foreign acquisitions worth more than US$10.7 billion.

- Last year's total was US$23 billion, more than five times the previous record and more than the investments made by foreigners in Indian companies. Today, 50 to 60 percent of world manufacturing output is actually organized within this globally integrated production circuit.

- In 1986 the total amount of foreign exchange transactions per day was 200 billion, a reasonably high figure. Today, it is 2 trillion—2 trillion foreign exchange transactions taking place every twenty-four hours. The daily value of financial derivatives, which didn't exist 20 to 25 years ago, has reached US$1 trillion a day. This gives us an idea of the degree to which today's financial markets are integrated. It also shows us the speed with which events take place: with one touch of a button on a computer you can transfer billions – if not hundreds of billions – of dollars from one part of the world to another.

Consider "soft globalization"—the globalization of ideas, access to the Internet, the sharing of knowledge, immediate communication, and the ease with which we can remain in touch with each other even when we are traveling or living far from our home base. Be they cellular phones, internet connections or other telecommunications links, all have exploded over the past decade. The 50 most populous countries average more than 95 televisions per 100 households. Information passes quickly from one country to another, from one household in Cairo to another in Seoul.

Global problems are also more visible today than they have ever been. We are living in a different world, one that is growing smaller each and every day. It is this increasing inter-connectedness that provides our strength and exposes our weaknesses. A natural disaster, a terrorist attack, a war, a virus will affect us all, because nothing happens in isolation. Also, because we are linked in so many ways, we need to consider global governance issues, global cooperation and multilateral planning if we hope to survive and prosper.

In his book *The World is Flat*, Thomas Friedman describes this unplanned cascade of technological and social shifts as having had a leveling effect and of "accidentally [making] Beijing, Bangalore and Bethesda next-door neighbors."[3] Friedman's list of "flatteners" includes: the fall of the Berlin Wall; the rise of netscape and the dotcom boom that led to a trillion dollar investment in fiber optic cable; the emergence of common software platforms and open source code enabling global collaboration; and the rise of outsourcing, offshoring, supply chaining and insourcing. These flatteners converged around the year 2000 and enabled the emergence of three huge economies – those of India, China and the former Soviet Union – whose "three billion people who were out of the game, walked onto the playing field."[4]

Bill Gates explains the meaning of this transformation best. Thirty years ago, if you had to choose between being born a genius in Mumbai or Shanghai and an average person in Poughkeepsie, you would have chosen Poughkeepsie because your chances of living a prosperous and fulfilled life were much greater there. "Now," Gates says, "I would rather be a genius born in China than an average guy born in Poughkeepsie."[5] I would suggest that one of the primary forces driving the flat world is actually the shifting attitudes and policies of governments around the world. From Brazil to South Africa to India, governments are becoming more market-friendly, accepting that the best way to cure poverty is to aim for high-growth policies.

This change, more than any other, has unleashed the energy of the private sector. After all, India had hundreds of thousands of trained engineers in the 1970s, but they didn't produce growth. In the United States and Europe, deregulation policies spurred the competition that led to radical innovation. There is a chicken-and-egg problem, to be sure: did government policies create the technological boom or did the technological boom transcend the walls of bureaucracy? I'll leave the answer to the experts.

The flat economic world has been created by an extremely uneven political world. The United States has dominated the globe like no other power since ancient Rome. It has been at the forefront, pushing for open markets, open trade and open politics. The consequence of these policies, however, will be to create a more economically and politically balanced world. If China grows economically, at some point it will also have to contend with the social aspirations and political ambitions of its citizens. If Brazil continues to surge, it will want to have a more influential voice on the international stage. If India gains economic muscle, history suggests that it will also seek the security of a stronger military.

Many scholars have argued that strengthened economic relations between states will be a powerful deterrent to war, which is true if nations act sensibly. But as we have seen in recent years, pride, honor and rage continue to play a large part in global politics.

While the metaphor of a flat world has been popularized, it goes too far. In fact, the world has not been leveled for several billion of today's population. Nearly 40 percent of the world's 6.5 billion people live in poverty, and in many countries there is an accelerating rate of inequality.

There is no easy answer to the challenge of how to reduce the growing gap between the "haves" and the "have-nots." As Joseph Stiglitz points out, education is important, but if there are no jobs for those who are educated, there can be little development or advancement. Similarly, we know it is important for developed countries to open their markets to poorer ones but if the poorer countries have no roads, ports or basic infrastructure, they will be unable to bring their goods to market and will be less likely to attract foreign investment. If developing countries have roads and ports but their farmers have poor productivity they will have no produce to sell. Should the developing countries have the products and the infrastructure to bring them to market they will not succeed if the developed countries continue to erect trade barriers to protect their domestic producers from competition.

Globalization is a word that evokes anxiety, troubling images and fears, even when it represents opportunities and new horizons. In the United States, some worry that economic globalization will threaten their livelihoods and that jobs will be exported to other countries. Public skepticism about open trade is rising in both rich and poor countries alike, and a host of major economic shifts, such as rising income inequality, are blamed on global integration. Furthermore, the Doha round of trade talks has long been stalled and the November 2006 mid-term elections in the United States brought in a clutch of lawmakers deeply opposed to freer trade.

To control this backlash, we have to be more sensitive to the negative impacts of this phenomenon. Globalization, some critics argue, creates a "race to the bottom" which leads countries to abandon protection for consumers, workers and the environment. Culturally, some are concerned that globalization will impose conformity and homogeneity and that their familiar, personal neighborhood coffeehouses and indigenous religious communities will be replaced by impersonal global identities.

There are also times when we have an irrational fear that globalization will threaten our security, as seen last year when the United States Congress objected to Dubai Ports World having any operational control over US ports. At the time, I joined my colleague, Admiral James Loy, to write an article in the *Wall Street Journal* expressing our conviction that our actions should not be based on fear, and that we should look at the facts surrounding this issue in a fair-minded and responsible manner.[6] Fear, however, prevailed.

I have mentioned both the good and the bad in discussing globalization. There is also the ugly—knowledge and information can be used to harm as well as help. The same technologies that are spreading prosperity can be used to cause mayhem and martyrdom.

President John F. Kennedy in his inaugural address said that the world had changed; that we held in our hands the power to abolish all forms of human poverty but also all forms of human life—the choice was, and continues to be ours to make. We can only succeed if we choose to live together and are prepared to work together, seeking balance, harmony and greater humanity.

GLOBALIZATION:
ECONOMIC FOUNDATIONS AND MANIFESTATIONS

1

Free Trade and Open Market Policies: Who Benefits?

Duane Windsor

This paper addresses the broad and ultimately difficult question of who benefits (and who loses) from free trade and open market policies in today's globalizing economy. "Economic globalization is a surprisingly controversial process. Surprising, that is, to the many economists and policy makers who believe it is the best means of bringing prosperity to the largest number of people all around the world. Proponents of economic globalization have had a tendency to conclude that dissent and criticism is the result of ignorance or vested interest."[1] However, there is an unsurprising backlash from various interests against globalization's effects;[2] and also increasing reservations expressed by some prominent economists.[3]

A deceptively simple solution to this debate is that, over some abstract "long run" time period, aggregate global real welfare should increase as a result of the operation of the principle of comparative advantage.[4] According to this principle, holding constant any other considerations, the world as a whole cannot ever lose from free trade and open markets.[5] This simple answer is well established in conventional mainstream economic theory (i.e., the classical and neoclassical tradition) and in the historical record of economic development and growth since 1776, the year in which Adam Smith's *The Wealth of Nations* was published.[6] The theory of, and evidence for, the broad benefits of free trade and open market policies are well founded. Over sufficient time, free trade in open markets pursuing comparative advantage can generate rising aggregate economic wealth. Douglas Irwin cites Harry Johnson to the effect that it is well established that free trade is on the whole more beneficial than protectionism.[7] This simple answer is supported by the strong empirical evidence associated with various bilateral and multilateral free trade arrangements undertaken since the end of World War II. The paper by Professor Jeffrey H. Bergstrand on "Regional and Inter-Regional Trade Agreements" (Chapter 2 of this volume) summarizes the body of empirical evidence as demonstrating that economic modelers frequently underestimate both the overall benefits of regional and inter-regional trade arrangements and the temporal rapidity of their appearance. Freer trade and open markets are typically strong drivers of economic development and growth.

Despite the well-established theory and empirical evidence favoring free trade and open market policies, there is both considerable popular unease over the immediate effects of "globalization" and open expression of important reservations by some prominent economists. In June 2007, the heads of government of the Group of Eight (G8) largest, advanced industrial nations held their annual summit meeting in Heiligendamm, Germany.[8] The official agenda concerned "Growth and Responsibility" with respect to the global economy, Africa and climate change. Specific emphasis was placed on the increasing responsibilities of Brazil, China and India as large developing economies. As is now commonplace at the summits of the G8 and the World Trade Organization (WTO), there was a strong turnout of anti-globalization, pro-green and pro-developing-country activists held back from the meeting site by German police. These demonstrations, while plainly orchestrated by activists for public effect, are in perspective simply the tip of the iceberg of popular unease.[9]

Alan Blinder argues that economists defending freer trade tend to underestimate "... both the importance of offshoring [i.e., offshore outsourcing] and its disruptive effect on wealthy countries."[10] Paul

Samuelson comments that, "Most non-economists are fearful when an emerging China or India, helped by their still low real wage rates, outsourcing and miracle export-led developments, cause layoffs from good American jobs. This is a hot issue now, and in the coming decade, it will not go away."[11] The "short run" reality is that globalization has negative as well as positive impacts (economic and non-economic) on both developed and developing countries. These short run effects are direct as well as immediate, while long run benefits are indirect as well as distant in time. Paul Krugman, well known as a pro-free trade economist, conceded in January 2007 that "... those who are worried about trade have a point, and deserve some respect."[12] It should be noted that Krugman argued that the chief justification for free trade was to assist with the global development process—which could come at some cost to the developed countries. Krugman advises that developed countries must strengthen their social safety nets.

Globalization is therefore not automatically popular.[13] Both Blinder and Samuelson made immediate reference to remarks in February 2004 by Dr. N. Gregory Mankiw, Chairman of the US Council of Economic Advisors.[14] Mankiw's comment that moving US service jobs abroad was "just a new way to do international trade" predictably ignited a political firestorm. Mankiw subsequently stated that he had been misunderstood: "Economists and non-economists speak very different languages ... some of the comments I made about the benefits of international trade were far from clear and were misinterpreted."[15] He then linked job loss abroad to job creation at home and job retraining efforts. The vital lesson is that in this instance the deceptively simple answer is not automatically popular or easily communicated.[16]

As this paper undertakes to explain, a useful, realistic answer to the question of who benefits is ultimately quite complicated, for several reasons. Economic theory and evidence are reasonably clear and mutually reinforcing with respect to long run aggregate world real welfare. But there are practical difficulties in the deceptively simple answer of comparative advantage, in which unequal distribution of gains (i.e., benefits) and losses (i.e., burdens) shifts controversy over free trade and open markets from the economics textbook to the real world of political economy—where economics and politics meet over distribution of real welfare within and between countries.[17] Benefits and losses will be unevenly distributed. There is no guarantee of continuing advantage for advanced economies. Markets may help the poor at the "bottom of the pyramid"[18] but arguably not "globalization's missing middle."[19] Adam Smith's classical economic growth model can end in a zero-growth stationary state. A general and long run theory does not take account of practical difficulties on a very uneven playing field.

First, the "long run" is an abstraction that is awkward to delimit concretely.[20] Professor Bergstrand reports the evidence that regional and inter-regional arrangements show quick returns. But how much time is required for the aggregate real welfare effects to appear with globalization? This time period may exceed the impatience of employees losing their jobs in developed countries, the impatience of consumers and potential employees in developing countries, and the impatience of activists.

Second, the distribution of benefits and burdens may differ markedly from an average increase in real welfare. There can be rising total welfare and also painful distributions of losses. Aggregate and average indices mask disparities. The deceptively simple answer is true if everyone gains, or if there are far more winners than losers and if the gains markedly exceed the losses. Distribution is then theoretically irrelevant. As Mankiw's comments indicate, the economic betting is that as international trade generates old job losses through one door (i.e., imports) it generates new job increases through other doors (i.e., exports and domestic wealth gains).

Third, under the proposed principle of hypothetical compensation, the winners could in theory compensate the losers and still be better off than before.[21] In reality, the upwardly mobile in developing countries may not

[26]

favor globalization or compensation to losers.[22] Mankiw refers to job retraining investment, for example. However, such compensation remains by and large hypothetical even in developed countries: who wants to give up their welfare gains to correct the misfortunes of others?—especially in a free trade regime where everyone competes on the basis of dynamic comparative advantage.

There are likely to be highly dissatisfied losers from globalization, while winners may not be as intensely concerned. Irwin cites John Stuart Mill to the effect that, while protectionism has been defeated intellectually in general, there are repeated attempts to develop specific cases for protectionism.[23] Indeed, there is reason to suppose that individuals attach greater psychological significance to losses than to gains—especially if the losses are immediate and the gains are potential and in the future.

Fourth, the timing of gains and losses could be unhelpful. More losses might occur immediately in the short run with the bulk of the gains arriving later. This time profile fits, for example, the empirical studies undertaken by Karl Marx and Friedrich Engels concerning the at least temporary negative effects of the first industrial revolution in the 19th century.[24] This time profile poses serious political difficulties.

Fifth, real welfare is a compound of multiple dimensions (leaving aside technical considerations of proper definitions and measurements). Real income gains may be offset by world ecological declines and population growth. Economic development and growth may generate various unpriced negative externalities, which are real costs borne by someone without compensation. The true effects of such negative externalities may not become recognized until some time in the future. Therefore, the real welfare measured in economic terms at a given point in time may have to be discounted significantly for these unpriced negative externalities. Climate change is a case in point. Technological progress and population growth may destroy the planet's natural resources and habitability.

Economic globalization – market interconnectedness – is far from complete, rendering predictions unreliable. The potential effects of full globalization include lack of local self-sufficiency and inability to buffer against distant events. For example, in February 2007, when the Shanghai Composite Benchmark and the Shenzhen Component Index suddenly dropped about 9 percent (averaged together) in one day following a record high, European, Asian and US markets declined in immediate response. The Dow Jones industrial average dropped just over 416 points (3.3 percent), with all 30 stocks falling.

WTO progress has stalled since 2001 on the Doha round, postponed from the 1999 Seattle meetings thwarted by demonstrations. The stalemate is partly a North–South divide between advanced economies (Europe, the United States and Japan) and developing economies, especially the Group of 20 led by Brazil, China and India. Adequate "rules of the game" are not in place. There is, at best, a patchwork of partial international policy regimes and institutional arrangements barely in place that do not amount to adequate "rules" for international commerce and relations.[25] Economic changes and volatility involve serious transition costs and stresses. Distribution of wealth differs from aggregate wealth production; acceptable shares for all stakeholders are not guaranteed. There is considerable corruption in various governments and international efforts to combat such corruption are not yet widely effective.[26] Globalization may adversely affect the poor and the self-sufficient; and foster larger multinational businesses. State-influenced enterprises, as is characteristic of the present Chinese economy for example, violate the general theory. A rational game theorist prefers open markets abroad and closed markets at home. This preference is reinforced by agricultural and other subsidies in advanced economies (illustrated by South Korean concerns about rice imports) and well-founded concerns that jobs will shift away to other locations (illustrated by Citigroup's recent offshoring announcement discussed below). Estimation of timing and distribution of benefits and losses involves assertion of a moral dimension concerning poverty alleviation and equity. Brazil, China and India are exempted from the Kyoto Protocol so as to help raise the living standards of their growing populations.

The remainder of this paper is organized as follows. The section following this introduction explains the theory of comparative advantage specialization. Emphasis is placed on why the theory is deceptively simple when compared to the complex phenomenon of economic globalization. The next section explains the nature of Joseph Schumpeter's theory of creative destruction in relation to economic development and growth. It is the creative destruction process that generates dynamic or kaleidoscopic advantage in a continually changing world economy. The effects of kaleidoscopic advantage are complex and difficult to predict. The paper goes on in the subsequent section to discuss possible outcomes in terms of types of countries and types of populations. Present information suggests that Brazil, China and India will tend to advance in a globalizing economy, while the current advanced economies will have to work harder to stay ahead in the race and middle income countries may lose out over time. The penultimate section examines the problem of increasing real welfare in the face of continuing population growth and declining global natural resources and ecology. Technical progress is both the key to sustainable development and a grave threat – along with population growth – to sustainable development. Two key risks are: there may not be sufficient world resources; and world economic development might pass a global ecological tipping point. Finally, a brief concluding section summarizes the paper's key arguments.

Appreciating Comparative Advantage Specialization

Free trade is essentially the open movement of goods and services in unrestricted (i.e., relatively ideal) markets operating between and within countries, whereby resources should flow to the most economically valuable uses. This increased efficiency is an important source of real welfare improvement. These countries are, however, sovereign political jurisdictions with the ability to restrict such movement through various forms of protectionism. Freer trade is an improvement in arrangements moving away from any existing restrictions and toward the ideal of free trade. Open markets are relatively ideal conditions in which there are no "trade" or "non-trade" barriers to the international and domestic movement of goods and services, capital (i.e., financial investments) or labor. Full globalization would essentially mean free trade and open markets worldwide. Even with the efforts of the WTO, the world is nowhere near such a state of full globalization. Freer trade efforts tend to focus on trade and investment rather than on labor movement. Migration of labor from developing countries is a controversial policy issue in the United States and Western Europe. A key reason for this controversy is the question of citizenship rights for temporary (i.e., visa) workers who seek to obtain permanent residency status.[27]

The wealth-generating capabilities of free trade and open markets are a result of the operation of the principle of comparative advantage.[28] There are three types of advantage: *absolute*, *comparative* and *dynamic* (or *kaleidoscopic*).

Absolute (i.e., simple cost) advantage occurs when any country or population segment or entity can produce a product or service at a lower cost per unit than another. So, for example, country A might produce corn (i.e., maize) more cheaply with mechanized and biogenetic agriculture than country B can with manual and conventional agriculture. Corn is an important example, because it is a basic feedstock used for animal feed, human food, ethanol and a variety of other purposes. In Mexico, corn is a staple. The price of corn has been rising there due to increased ethanol demand in the United States.[29] If, correspondingly, country B were to produce tequila more cheaply per unit than country A can, there is a basis for trade between A – which exports corn and imports tequila – and country B—which exports tequila and imports corn. There are mutual gains from trade in this instance: both A and B become wealthier (on an aggregate measurement) since they voluntarily exchange corn and tequila for mutual benefit.[30]

[30]

The gains from absolute cost-based trade are, however, fairly limited. What the principle of *comparative* advantage dramatically demonstrates is a much more powerful basis for trade. What matters far more than absolute advantage is the relative opportunity cost of, for example, gasoline production.[31] Even if A can produce gasoline more cheaply absolutely, it may be still better to export something else (such as corn, with which A has an even greater advantage) and import gasoline from B (say in this instance Venezuela).

The global economy, operating in accord with comparative (or relative) advantage, increases specialization and thus trade. Specialization is the source of even greater trade gains than absolute cost advantage. The great importance of this effect, first described by Robert Torrens[32] and named by David Ricardo[33] in a more famous illustration,[34] is emphasized by Samuelson.[35] The illustration of comparative advantage by Ricardo for England (cloth, for example) and Portugal (wine, for example) is a relatively simple two-by-two scenario. There are two countries and two products. The principle is powerful, because it applies to all voluntary trade (between any two people, two countries, and so forth).

Samuelson argues that this principle, while fully valid in simple conditions, cannot be demonstrated to be automatically true under conditions of *dynamic* comparative advantage.[36] Jagdish Bhagwati refers to *kaleidoscopic* comparative advantage.[37] Dynamic comparative advantage in a changing global economy should increase worldwide real per capita well-being, so that gainers can hypothetically compensate losers. However, that condition does not guarantee that in each region (or country) of the world there will be more gainers than losers. A region or country could lose overall, even if some proportion of the population gains. In effect, comparative advantage keeps shifting around rather than being relatively stable—and stability is the condition in Ricardo's classical example of England and Portugal, long-trading partners and allies. The problem arises with a shift in circumstances to a complex N-by-N scenario. Instead of two countries and two products, there are multiple (i.e., N) countries and products (and services and information) engaged in complex trading operations. With information, knowledge and learning dynamically changing,[38] relative advantage may shift continually among countries as a result of changes in three underlying economic conditions: (i) long run world prices for key resources, such as hydrocarbons; (ii) the opportunity costs of factors of production, such as capital and labor; and (iii) technical progress (i.e., innovation) in production methods. The distribution of effects is likely quite uneven across and within countries. As Samuelson notes, complex conditions do not rule out gains from trade on an aggregate basis or even for all countries; but under complex conditions, economic theory can no longer guarantee gains from trade for all participants (i.e., all stakeholders) in the global economy. Thus, the situation becomes considerably more uncertain and volatile.[39]

Popular unease arises, in effect, in this uncertainty and volatility, and therefore is more than just inaccurate "folk economics."[40] Blinder summarizes the forecast as follows: "… we should not view the coming wave of offshoring as an impending catastrophe. Nor should we try to stop it. The normal gains from trade mean that the world cannot lose from increases in productivity, and the United States and other industrial countries have not only weathered but also benefited from comparable changes in the past."[41] Nevertheless, there will be "massive, complex and multifaceted challenges" requiring national adaptations that are not in fact occurring.[42] Just as every investor should understand that the past is not automatically a guide to future performance, so "… the nature of international trade is changing before our eyes," from tradable goods to electronic service delivery.[43]

It is possible analytically to reduce N-by-N comparative advantage to two-by-two comparative advantage. The simple method is to consider country A and then group together all other countries of the world and consider them country B. This approach is, however, what landed Dr. Mankiw in political hot water: the N-by-N conditions cannot be automatically guaranteed to result in the two-by-two outcomes.

The Process of Creative Destruction

As Samuelson emphasizes, dynamic comparative advantage is closely linked to Schumpeter's theory of creative destruction.[44] Schumpeter argued that economic development results from entrepreneurship (defined as risk-bearing innovation) operating on the supply side of markets. The creation of new economic wealth through innovation generating new monopolies is simultaneously the destruction of old economic wealth from established monopolies that are driven out of business. The new wealth is more valuable than the old wealth. (For example, the automobile eliminated most horse-drawn conveyances.) This creative destruction theory has resisted formalization for mathematical treatment, because it is not a model of prices or markets but rather is an exposition of the important role of the entrepreneur who drives technical progress in production.[45] The process of creative destruction driving dynamic comparative advantage is endless.

Figure 1.1 depicts in very simplified form the classical world of Adam Smith (1776) and David Ricardo (1817). The vertical axis is per capita (i.e., average) real well-being, measured in Figure 1.1 effectively as gross domestic product (GDP)—although this approach involves some technical difficulties. ("Real" already accounts for nominal inflation in prices over time.) The horizontal axis is time. The GDP line shown as a function of the two axes is a time-dependent path of economic development and growth. The third axis involves population dynamics defining how many people are in the changing denominator for computing per capita real well-being. (The computation is aggregate real well-being divided by population to yield per capita real well-being.) Initially, it is simpler to ignore population dynamics by assuming that GDP is increasing faster than population rises. In stylized form, the classical economy begins with exogenously fixed resources and population in each country. The initial distribution across countries is effectively random.[46] What free trade between and within countries based on comparative advantage specialization achieves is higher per capita real well-being from fixed

[33]

resources than can occur from simple absolute cost advantage. What the WTO in effect accomplishes is faster achievement of the gains from comparative advantage specialization through reduction of artificial trade and non-trade barriers erected by political jurisdictions as forms of protectionism. Figure 1.1 depicts the WTO operating in a zone between fixed resources and the limit to economic development and growth with such fixed resources.

Figure 1.1

The Classical World of Adam Smith and David Ricardo

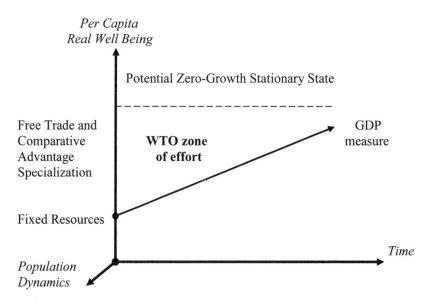

The classical approach to economic development and international trade approaches a ceiling or limit, expressed in Figure 1.1 as a zero-growth stationary state. Without technical progress of some sort, specialization and trade can accomplish only so much (however large that gain may be empirically). *The Limits of Growth* study prepared more than three decades ago for the Club of Rome posited roughly fixed limits of this sort.[47]

The classical scenario permits population growth, because higher social welfare and higher population can occur jointly over time. Thomas Malthus pessimistically cautioned, however, that problems could arise if population for some reason(s) expanded significantly faster than the rate of economic growth.[48] This problem is solved by technical progress (as will be discussed below). Otherwise the third axis for population dynamics becomes critically important.

Figure 1.2

Schumpeter's World of Creative Destruction

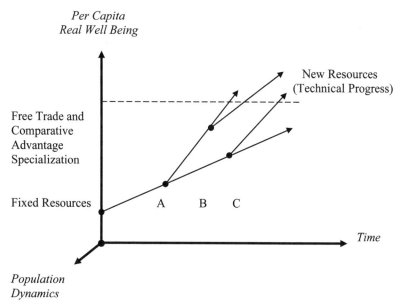

Figure 1.2 depicts in very simplified form the creative destruction solution proposed by Schumpeter.[49] In effect, technical progress continually creates new resources (again measured as GDP roughly). The resource situation thus continually moves up the vertical axis with a rising effective limit. As a result, any zero growth stationary state of Figure 1.1 is continually postponed, so that for practical purposes it is never reached.

[35]

New resources (including renewable resources) can outpace population growth. Thus the numerator increases faster than the denominator in the per capita index. There may be, however, ultimate planetary resource constraints; but, if so, these constraints are greatly postponed relative to the classical scenario. At the same time, however, this process of creative destruction is the source of dynamic or kaleidoscopic competitive advantage. How does a particular country stay ahead in a situation of continually changing advantage? Samuelson argues that the outcome cannot be guaranteed theoretically. A may lead; then B may lead; then C may lead—as illustrated in Figure 1.2 above.

Forecasting Outcomes for Countries and Populations

While economic theory and economic history generally support Adam Smith's thesis that free trade and open markets alleviate poverty, this theory of economic development and growth is both general and long run. Generally, over sufficient time, most people and countries should (and likely will) benefit from free trade and open markets. On the whole, relatively free and open markets are the best driver of economic performance. Nevertheless, the nature of the creative destruction process is such that rising real well-being is not strictly guaranteed for everyone: there can be losers as well as gainers. Presently, there is no mechanism for implementing hypothetical compensation as real compensation from gainers to losers.

Following the general approach taken by Geoffrey Garrett, one might classify countries or populations within countries into several relevant types.[50] In Figure 1.3, key types are shown as technically advancing, resource endowed, low labor cost, and middle income. In addition, there may be countries so poor or so underdeveloped that no absolute progress or decline is even likely. Such countries are excluded from consideration here, as they are largely candidates for foreign aid transfers. The size of the circle in Figure 1.3 can be understood as the size of the global economic pie in terms of aggregate wealth and welfare. The larger the pie, the more the successful countries (or populations) can afford to assist those countries (or populations) in truly desperate need.

Figure 1.3

Types of Countries and Populations Sharing the Global Pie

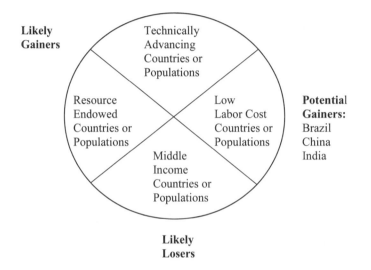

Likely Gainers

Technically Advancing Countries or Populations

Resource Endowed Countries or Populations

Low Labor Cost Countries or Populations

Potential Gainers:
Brazil
China
India

Middle Income Countries or Populations

Likely Losers

Some 62 countries account for 96 percent of global GDP and 85 percent of the world's population.[51] The likely gainers from globalization are technically advancing countries (or population segments) and resource-endowed countries (or populations segments). These countries are most likely to trade with one another. Trading and investment patterns in the global economy tend to be among the advanced countries, and between advanced and resource-endowed countries.

A country's sustainable access to valuable natural resources or knowledge appears to be the key driver of economic performance over time. Whether a particular resource or knowledge is valuable depends on consumer demand for what is a derived factor of production. Natural resources are more or less randomly distributed (i.e., exogenously determined). Some countries are resource rich, while others are resource poor. For example, oil and gas are valuable, and Saudi Arabia and Iran benefit from that circumstance, while North America and Western Europe are well watered for agriculture. The United Arab Emirates (UAE) has energy resources and more importantly is well positioned geographically for international commerce. These types of countries and populations are likely to enjoy high incomes. The distribution of income and wealth within a country is a different matter. Garrett suggests that relatively low labor cost countries – Brazil, China and India – or populations have a different kind of advantage. Labor-intensive jobs (manufacturing or long-distance services) are likely to move to such locations or populations. Garrett suggests that middle income countries or populations are likely to lose out over time. They typically lack resources, knowledge or skills and cannot be low cost.[52] There will be population-serving jobs in all economies, but such jobs are likely to receive relatively low wages.[53] Dynamic comparative advantage means that production and jobs may shift among countries. Massive transition and adjustment costs are more likely than massive unemployment.[54] Nevertheless, a country's share of the global work force may decrease, and the situation may not be corrected simply by skill development.[55]

There is a recent analysis of income distribution effects in the United States by economists Emmanuel Saez (University of California at Berkeley) and Thomas Piketty (of the recently founded Paris School of Economics).[56] Using tax data for 2005, they found that total reported income increased by almost 9 percent over the previous year. The top 1 percent and top 10 percent received the largest shares of national income since 1928. Per capita, the top 300,000 Americans received 440 times as much as the average person in the bottom half; this ratio has doubled since 1980. While the top 1 percent experienced an average gain in income of more than $139,000, average income for the bottom 90 percent dropped by $172 (-0.6 percent). While the drop is minor (and perhaps not statistically very significant), the movement is in the wrong direction. The distribution of national income is becoming more inequitable between the top and bottom segments. This data is subject to various criticisms (e.g., one year only, year could be abnormal, and so forth); but income distribution in the United States is not looking terribly robust in this quick view.

Foreign competition to the United States is likely to occur in two phases. The first phase is the rise of China (PRC) as a manufacturing country. The second phase is the rise of India as a long-distance service provider. Blinder suggests that India, rather than China, will be the more significant competitor to the United States in the third industrial revolution of the information age.[57]

China presently has the largest trade surplus with the United States, constituting about one-third of the US trade deficit. In 2007, according to the WTO, China will likely move from third to second in terms of money value of exports, putting it ahead of the United States. In 2007, China might overtake Germany to take the top spot in terms of exports. Chinese imports and import growth lag behind Chinese exports and export growth. China has already announced plans to begin building large commercial aircraft in the near future. The PRC has the world's largest foreign reserves (about $1.2 trillion) – ahead of Japan (about $909 billion) – and the PRC has announced it will form a state-owned enterprise, modeled on Singapore's Temasek Holdings, to begin investing surplus reserves abroad.

Increasingly there are concerns about the income and wealth effects of globalization trends on the United States.[58] As Mortimer Zuckerman points out, "Even Americans who went to college are now experiencing the kind of income instability high school dropouts faced in the 1970s."[59] Record profits appear to be associated with stagnant wages and business investment in the United States.[60] Toyota and General Motors (GM) are in close contention for the number one position in global auto sales, although GM reportedly sold about 1.1 million more vehicles in the United States during 2007. If human capital is the key causal factor in US economic development, then continuing investment in such human capital becomes essential but increasingly costly as a social investment.[61]

In March 2007, Halliburton Co., headquartered in Houston, Texas, announced that it would soon move its corporate headquarters to Dubai, where the CEO relocated in mid-May.[62] In 2006, perhaps 35–38 percent of the firm's $13 billion in revenues and 16,000 of its 45,000 employees were based in the Eastern Hemisphere.[63] The firm will seek a share listing on Dubai's new international stock exchange, begin hiring thousands of new employees in the Arab and Asian countries, and shift as much as 70 percent of future capital spending to the Eastern Hemisphere.[64] Halliburton is the first major multinational firm from the West to locate its chief executive in Dubai.[65] CEO David Lesar stated that the intention is to obtain a 50–50 split in revenues between the Western and Eastern Hemispheres.[66] The firm will reportedly continue to pay US taxes on its global earnings.[67]

In April 2007, Citigroup, the largest US financial company, announced a cut of 17,000 jobs (roughly 5 percent of the total 327,000) and a shift of another 9,500 jobs to "lower cost locations" outside the United States. Citigroup is reportedly seeking to raise international revenues from 44 percent to 60 percent of its total.

The WTO is far from an economic constitution for a globally integrated economy. WTO rounds must be regarded as hardball bargaining among rational game theorists, who prefer open markets abroad and protected markets at home. WTO progress has stalled since 2001 on the Doha (Qatar) round, postponed from the 1999 Seattle meetings thwarted by anti-globalization, pro-labor and pro-environment demonstrations. The stalemate is essentially a North–South divide between advanced economies and developing economies (the Group of 20 lead by Brazil, China and India). Part of the stalemate concerns continuing large-scale subsidy by the United States, Western Europe and Japan of agricultural interests. In October 2005, the Bush administration offered to cap such subsidies at $22 billion. In June 2007, Geneva, Brazil and China challenged the United States to offer "real" (i.e., additional) cuts in subsidies.

Globalization tends to drive up prices, for example of oil and gas.[68] There are competing models of economic development in the globalizing economy. In contrast to the liberal (or libertarian) model of free markets,[69] China is following a path that is neither democratic nor free market[70] and socialism may be staging a comeback in Latin America.[71]

In March 2007, free trade area talks between the United States and South Korea (long-time military allies) were delayed by South Korean protestors concerned, understandably, about potential job losses and imported rice. The United States and India have also been discussing possibilities for freer trade. The United States bans Indian mangoes (due to pesticide use) and India maintains stringent emissions standards and tariffs (greater than 90 percent) for heavy motorcycles. Mangoes can now be irradiated for import into the United States, and India may agree to accept "Euro 3" standards for heavy motorcycles, such as US manufactured Harley-Davidsons.[72] However, there is reported resistance in the US Congress to proposed free trade agreements with Colombia, Panama, Peru and South Korea.

The United States has imposed tariffs on Chinese high-gloss paper, alleging illegal government subsidies. Furthermore, in April 2007 it filed two new WTO complaints against China concerning copyright infringements and restrictions on the sale of American movies, music and books. In June 2007, China (as it is entitled to do) rejected a shipment of US pistachios allegedly containing ants.[73] It also ordered some US health supplements and raisins returned or destroyed for not meeting China's safety standards. Similarly, there have been reports of unsafe food additives at Chinese sources being shipped to the United States and toothpaste containing antifreeze being shipped to Panama from China.

Another key debate concerns the effect of globalization on the world's poor.[74] C.K. Prahalad presents the case for how markets and businesses can improve the lot of those at the "bottom of the pyramid."[75] Markets are

[41]

not strictly speaking the same thing as globalization. So it is conceivable that freer markets will tend to help the poor, while open market policies will tend to hurt the poor. The net effects could be relatively negligible over time. The theory of economic development is itself a matter of considerable controversy and is constantly evolving.[76] It is still not clear that we know how to move societies from a condition of underdevelopment to a process of economic development and growth. The general consensus seems to be that during much of the twentieth century (1900–1980), there was a major rise in global inequality.[77] The controversy concerns what has happened since 1980.[78] Sutcliffe suggests that while overall inequality has tended to fall, the global gap between the very top and very bottom incomes has tended to increase. He proposes that various approximate measures are need to, in effect, triangulate the matter.[79] A key difficulty is that neither trade liberalization nor poverty is readily measured in order to establish their likely relationship.[80] The evidence favors trade liberalization,[81] but corruption in developing and transition countries may undermine the general benefits.

Ecological Tipping Points

The effects of economic globalization on the natural environment are debatable.[82] Time is, however, operating against sustainable development. The term "sustainable development" encompasses three related effects. There must be continuing economic development to raise overall global wealth and improve conditions for the world's poor. This wealth increase must occur without adversely harming the natural environment of the planet.

The world's population will tend to keep increasing, from about 6.6 billion in June 2007 to 9 billion at mid-year 2042. World population may continue to grow beyond 2050, although the rate of increase is slowing. World population doubled over 40 years from 3 billion in 1959 to 6 billion in 1999. By 2042, world population will have increased over 43 years by 50 percent to 9 billion.[83] Population growth must inevitably place stress on both resources and the natural environment.

The problem is not barriers to growth in the form of resource constraints relative to population growth,[84] as technical progress increases resources relative to population. Instead the fundamental problem is that both technical progress and population growth tend to degrade the planet itself. There may be ecological tipping points both locally and globally that are effectively irreversible once reached. Environmental degradation is a set of negative externalities not properly priced in economic choices. The tropical rain forests are being reduced in a number of countries. Ocean fish populations appear to be declining. The climate is warming in various locations. Rain patterns are shifting. The effects of these negative externalities are postponed to the future.

A key problem is global warming and its potential effects on human populations and their living environments. The UN recently issued a series of important reports on this problem.[85] One potential effect is the melting of ice sheets resulting in sea level rise. Susmit Dasgupta et al. provide estimates for the impact of sea level rise on 84 developing countries.[86] Large proportions of the world's population live near the sea. They base their estimates on a range of 1 to 3 meter rises in the 21st century, which could go up to 5 meters if the Greenland and West Antarctic ice sheets broke up unexpectedly.[87] This rise would cause large-scale population displacement and severe economic and ecological damage affecting hundreds of millions of people. Severe impacts are likely to be limited to a relatively small number of countries, especially Vietnam, Egypt, the Bahamas and other island nations particularly exposed to rising sea levels. China would experience fairly large absolute impacts due to the size of populations in affected areas. The US Gulf Coast would also be affected. Many developing countries would likely experience limited impacts. East Asia, the Middle East and North Africa would experience the greatest relative impacts of this group.

Brazil, China and India – the leaders of the Group of 20 – are exempted from the Kyoto Protocol, which the United States and Australia have so far declined to ratify. The Kyoto Protocol may be, at best, seriously flawed in design despite its importance.[88] In 2006, China reportedly became the top producer of carbon dioxide emissions, ahead of the United States, according to a report from the Netherlands Environmental Assessment Agency.[89] Consequently, the Bush administration declined to ratify the Protocol. In any event, it is unlikely that the Republican-dominated Senate would have ratified the Protocol.[90] At the 2007 G8 summit, the Bush administration indicated a willingness to accept a compromise that would move toward halving global emissions by 2050 through a collaborative process involving China and India.[91] This process would substitute flexible cooperation for the allegedly (but not in reality) "binding" targets accepted in Kyoto.[92]

Conclusions

In the short run, it is possible that many people and at least some countries overall could lose from freer trade and more open markets. There are potentially significant transition and adjustment difficulties imposed by economic globalization. Generally, the empirical evidence supports the expectation that overall benefits occur from freer trade arrangements among and within countries. However, this pattern does not guarantee that there will be no losers. Welfare and wealth effects may differ from one another. Happiness is even more subjective. Compensatory transfers from winners to losers remain largely problematic. The longer the time horizon over which aggregate benefits are created, the greater the likelihood of encountering both increasing world population (rising from about 6.6 billion in June 2007 to about 9 billion in mid-year 2042 on present forecasts) and potentially irreversible ecological tipping points at least locally if not regionally and globally.

Essentially, what we do know is that technical progress (i.e., innovation) through entrepreneurship is the key to sustainable development. On the one hand, creative destruction leading to dynamically changing comparative advantage is the source of aggregate real wealth increase—on the whole, more people and countries are likely to benefit than to lose. But the aggregate results are not guaranteed to work for everyone in the global economy. Geoffrey Garrett suggests that a likely scenario is increasing wealth for Brazil, China and India, while the presently advanced countries will have to work harder.[93] Alan Blinder suggests that India will tend to succeed China as a chief competitor to the United States over time.[94] Countries with valuable resources (e.g., oil and natural gas) will tend to prosper, while middle income countries may lose out in the global competition. On the other hand, both technical progress and rising world population may undermine sustainable development by eroding the planet's capacity to handle local, regional and global ecological tipping points.

Regional and Inter-Regional Trade Agreements: Examining their Role for the Middle East

Jeffrey H. Bergstrand, Scott L. Baier and Patrick A. McLaughlin[*]

The Middle East is at a crossroads in terms of the process of globalization. A few countries in the region – such as the United Arab Emirates (UAE) – are ranked among those with the highest per capita income in the world and enjoy extensive international trade, investment and migration compared to the rest of the world. Unlike most countries in the Middle East, UAE trade is extensive, although it remains at about 85 percent below its "potential" (an estimate that will be presented below). The UAE requires fewer signatures on export and import documentation than most other Middle East countries, has delivery times that are among the shortest in the world, and has infrastructure for international trade that rivals that of large industrialized countries.[1] The UAE's overall ranking in facilitating international trade is the 73rd percentile, above the 47th percentile average for all Middle East and North African (MENA) countries.[2] Policy makers in the UAE are highly sensitive to the process of globalization, being strong proponents of the continued development and strengthening of the Gulf Cooperation Council (GCC), including the GCC's planned emergence into a customs union; negotiation of a free trade agreement (FTA) between the GCC and the European Union (EU);

[*] Jeffrey Bergstrand and Scott Baier are grateful for financial support from the US National Science Foundation under grants SES 0351154 (Bergstrand) and SES-0351018 (Baier).

negotiation of a UAE FTA with the United States; and membership of the World Trade Organization (WTO).

By contrast, many other countries in the Middle East are isolated from the process of globalization and focus instead on internal strategies for development. As a consequence, they continue to fall behind in raising standards of living relative to countries that are highly interconnected with the world economy. For example, Syria ranks in the 11th percentile in trade facilitation measures by the World Bank, Iran ranks 18th and Algeria ranks 35th.[3] Not surprisingly, all three countries trade well below their "potentials" and many MENA countries trade at half of what standard trade models would predict—most likely due to extensive barriers to trade.[4] Even Oman and Qatar trade considerably less than their respective potentials relative to the EU.[5] Moreover, Iran has no economic integration agreements with other countries, near or far, and is not a member of the WTO.

This paper examines conceptually and empirically the role of trade agreements – such as FTAs – in facilitating globalization and providing potential opportunities for countries to develop further and raise their standards of living, especially in the Middle East.

The discussion is structured around four themes; first, in order to focus the discussion, we offer a concise and tractable definition of "globalization." While much anecdotal evidence indicates that globalization is progressing, we step back and try to take a "bird's-eye view" of how inter-connected the world really is and argue that, while globalization *has* advanced, the world still has a considerable way to go before it becomes "flat"—to use Thomas Friedman's metaphor. In particular, we will examine how "flat" the world is from the perspective of international trade flows.

Second, the growth in the number of parties to the WTO (currently 150) and the more modest declines in countries' non-tariff barriers to international trade (relative to tariffs due to more difficulty in lowering non-tariff barriers) have lowered the *relative* economic and political costs of forming bilateral and regional – and perhaps even inter-regional – trade agreements. The number of FTAs has exploded, and at a pace rivaling that of the speed of globalization itself. There exists an intricate and seemingly chaotic web – the so-called "spaghetti bowl" – of bilateral, regional and inter-regional FTAs in the Americas and Asia. We will argue that this has created not a "spaghetti bowl" of FTAs but rather a *market* for trade agreements. FTAs – like trade flows – are likely determined under competitive conditions (so-called "competitive liberalization") and recent empirical evidence now shows they can be well predicted based on countries' economic characteristics.

Third, having now experienced 50 years of FTA formation throughout the world and with the development of better statistical techniques, policy makers can examine with actual data the *ex post* gains from economic integration agreements (EIAs). Evidence indicates that the gains from FTAs are much larger than economists' *ex ante* analyses (using "computable general equilibrium models") previously have suggested. We discuss what we conjecture is the *first ex post evidence* of the impact of the GCC's free trade agreement on the member nations' trade, and compare these estimates to those for FTAs in other parts of the world (estimated using similar techniques).

Finally, the paper concludes by arguing that the worldwide "market" for FTAs is now a fact and the market will likely continue to grow in step with globalization. Regions of the world that have not – and will not – form economically-rationalized FTAs and participate in this market will likely lose in relative economic terms, continuing to suffer from falls in relative per capita income and experiencing increased economic and political instability. We address the plausibility of broadening economic integration within the wider Middle East, a potential FTA between the GCC and the European Union, and potential FTAs between the GCC countries and the United States.

Globalization

The starting point is first to define the term "globalization." Thomas Friedman's book *The World is Flat* has widened the world's understanding of the breadth and prevalence of globalization. The term globalization is widely used, but often has different interpretations. The view taken here is that – put as simply as is possible – globalization is the process of "increasing interaction" among people of different nations.[6]

How does one define interaction? In our view, an interaction requires a "flow." For instance, one of the most common measures of international interaction is the flow of goods (or services) from one country (i) to another country (j). These are commonly called "trade flows." While a trade flow is not a direct interaction between two nations' peoples, it is an indirect one; it is a proxy for the time and resources of the people of one nation (i, using the services of their labor, human capital, physical capital and/or natural resource endowments) to produce a product and sell it to another nation's people (j) where the product is valued (in economic terms, the product provides "utility" to the consumers or is useful as an intermediate in production by firms in j). Thus, an important component of globalization is increased international trade flows. Certainly, the increased share of nations' gross domestic products (GDPs) since World War II that are being exported and imported internationally is evidence of globalization.

However, globalization is much wider in scope than simply increased international trade. The people of different nations can exchange claims to wealth in the form of international investment flows. When a multinational firm owned by people in nation i uses its human and/or physical capital in nation j to set up an affiliated plant and to produce goods (or services) in nation j, this foreign direct investment flow from i to j is a measure of globalization. Similarly, portfolio investment flows of financial capital from country i to country j are an international interaction of the people of different nations.

A more direct interaction of two nations' peoples is a migration flow from i to j. This physical flow of people has numerous potential motivations, ranging from family reasons to economic and political reasons. Economists often find one of the major motives for migration is a higher relative wage or income in the destination country relative to the country of origin. Migration flows – as a percent of countries' GDPs – tend to be much lower than trade and investment flows because the cost of the flow (the migration) is much higher than that of international trade and investment. However, despite the high immediate costs that an individual faces when migrating to another country, once in the new host nation that individual can potentially benefit from years of relative economic gains.

Globalization, however, goes beyond just the traditional international economic flows of goods, services, capital and labor. Globalization encompasses flows of culture, values and information (through electronic or non-electronic "flows"). Increased globalization is simply an increased volume of international interactions of innumerable types. Thomas Friedman has argued that the reduced cost of international exchanges and flows of goods, services, labor, capital, culture, values, information, etc., due to falling "natural" barriers to such flows (non policy-related barriers such as the usage of resources to actually transport a product from country i to country j), as well as reduced policy-related barriers (such as tariffs), have increased such interactions and consequently made the world "flat."

Is the World "Flat"?

A comprehensive analysis of the innumerable declines in barriers that have enabled the advance of globalization is beyond the scope of this paper and would form the potential subject of an entire book, or books. However, for the broad audience that Thomas Friedman's *The World is Flat* was intended to address, his title provides extensive and persuasive anecdotes that suggest that the barriers to the international exchange of goods, services, capital, labor, culture, information, etc., have likely declined substantially, and such declines are important – if not the primary – determinants of globalization's advance.

Since this paper concerns regional and inter-regional trade agreements, we must narrow our scope to international trade only. Throughout this analysis, we use the terms "natural" barriers and "policy-related" barriers to trade, and therefore offer some clarification. These two terms are intended to be exhaustive; for instance, we could have used the terms "natural" and "unnatural" (or "man-made") to emphasize that all barriers fall into one category or the other. However, "policy-related" more aptly describes the "man-made" barriers to trade. "Natural barriers to trade" refer more precisely to costs that firms (or households) incur to ship goods (or services) from where they were produced to where they are consumed. In almost all cases, these trade costs require "factors to production" (labor, physical capital and/or human capital) to transport goods; in the absence of these barriers more products could flow across borders, lowering transaction costs, and raising consumer welfare even further. Distance is an enormously important factor deterring trade and constitutes one such "natural" trade barrier, raising both the costs to transport goods as well as to even locate them (i.e., informational trade costs). "Policy-related" barriers to trade refer to government policies that create an additional "cost" of international trade. Tariffs imposed by governments on imports are a classic example. However, non-tariff barriers imposed by governments in many cases can have as great an effect – more so in some cases – as tariffs in reducing international exchanges.

Friedman's book argues that the decline in these two types of barrier has contributed to making the world – in economic terms – virtually flat. His argument suggests that these barriers have now become so trivial that international interaction is virtually costless; that is, international exchange is "frictionless."[7] While two of this paper's authors have argued previously that both types of barriers have declined dramatically in the post-World War II period and the world has become flatter,[8] we argue here that the world is still far from "flat" or "frictionless" in an *absolute* sense. Despite falling transport costs, natural barriers to trade are still not trivial. Despite lower world tariff rates, policy-related barriers to trade are also still not trivial. In fact, in one recent seminal article in the literature on international trade, Anderson and van Wincoop argue that the additional cost to trade the typical good between a producer in one country and a consumer in another (including natural and policy-related barriers) is on average 170 percent of the cost of producing the good.[9] That is, the final cost to a consumer in a final destination of a typical product is almost three times the price at which the producer sold it on the market in the country of origin. A recent paper supporting these arguments is Brakman and van Marrewijk.[10]

Moreover, we will show that an economy such as the United States, which produces 25 percent of the world's GDP, should – in a frictionless world – export and import 75 percent of its GDP. However, the United States exports and imports only 15 percent of its GDP, considerably less than it should in a frictionless world. In a more comprehensive study, Eaton and Kortum provide evidence that the world is far from operating in a setting with no frictions (i.e., a "zero-gravity" economy), adding that the world is likely closer to autarky (i.e., a world of trade barriers that prohibit trade), which hardly suggests a flat world yet.[11] More importantly, however, it suggests that there remains considerable room to further lower natural and policy-related barriers to trade.

Determinants of International Trade Flows

In order to understand the growth in the number of regional and inter-regional FTAs in the world economy, one must first understand the determinants of international trade flows—a major factor in globalization. First, we discuss the economic factors that influence international trade flows. By analyzing empirically what determines trade flows between countries, we can ascertain countries' "potential" trade flows, and then compare these against their actual trade flows. Using the model to predict (potential) trade flows, it suggests for certain countries that "difficult-to-quantify" non-tariff barriers can help explain why numerous countries trade below their potential. Moreover, this explanation further helps us to understand what we believe is a *major rationale* for the growth in regional and inter-regional trade agreements.

The modern theory of international trade usually emphasizes that the main economic rationale for international trade is the "Law of Comparative Advantage," i.e., nations gain by producing goods at relatively low costs and exchanging their products for different goods produced by others at relatively low costs. Therefore, mutually beneficial exchange is possible whenever relative production costs differ prior to trade. For instance, both the UAE and the EU benefit from the UAE specializing in the production of oil (and natural gas) and the EU specializing in the production of manufactures (their respective "comparative advantages"), and the UAE trading oil for manufactures and the EU trading manufactures for oil. This is called *inter-industry trade*. Clearly, both the UAE (and other GCC countries) and the EU could potentially benefit from liberalizing fully their trade policies relative to each other—that is, an EU–GCC free trade agreement. Such a FTA would help both countries to expand upon current production and consumption opportunities. Economists have constructed detailed numerical models of world economies to further predict by what percent trade, national outputs, and consumption levels might increase from such agreements. However, these *ex ante* estimates are typically quite small, an issue to which we will return.[12]

While the Law of Comparative Advantage is very useful to understand trade flows between GCC countries and either the EU or the United States, will it work well to explain the largest trade flows in the world, that is, aggregate trade flows between the EU and the United States? Treating the EU as a "country," the EU and United States have very similar industrial structures, very similar technologies, and very similar

[54]

relative factor endowments (both are relatively abundant in human and physical capital, and relatively scarce in unskilled labor), especially prior to the expansion of the EU from 15 to 27 countries. Why should they trade?

The main type of trade between the EU and the United States is *intra-industry trade*, i.e., the exchange of products belonging to the same industry. The primary motivation for such trade is that consumers in any country have a taste for the "varieties" of goods they consume. If two similar countries (in terms of tastes, technologies, and relative factor endowments) can produce different varieties of the same "good" under economies of scale (that is, lower average production costs with larger production volumes), they can each specialize their production, trade their different varieties with each other, leaving both countries better off.[13] For example, Boeing and Airbus both require large plant setups and incur economies of scale in production. Each jet is produced in one country, but both firms sell their slightly differentiated jets in both markets. More variety enhances welfare, either for final consumption goods or intermediate products for producers.

Both sources of trade can be captured empirically in one simple (statistical regression) equation that has come to be called the "gravity equation" in international trade, owing to its similarity to Newton's "Law of Gravitation." A representative gravity equation in international trade is:

(1) $$X_{ijt} = \beta_0 \left(GDP_{it}\right)^1 \left(GDP_{jt}\right)^1 \left(\left|RFE_{ijt}\right|\right)^\alpha \left(tc_{ijt}\right)^{1-\sigma} \left(P_{it}^{\sigma-1} P_{jt}^{\sigma-1}\right) \varepsilon_{ijt}$$

where X_{ijt} is the real value (in constant prices) of the merchandise trade flow from exporter i to importer j in year t; GDP_{it} (or GDP_{jt}) is the level of real gross domestic product in country i (or j) in year t; $|RFE_{ijt}|$ is the absolute value of the difference in relative factor endowments of countries i and j in year t; tc_{ijt} is a variable (or set of variables) representing any natural or policy-related barrier (or "trade cost") between countries i and j in year t; P_{it} and P_{jt} are "multilateral" price terms that account for trade costs that agents in countries i and j face from all (N) countries (including at home);

[55]

and ε_{ij} is assumed to be a log-normally distributed error term. The theory suggests that $\alpha > 0$ and $\sigma > 1$, so that $\sigma - 1 > 0$.

Equation (1) allows aggregate trade from country i to country j to be influenced by both intra- and inter-industry trade. As shown in Helpman and Krugman, in a frictionless world with N countries and identical relative factor endowments, the trade flow from i to j will be determined *uniquely* by the product of their GDPs; both the economic size and *size similarity* determine the volume of trade from i to j.[14] This explains the vast bulk of trade between, say, the EU and the United States. The theory suggests that the coefficient estimates for GDPs should be unity. Equation (1) also allows for inter-industry (Comparative Advantage) trade, influenced by relative factor endowments. This explains the large amount of trade between the GCC and the EU and between the GCC and the United States, with $|RFE_{ijt}| > 0$. Natural and policy-related trade barriers influence trade flows via two channels. One channel is the bilateral trade cost (tc_{ij}); lower bilateral trade barriers increase bilateral trade. But the bilateral trade flow from i to j can be reduced if any relevant factor lowers the overall "multilateral" price terms in either i or j; $(P_{it}^{\sigma-1} P_{jt}^{\sigma-1})$. P_{it} (or P_{jt}) is an index of the overall multilateral level of resistance that country i (or j) faces. For a given bilateral trade cost (tc_{ijt}), a fall in overall multilateral (price) resistance for country i (P_{it}) will tend to raise the relative price of goods from i to j, thus tending to reduce the flow from i to j. A detailed analysis of the theoretical foundations for a properly-specified gravity equation are found in Anderson and van Wincoop and Baier and Bergstrand.[15] In econometric work that follows, we will not need to measure P_{it} and P_{jt}, as we will control for variation in these factors using binary country-time (it, jt) dummy variables.

Estimation of equation (1) using cross-section or pooled cross-section time-series (i.e., panel) data requires data on trade costs (tc_{ijt}) for every pair of countries. Several studies have found a fairly large number of economic variables that influence tc_{ijt}, cf., Rose (2004). Several of the variables do not vary over time (i.e., "time-invariant" factors), such as bilateral distance between the countries, the product of their land areas, and binary (dummy) variables representing the presence or absence of a common land border, common language, or common colonizing country, cf., Rose (2004). However, other variables influencing tc_{ijt} vary across country pairs ij and across time (t), such as the presence or absence of a free trade agreement, a currency union, or common membership in the General Agreement on Tariffs and Trade (GATT)/WTO.

Equation (2) below is a gravity equation estimated using trade flows among 103 countries in the world using the most important variables typically used:

(2) $\ln (X_{ijt} / GDP_{it}\, GDP_{jt}) =$

$$\beta_0 + \beta_1\, |K/L_i - K/L_j| + \beta_2\, (\ln DIST_{ij}) + \beta_3\, (ADJ_{ij}) + \beta_4\, (LANG_{ij}) + \beta_5\, (FTA_{ijt})$$
$$+\, a_{it} + c_{jt} + \varepsilon_{ijt}$$

where $|K/L_i - K/L_j|$ is the absolute value of the difference in capital-labor ratios of the two countries and the variables representing trade costs (tc_{ijt}) include *time-invariant* (logarithm of) bilateral distance ($\ln DIST_{ij}$), a dummy variable for adjacency *(ADJ_{ij})* which assumes the value 1 (or 0) if the two countries share (or do not share) a common border, and a dummy variable for language *(LANG_{ij})* which assumes the value 1 (or 0) if the two countries share (or do not share) a common language, and a *time-varying* dummy variable for the presence or absence of a free trade agreement *(FTA_{ijt})* which assumes the value 1 (or 0) if the two countries share (or do not share) a FTA. Variables a_{it} and c_{jt} are country-time fixed effects to account for variation in the theoretically-motivated time-varying multilateral price resistance terms P_{it} and P_{jt}. The parameters denoted by β will be termed "coefficient estimates."

We provide representative cross-sectional estimates of variables' coefficient estimates for two years, 1970 and 2000, for reasons that will be discussed in detail later:[*]

---

[*] Note that below each coefficient estimate is the estimate's t-statistic in parentheses.

1970:

(3) $\ln (X_{ijt} / GDP_{it} \, GDP_{jt}) = -12.49 + 0.000006 \, |K_i/L_i\text{-}K_j/L_j|$

$\qquad\qquad\qquad\qquad (-8.25) \quad (2.75)$

$- 0.89(\ln DIST_{ij}) + 0.35(ADJ_{ij}) + 0.84(LANG_{ij}) + 0.61(FTA_{ijt}) + a_{it} + c_{jt} + \varepsilon_{ijt}$

$(-21.58) \qquad\quad (2.38) \qquad\quad (8.33) \qquad\qquad (3.27)$

Within $R^2 = 0.43$; RMSE $= 1.5025$; number of observations $= 4030$

2000:

(4) $\ln (X_{ijt} / GDP_{it} \, GDP_{jt}) = -12.76 + 0.000004 \, |K_i/L_i\text{-}K_j/L_j|$

$\qquad\qquad\qquad\qquad (-27.18) \quad (3.12)$

$- 1.46(\ln DIST_{ij}) + 0.59(ADJ_{ij}) + 0.97(LANG_{ij}) - 0.14(FTA_{ijt}) + a_{it} + c_{jt} + \varepsilon_{ijt}$

$(-35.79) \qquad\quad (4.09) \qquad\quad (9.78) \qquad\quad (-1.36)$

Within $R^2 = 0.38$; RMSE $= 1.7851$; number of observations $= 7302$

Three important results are worth noting. First, the coefficient estimates for the time-invariant trade cost variables are signed as expected; distance has a negative effect on trade and sharing a common land border (language) raises trade. Interestingly, distance has an even *larger* (more negative) effect on trade in 2000 relative to 1970. Second, the presence of a FTA has an economically and statistically significant positive (partial) effect on two members' bilateral trade in 1970, but an economically and statistically insignificant effect in 2000. The 1970 *FTA* coefficient estimate suggests that trade agreements that existed by 1970 – notably, the European Economic Community (EEC), European Free Trade Association (EFTA), Central American Common Market (CACM), and Caribbean Free Trade Agreement (CARIFTA) – had on average *doubled* two representative members' international trade.[16] This result is quite plausible. However, the year 2000 results suggest that – even though there were at least 200 trade agreements in the world by 2000 – the effect of a FTA was *negligible*. This result seems implausible. Third, relative factor endowments have the expected positive effect on the ratio of trade relative to GDPs. This agrees with the fact that differences in relative factor endowments generate inter-industry trade, due to comparative advantage.

Following Baier and Bergstrand, we argue that the coefficient estimate for *FTA* in 2000 is biased downward because of the endogenous self-selection of countries into FTAs, the so-called "competitive liberalization" of countries' trade policies in the world due to the onslaught of globalization.[17] The *FTA* coefficient estimate for 1970 is credible because the EEC, EFTA, etc. were formed for exogenous reasons; for example, the EEC was formed for political and security reasons in the post-World War II era. However, since 1970, competitive liberalization among countries makes inferences about the *ex post* effects of FTAs more difficult to uncover. We now address why.

Understanding the Causes and Consequences
of the Growth of Regionalism

International economists have long argued on behalf of the benefits of globalization, most often in the context of the benefits of specialization arising from reducing trade barriers and enhancing international trade. For instance, most economists argue that reduced trade barriers will allow countries to either specialize production in those products for which they have a natural comparative advantage (either in terms of a relative productivity advantage or a relative factor endowment advantage, such as oil in the UAE) or an "acquired" comparative advantage (products in which the countries' firms incurred fixed setup costs and experience economies of scale in production, such as aircraft in the United States). The main argument is that reduced trade barriers will enhance production specialization within countries, trade between countries, and therefore the per capita incomes of all countries involved (all other things being constant). The latter is the main argument for globalization.

While such reasons argue for reducing trade barriers, they do not explain why governments have increasingly pursued regional and inter-regional trade agreements and foregone emphasis on multilateral trade liberalization. As economists have long argued, preferential (regional and inter-regional) trade agreements by definition exclude some countries, therefore "creating trade" but also "diverting trade" from other producers, and can potentially reduce welfare for participating members. By contrast, multilateral liberalization is nondiscriminatory, and as such does not create that risk. So why pursue preferential trade agreements?

Two prominent reasons have surfaced over the decades. While the GATT has been successful in lowering world tariffs dramatically since World War II and creating trade without "diverting" trade, the relative costs of further multilateral liberalization under the WTO have become very large. The first reason for this is that the number of parties (150) is now more than six times that of the first round of tariff cuts under the GATT in 1947 (23). This has made the costs of negotiation under one umbrella that requires consensus almost prohibitive.

The second reason is that the first eight rounds of GATT reductions focused on reducing the readily observable and easily quantifiable tariff rates. This made coordination of negotiations transparent and accountable. However, this was the easy part. Robert Lawrence distinguishes between "international policies" that deal with border barriers, such as tariffs, and "domestic policies" that are concerned with everything "behind the nation's borders, such as competition and antitrust rules, corporate governance, product standards, worker safety, regulation and supervision of financial institutions, environmental protection, tax codes ..." and other national issues.[18] The GATT and WTO have been remarkably effective in the post-World War II era in reducing border barriers such as tariffs. However, these institutions have been much less effective in liberalizing the domestic policies named above. As Lawrence states, "Once tariffs are removed, complex problems remain because of differing regulatory policies among nations."[19] He argues that in many cases, FTA "agreements are also meant to achieve deeper integration of international competition and investment."[20] Gilpin echos this argument: "Yet, the inability to agree on international rules or to increase international cooperation in this area has contributed to the development of both managed trade *and regional arrangements*."[21] Preeg notes:

> [Free] trade agreements over time, however, have tended to include a broader and broader scope of other trade-related policies. This trend is a reflection, in part, of the fact that as border restrictions [tariffs] are reduced or eliminated, other policies become relatively more important in influencing trade flows and thus need to be assimilated in the trade relationship.[22]

Richard Baldwin[23] and C. Fred Bergsten[24] noted more than a decade ago that there were seemingly strong competitive pressures in the world economy – sensed by nations' governments – that induced governments to liberalize trade both bilaterally and regionally. Governments are pressured by individual voters and firms' lobbies to provide a framework of policies well-suited to both constituencies' interests (maximizing economic welfare and economic profits, respectively). In the face of these pressures and an impasse in multilateral trade and investment liberalization at the WTO level, governments have sought alternative policy changes to improve economic welfare and firms' profits. One alternative – potentially a "building block" for further multilateral liberalization – is regional economic integration agreements (which include bilateral agreements). As mentioned earlier, the proliferation of EIAs over the past fifty years has created what economists refer to as a "spaghetti bowl" of EIAs.

However, the metaphor of a "spaghetti bowl" may be a misleading one, as it suggests that the web of arrangements arose randomly. This could not be further from the truth. As Baier and Bergstrand noted, the determinants of FTAs can be explained theoretically and empirically by a small handful of economic variables and are consistent with the notion of "competitive liberalization" by nations' governments.[25] Pairs of countries (theoretically and empirically) tend to form FTAs the larger and more similar their economic size (GDP), the closer they are to each other, the more remote the two countries are from the rest of the world, and the greater their relative factor endowment differences from each other.[26] However, closer inspection reveals that these are the same factors that determine countries' bilateral trade flows, as discussed in the previous section. Thus, we have systematic evidence that pairs of countries that enter into free trade agreements are countries that trade extensively anyway, which limits the amount of trade diversion from non-member countries. The empirical model predicts correctly 85 percent of the 286 FTAs among pairings of 54 countries in 1996, and 97 percent of the remaining 1,145 country pairs with no FTAs. On net, this suggests that countries that select free trade agreements have "chosen well."

While Baier and Bergstrand provide some guidance for determining which pairs of countries' "bilateralism" (in terms of FTAs) has been "excessive" and which pairs' has been insufficient, an interesting question arises as to whether the proposed FTA between the GCC and the EU would be – in the context of Baier and Bergstrand – "excessive." Moreover, what about a FTA between the GCC and the United States? Are the economic and geographic characteristics of these pairs of economic entities such that – in the context of the theory and empirical model – a FTA would be a "good choice"? We will address this in the final section of the paper.

Ex Post Evaluation of FTAs

The logic behind the argument for trade liberalization is now well accepted in many – if not most – regions of the world. However, while the theory behind the benefits of international trade is well known and widely accepted, quantitative support for large trade, output and welfare effects from trade liberalization is still limited. First, the standard approach to quantifying, *ex ante*, the trade, output and welfare gains from trade liberalization are numerical versions of "general equilibrium" models of economies, such as Purdue University's "Global Trade Analysis Project (GTAP) Model" and the University of Michigan's "Michigan Model."

DeRosa and Gilbert recently summarized some typical predicted trade estimates from implementation of the North American Free Trade Agreement (NAFTA) and South America's Mercado Comun del Sur (Mercosur) using the GTAP model. DeRosa and Gilbert find that this model (arguably) has tended to *underpredict* considerably the trade effects of these two FTAs; such results are common.[27]

As discussed above, *ex post* estimates of the trade effects of FTAs can often be implausibly small. While our results for 1970 are quite plausible, the results for 2000 are implausibly small, given the enormous growth of regional and inter-regional FTAs over the past two decades. Similarly small or theoretically implausible results have been found using more systematic techniques.[28] The natural question to ask is: If the trade effects are so small, why do countries' governments pursue these trade agreements?

Empirical evidence supporting the welfare gains from increasing trade is not very well established. The lack of empirical support for the benefits of trade can be categorized along two lines. First, there is the looming methodological issue in social science of how to actually quantify, *ex post,* the effects of trade-barrier reductions on trade flows, and then the effects of more trade on per capita incomes. Unlike the natural sciences where researchers can conduct "controlled" experiments, social scientists face the problem of identifying the "counterfactual." For example, trade among the six GCC members before 1983 (the year the GCC FTA went into effect) can be measured. Also, trade among the GCC countries after 1983 can be measured. On average, trade increased across country pairs between the two periods. However, that is not necessarily due to the formation of the GCC. The dilemma is that one cannot ever measure *either* pre-1983 trade among GCC countries *in the presence* of the GCC FTA (counterfactual #1), or post-1983 trade among the GCC countries *in the absence* of the GCC FTA (counterfactual #2). The difference between either actual pre-1983 trade and counterfactual #1, or between actual post-1983 trade and counterfactual #2, would provide an estimate of the "effect" of the FTA on members' trade. So the standing methodological dilemma is generating a credible "counterfactual" (a standing issue for *ex post* policy evaluation in any of the social sciences). This issue is behind the seemingly low value of the *FTA* coefficient in equation (4) in the previous section.

The solution then for the first problem (the second problem will be identified shortly) is to try to motivate, ideally based upon sound theory, a *credible* empirical counterfactual. This is where theoretical foundations for the gravity equation surface as important. The gravity equation provides a theoretically-rationalized model for predicting trade flows. Moreover, it works extremely well empirically. In general, R^2 values range from 70–90 percent ($R^2 = 100$ percent implies that the model predicts all bilateral trade flows *exactly*). In fact, applying the model to the UAE's (non-zero) trade flows with more than 100 countries, the R^2 between actual and predicted trade flows was 95 percent.

The second issue is that the *FTA* variable may be endogenous in equations (3) or (4). As discussed earlier, the country pairs that have selected FTAs have "chosen well," in the sense that the economic characteristics that explain FTA_{ijt} also explain trade flows. This raises problems for estimating the "effect" of FTA_{ijt} on X_{ijt}. We believe that this is not a problem for cross-section estimates for 1970 or earlier because competitive liberalization was not present before 1973. By many accounts, the original European Economic Community (EEC) was formed in 1957 for national security (i.e., Cold War) reasons and to secure positive political relations between France and Germany; these are exogenous reasons. The formations of the Central American Common Market (CACM) in 1961 and the Caribbean Free Trade Association (CARIFTA) in 1966 were not endogenous events either, since both regions are remote from Europe. The only agreement that was arguably endogenously created was the European Free Trade Association (EFTA), created in 1961 largely in response to the EEC (for countries that wanted to maintain political independence). Consequently, it is reasonable to argue that the coefficient estimate for *FTA* in 1970 was an unbiased estimate of the "average treatment effect" of a FTA on members' trade; an estimate of 0.61 implies that a FTA increased trade by 86 percent ($e^{0.61}$ = 1.84) or roughly 6 percent per year (over 10 years).

However, the cross-section coefficient estimate for *FTA* in 2000 was negative. Did membership in a FTA actually *decrease* two members' trade? This seems unlikely. We argue that this coefficient estimate is biased downward for the following reason. Suppose two countries have extensive unmeasurable domestic regulations (e.g., internal market shipping regulations) that inhibit trade (causing the actual trade flow to be well below what the gravity equation would predict). The likelihood of the two countries' governments selecting a FTA may be high if there is a large expected welfare gain from potential bilateral trade creation, if the FTA deepens liberalization beyond tariff barriers into domestic regulations (and other non-tariff barriers). Thus, FTA_{ijt} and the intensity of domestic regulations may be positively correlated in a cross-section of data, but the gravity equation error term (representing how much the actual trade flow is below its potential) and the intensity of domestic regulations may be negatively correlated. This reason suggests that FTA_{ijt} and the gravity equation error term are negatively correlated, and the *FTA* coefficient will therefore tend to be *underestimated*.

Fortunately, panel techniques allow a method for avoiding the endogeneity bias. If decisions to form FTAs are slow-moving (as is often the case), they are likely related more to the level of trade than to recent changes in it. Thus, the determinants of *FTA* are likely to be slow moving. Consequently, as shown formally in Baier and Bergstrand, estimation of equation (2) using bilateral fixed (*ij*) effects and country-time effects for exporter (*it*) and importer (*jt*) will likely yield unbiased estimates of the effects of FTAs on trade flows.[29]

Table 2.1 presents the results of estimating such a gravity equation, including a variable for the GCC FTA (*GCC*) and a separate variable for all other FTAs (*FTA_other*). Column (1) of Table 2.1 provides two coefficient estimates, one for *GCC* and one for *FTA_other* (as well as an intercept estimate, which we ignore). We discuss first the coefficient estimates for *FTA_other*. The coefficient estimate for *FTA_other* implies that over the period 1960 to 2000 a typical FTA (other than that of the GCC) increased trade by 57 percent ($e^{0.45} = 1.57$, implying a 57 percent increase). It is worth noting that this is virtually identical to that found in Baier and Bergstrand, using similar techniques (there, $e^{0.46} = 1.58$).[30]

Table 2.1

Panel Gravity Equations with Bilateral Fixed and Country-Time Effects*

Variable	(1)	(2)	(3)	(4)
FTA_other$_{ijt}$	0.45 (8.73)^c	0.24 (3.53)^c	0.24 (3.23)^c	0.31 (3.20)^c
FTA_other$_{ijt-5}$		0.39 (4.79)^c	0.29 (2.89)^c	0.19 (1.76)^b
FTA_other$_{ijt-10}$			0.22 (2.30)^b	0.13 (1.27)
FTA_other$_{ijt+5}$				-0.01 (-0.19)
GCC$_{ijt}$	1.15 (5.66)^c	0.79 (2.57)^c	1.00 (3.18)^c	1.04 (2.97)^c
GCC$_{ijt-5}$		0.45 (1.52)^a	0.42 (1.13)	0.27 (0.75)
GCC$_{ijt-10}$			0.05 (0.16)	0.46 (1.32)^a
GCC$_{ijt+5}$				-0.46 (-1.46)^a
Constant	6.92 (208.74)^c	7.91 (323.18)^c	8.28 (255.42)^c	7.81 (336.46)^c
Total FTA_other	0.45	0.63	0.75	0.50
Total GCC	1.15	1.24	1.47	1.31
Overall R^2	0.1757	0.0672	0.0509	0.0471
Within R^2	0.5169	0.4170	0.3082	0.4192
No. observations	52639	45421	40354	37469

*t-statistics are in parentheses. The dependent variable is the (natural log of the) real bilateral trade flow. a, b, c denote statistical significance at 10, 5, and 1 percent levels, respectively, in one-tailed *t*-tests. Coefficient estimates for bilateral fixed and country-and-time effects are not reported for brevity. "Total" is the sum of the (statistically significant) coefficient estimates for the corresponding FTA.

However, we argue that this estimate of the effect of a typical FTA is low. First, since the data are for five-year intervals (1960, 1965, ... 2000), the coefficient estimate reflects only a five-year trade change. Since most agreements take about 10 years to phase in, and the effects on terms-of-trade may be lagged, we argue that this effect should be spread out over 15 years. This implies that one or two lagged values of the dummy variables should be included as well. Columns (2) and (3) provide estimates including one and two lags, respectively. The sum of the coefficient estimates in column (3) (which are all economically and statistically significant) is 0.75. This estimate implies that after 15 years, the typical FTA increases trade by 112 percent ($e^{0.75} = 2.12$, implying a 112 percent increase), or approximately 5.1 percent per year for 15 years. Finally, column (4) provides estimates adding a *future* level of the trade policy, to determine "causality." This helps to confirm the absence of "feedback' effects from trade to *FTA_other*. The negative and statistically insignificant coefficient estimate for the future level of *FTA_other* implies that there is no reverse causality in the findings; the causality is running from trade policies to trade flows.

The 5.1 percent annual increase in trade – totaling 112 percent over 15 years – is a much larger effect than typically found in *ex ante* computable general equilibrium (CGE) models by economists. For instance, DeRosa and Gilbert indicated that the GTAP estimates of the trade effects of the North American Free Trade Association (NAFTA) were only about one percent for Canada and Mexico, and were negative for the United States after five years (the longest period examined).[31] For Mercosur, GTAP predicted about a 54–63 percent increase in trade for the member countries (Argentina, Brazil, Paraguay and Uruguay). However, it should be noted that the 112 percent increase we found using the gravity model does not include feedback effects on multilateral price resistance terms that on average tend to dampen the partial effect by about 20 percent. Thus, a reasonable "general-equilibrium" effect on trade from a FTA is about 90 percent over 15 years (or about 4.4 percent annually) when including "feedback" effects. However, at 90 percent, this effect for the average FTA is at least 50 percent larger than that suggested for Mercosur by the GTAP model.

In reality, the effects of any two FTAs are unlikely to be the same. Recall the coefficient estimate for *FTA_other* was an "average" effect. Consider now the effect of membership of the GCC. Columns (1)–(4) provide a set of coefficient estimates for *GCC*. Ignoring phasing in of the FTA (which began in 1983) and any lagged terms-of-trade effects, column (1) suggests an effect of 216 percent ($e^{1.15}$). With various lags, columns (2)–(4) suggest effects of 246 percent ($e^{1.24}$), 335 percent ($e^{1.47}$) and 271 percent ($e^{1.31}$) respectively. Since the coefficient estimates for the lagged terms in columns (3) are statistically insignificant from zero, we believe that the columns (2) and (4) estimates are conservatively the most reliable ones. The estimate of a 246 percent increase in trade over the 17 years of the GCC FTA from column (2) implies an average annual increase in trade from the GCC of 7.6 percent.

This estimate is 50 percent larger than that for the average (non-GCC) FTA. Is this plausible? We believe it is for two reasons. First, many of the GCC countries had very high tariff rates and cumbersome non-tariff barriers at the time of its formation. This can potentially contribute to a much larger impact than for many developed countries that had already experienced considerable trade liberalization under the GATT.

Second, this estimate is well within the range found for FTAs signed among similar natural-resource-based economies. In another recent paper by the authors, Baier, Bergstrand and Vidal calculated using similar techniques the trade effects of FTAs over the period 1960–2000 for all of the countries in the Americas.[32] For the CACM, we found a trade effect of 6.3 percent annually. For Mercosur, we found a trade effect of 8.0 percent annually, and for the Group of Three (Colombia, Mexico, and Venezuela) we found a trade effect of 14 percent annually. Thus, the 7.6 percent average annual increase in trade for the GCC is well within the range of estimates for trade effects of FTAs for similar natural resource-based economies that also reduced trade barriers substantially.

Overall, we believe that the *ex post* evidence of the effects of FTAs on trade flows explains the growth of regional and inter-regional FTAs over the past quarter century. The trade effects are often double the size of the *ex ante* estimates generated by economists using standard CGE models. The results for the GCC's FTA are in line with estimates found using the same technique for FTAs in the Americas. Often, FTAs add 6–14 percent average annual growth in trade during periods of transition that can last 10–15 years. The GCC's estimate of 7.6 percent suggests that the GCC FTA had a substantive effect on intra-member international trade.

The Future

As the process of "competitive liberalization" via regional and inter-regional trade agreements continues, countries in the Middle East will need to join this "market" or be left behind in the process of globalization. At stake is a potential decline in per capita incomes, similar to that which occurred during the period 1980–1995 when the Middle East and North Africa (MENA) countries' per capita incomes were stagnant in absolute terms and fell relative to that of the rest of the world. With growing political unrest in many parts of the Middle East, these countries can ill afford stagnant or declining relative per capita incomes. Joining the market for competitive liberalization of trade policies seemingly offers an opportunity for growth that cannot be sacrificed.

Where are the potential opportunities for the Middle East? An analysis for all these opportunities is well beyond the scope of this paper. However, for the GCC countries, two major opportunities are possible. First, since the beginning of this century, the EU and GCC have been in the process of negotiating a FTA. As discussed earlier, the literature now provides more "guidance" as to geographic and economic factors that can help identify FTAs that have the potential to improve the welfare of country pairs. While the GCC countries are quite distant from the economic center of the EU, they are not outside a feasible range. This is illustrated by the example of Turkey, which is not notably closer to the EU than the GCC countries, but yet has a customs union with the EU, and is a serious economic candidate for EU membership. While the GCC's economic size is small relative to the EU, this economic factor is offset by the difference in relative factor endowments that enhance the relative benefits of a FTA. When put into the empirical model of Baier and Bergstrand, our results suggest that the probability of an EU–GCC FTA is 69.6 percent, suggesting that on net the two economic entities would benefit from a FTA.[33]

Regarding the United States, the Bush administration has been pursuing individual FTAs with members of the GCC, such as the UAE. Based upon our economic analysis, we would argue that it is more economically beneficial to pursue a GCC–USA FTA rather than individual bilateral agreements. According to our model, the small economic size of the individual GCC countries and distance from the United States suggests that the amount of trade diversion from individual bilateral agreements would likely offset the trade creation. Moreover, individual agreements between the United States and various GCC countries violate the most recent GCC articles and weaken the operation of the GCC and its commitment to enforcement. Thus, more work needs to be done to evaluate the economic benefits of a GCC–USA FTA.

Conclusions

In concluding this paper, we note several caveats. First, much of the gains from specialization and trade are premised upon the notion that an economy's winners from free trade (e.g., highly skilled workers in developed economies) can compensate the losers from free trade (e.g., the lower skilled workers in developed economies) and still be better off. However, many countries that have pursued trade liberalization have neglected the consequent – and *expected* – redistributions of income. Trade theory – especially that based upon the Law of Comparative Advantage – has long recognized that specialization can lead to large income gains for those employed in the industries where countries have a comparative advantage. However, it can also lead to real income losses for those employed in the industries that have comparative disadvantages. It is the latter workers who are understandably apprehensive about globalization and trade policy liberalizations. However, this does not imply that globalization should not be pursued. Rather, it is the role of nations' governments to design tax policies to redistribute some of the gains of the winners from globalization to the losers in the same country, so that the latter are no worse off than before policy changes. To the extent that more trade generated is intra-industry in nature, the redistribution of income tends to be mitigated.

A second caveat is that – in a world with increased globalization – changing jobs and skill-upgrading become more frequent. Workers need to be prepared for lifelong education and retraining that can ease the adjustment costs between jobs. Many mainstream economists have recently curbed support for the rapid advancement of globalization because estimates of the adjustment costs have been shown to be much higher than previously thought. Whereas decades ago, economists thought the benefits to costs of globalization were 100-to-1, more current estimates put this ratio at 3-to-1. More complete estimates of the adjustment costs have sharply reduced this ratio. Again, it is the role of nations' governments to restructure tax and government expenditure policies to facilitate nations' adjustment to globalization, so that all may potentially benefit from its opportunities.

MIGRATION AND FREEDOM OF MOBILITY

Globalization, Migration and Challenges to States

Robert K. Schaeffer

W hat does globalization mean for international migration patterns? And what challenges does it pose to governments and states? It is difficult to provide a general answer to these questions because globalization is not a homogeneous process. Instead, globalization takes different shapes in different parts of the world. Because cross-border migration is shaped by political and economic developments specific to different regions and states, it is important to use an historical and comparative approach to identify developments that have contributed to migration and to assess the challenges that demographic change creates for origin and recipient states.

This paper first examines migration from dictatorships in southern Europe to democratic states in western Europe during the 1960s and 1970s, as well as the movement of people from dictatorships in East Germany, Cuba and Vietnam.

Dictatorship and Migration

In the 1960s, dictatorships in Portugal, Spain and Greece allowed male workers to migrate in large numbers to democratic states in western Europe, with workers from democratic states like Italy and Turkey also joining the exodus. Roughly 100,000 people migrated from each of these countries annually, and by 1970 about one million workers had migrated as "guest workers."[1] Demand for low-wage labor was strong in democratic European states because their economies were growing rapidly at this time.

Dictatorships in southern Europe allowed workers to leave because migration actually provided a number of benefits. First, migration reduced domestic unemployment, which was high because the economies of these countries were growing at a much slower pace than member states of the European Common Market. Second, migration was thought to reduce domestic dissent. Leaders of these regimes worried that if young, unemployed and unmarried men sat around in cafés complaining about their economic circumstances, they might develop into critical, political opponents of the government. Thus, sending young men abroad reduced the risk of political opposition. Third, migrant workers sent part of their wages home as remittances, amounting to approximately US$1 billion for each million migrants.[2] Remittances were an import source of hard currencies and used to import oil and manufactured goods by states facing persistent trade deficits.[3] Remittances, together with income from the tourist industries in these countries – what one scholar described as "Market Fascism" – enabled the dictatorships to sustain modest levels of economic development.[4]

However, global developments in the 1970s created problems for states that relied on migration as key to their political legitimacy and economic development. The 1971 dollar devaluation, Soviet grain shortages throughout the decade, and the 1974 OPEC oil embargo created a series of problems for dictatorships in southern Europe. These economic developments triggered a recession in western Europe where governments subsequently expelled many migrant workers. The recession also resulted in a decline in the numbers of tourists visiting southern Europe, which also resulted in a loss of income and increased unemployment in these states. In addition, returning workers meant reduced remittance income, raised levels of domestic unemployment and growing political unrest, as well as contributing to trade deficits. Altogether, these developments created a serious economic crisis for these regimes.[5] Added to this shared economic downturn were separate political crises – revolution in Portugal, the death of Franco in Spain, and the Greek military misadventure in Cyprus – that led to the collapse of dictatorships in all three countries during the mid-1970s.

For democratic states in Europe, the termination of guest worker programs and the expulsion of migrant workers were not wholly successful. Many migrants resisted expulsion and managed to stay on— for example, Turkish migrants living in Germany, who over the next 30 years established large groups of permanent residents without German citizenship.

During this period, Communist dictatorships in East Germany, Cuba and Vietnam also adopted policies to manage the exit of domestic migrants, largely to reduce dissent. Between 1949 – when Germany was partitioned (see discussion of partition below) – and 1961, 3.4 million East Germans (one-sixth of its population) left the country. In 1961, the regime sealed the inter-German border and built the Berlin Wall to stem the exodus, which had created labor shortages and threatened to bring the economy to a halt. However, even with the Wall in place the regime still managed a slow migration to the West, allowing 616,006 East Germans to leave the country between 1962 and 1988. It permitted another 29,670 political dissidents to leave the country in return for "ransoms" from the West German government, which paid about DM 100,000 for each migrant.[6] By 1989, another 500,000 East Germans had applied for official permission to leave the country.[7]

East German migration policies, like those in southern Europe, were designed to dissipate dissent and secure remittances and ransoms as income, but the collapse of the communist regime in Hungary and the opening of its borders in the summer of 1989, upset the East German government's migration management program. In 1989, 343,854 East

[77]

Germans left the country and by the end of the year, 50,000 were migrating each week. This rapid exodus brought the economy to a standstill. Demonstrators in Leipzig, who demanded the right to leave, created a political crisis that ultimately led to the collapse of the regime.[8]

The communist government in Cuba also adopted policies designed to manage outward migration. Between 1965 and 1973, the government allowed 250,000 people to leave the island and in 1980 permitted the departure of 125,000 more citizens from the port of Mariel. The regime in Vietnam, like that of Cuba, also allowed tens of thousands of "boat people" to exit the country after the war ended in 1975.

Regimes in Cuba and Vietnam allowed migrants to vent political dissent since they also reaped the economic benefits of remittance income. Although the migrants who left these countries opposed the government, they still sent money back to relatives, simultaneously providing regimes with the hard currency they needed to pay for essential imports and helping them to survive politically.[9]

For dictatorships in Portugal, Spain, Greece and East Germany, rapid demographic changes associated with cross-border migration created serious economic and political problems that contributed to their demise. The regimes in Cuba and Vietnam were more successful at "managing" migration, and have remained in power, but large migration flows have created severe economic and political problems for dictatorships around the world.

Partition and Migration

In the postwar period, partition in Korea, China, Vietnam, India, Pakistan, Palestine, Cyprus, Germany, Ethiopia, Yugoslavia, Czechoslovakia and the Soviet Union triggered large-scale migrations across newly created borders. For example, 17 million people crossed the Indo-Pakistani border in the six months following partition in India, which was the largest, fastest migration in human history. In Palestine between 700,000 and 900,000 people crossed borders following the UN partition in 1948.[10]

Partition-induced migrations led to a number of immediate and ongoing problems. Firstly, the great powers that partitioned these countries and the governments that emerged in divided states did not expect people to migrate in large numbers, and so were unprepared to deal with the related problems that emerged. Secondly, these migrations were extremely disruptive and led, in some cases, to conflict and violence. For example, one million people died in India and Pakistan as a result of partition and migration-related violence.[11] Thirdly, although many people migrated across newly drawn frontiers, groups of people stayed behind, creating large residual minority populations. For example, there are as many Muslims living in India as in Pakistan—an "Islamic" state. Fourth, governments in many of the divided states passed laws or adopted policies that effectively discriminated against residual minority populations, sometimes denying them citizenship in the country of their birth. This led to a fifth problem; disenfranchised minorities often protested their treatment by states and organized anti-government movements, which were supported by governments in neighboring states.

Problems associated with partition-related migrations are particularly evident today in Israel, the occupied territories and neighboring states. Partition-related migration led to the creation of refugee camps in neighboring states, cross-border conflicts between Israel and Palestinian insurgents, and conflicts between Palestinian insurgents and Arab governments in Jordan and later Lebanon. Migration contributed to conflict within and between states in the region, repeated Arab–Israeli wars, and to the wider economic and political problems associated with oil embargo and superpower intervention in the region.[12] Although these problems originated in 1948 (if not before), they continue to contribute to conflict in the region today.

Whilst some states were partitioned along secular, ideological lines (Korea, China, Vietnam, Germany), others were divided along ethnic-religious lines (India, Pakistan, Palestine, Cyprus, Yugoslavia, Czechoslovakia, Ethiopia and the Soviet Union). In Yugoslavia and the Soviet Union, the break-up of federal states led to civil war in some of the constituent republics (parts of Yugoslavia, republics in the Caucuses), the forcible expulsion of residents across newly created international borders, and intramural conflicts between governments controlled by ethnic majorities and residual ethnic minorities.

In extreme cases, such as in Rwanda, ethnic conflict was exacerbated by economic problems associated with globalization—the fall of world coffee prices and of export earnings for Rwanda. This led first to genocide and then to the exit of genocidaires into the Congo. Exiles in the Congo then launched cross-border raids on Tutsi forces in Rwanda. This cross-border conflict led to an invasion of the Congo by armies from Rwanda and Uganda, which in turn contributed to the collapse of the Mobutu regime and triggered a wider, multi-facetted civil war in the Congo. In a similar fashion, the exit of refugees from the Darfur region of Sudan into Chad as a result of ethnic conflict has created economic and political problems for governments in both countries, as well as for the international aid community.

Taken together, partition, ethnic conflict and genocide have triggered disruptive cross-border migrations that have created a series of ongoing problems for the states where they originate, neighboring states, and other states around the world.

Economic Development and Migration

In recent years, economic developments associated with globalization have contributed to migration and created both problems and opportunities for states that send and receive cross-border workers.

For small states, rapid economic development has encouraged the entry of large numbers of foreign workers. In Latvia, "foreign" workers make up 19.5 percent of the population; in Estonia, they make up 15.2 percent; in Singapore, they make up 42.6 percent; and in the United Arab

Emirates (UAE), they make up 71.4 percent.[13] In the Baltic states, the issue of "foreign" workers is complicated by the fact that most of the Russian residents were born in the country and were defined as "foreign" only after these states became independent of the Soviet Union in 1992, although the outward migration of citizens from the Baltics to other states in the European Union (EU) has also been accompanied by a new influx of workers from the former Soviet Union.[14]

For Singapore and the UAE, rapid economic growth has encouraged the entry of foreign workers from various countries. Migrants to Singapore come from the Philippines, Malaysia and Indonesia. Migrants to the UAE come from Pakistan, India, Bangladesh, Yemen, Jordan and also from the Philippines. Some demographers estimate that the number of illegal migrants in Singapore is much higher than official reports suggest.[15]

Both Singapore and the UAE benefit from the influx of low-wage workers and their willingness to take jobs that domestic workers, who are in short supply, are unwilling or unable to perform. The sending countries benefit from worker remittances, which are a source of foreign exchange earnings and of capital that contributes to domestic economic development. India received US$9 billion in remittance income in 2002, a sum greater than all direct foreign investment in the country, while Bangladesh received US$2 billion.[16] In the Philippines, the migration of workers to Singapore, the Middle East and the United States provides an important source of foreign exchange and domestic capital.

Migration to Singapore and the UAE differs in one important respect: women make up the majority of migrants to Singapore, while most of the migrants to the UAE are male. This is significant because women employed as domestic workers (maids and nannies) in Singapore work in relative isolation and under close supervision; whereas men employed in service and manufacturing industries in the UAE work in groups. The latter setting is more conducive to collective action than the former, although the ability of men to organize collectively is weakened by the fact that they are drawn from different countries and speak different languages, which inhibits their ability to collaborate.

The large scale of migration to small states poses challenges both for receiving and sending states. For Singapore and the UAE, the large number of foreign workers can challenge the linguistic and cultural identity of domestic citizens and means that governments have to devote considerable resources to managing and policing large immigrant populations. Although they prefer to allow only unmarried men and women to immigrate, foreign workers still bear children who, potentially, have some claim to rights that the initial immigrants do not possess. There is also the problem of expulsion. In the event that economic growth slows, or they experience an economic recession associated with the cyclical effects of globalization, governments may want some foreign workers to exit. (The Saudi Arabian government, for example, has said it wants three million guest workers to leave by 2013.) But this may be difficult to achieve, as in western Europe, where many Turkish workers stayed in Germany despite government efforts to persuade them to leave, a problem also evident in the United States.

For sending states, slowed economic growth and the expulsion of workers from Singapore or the UAE would reduce remittance income and foreign exchange and increase domestic unemployment—problems that in the 1970s contributed to economic crises for dictatorships in southern Europe.

Finally, there is the possibility that sending countries might take a protective, political interest in workers migrating to other states, becoming advocates on their behalf. Russia does this in the Baltic states, putting political and economic pressure on the small republics to improve the status of Russian residents there. The United States has done the same, putting political and economic pressure on the Cuban government. Likewise, the government in the Philippines has, in the past, made a political issue of the treatment of Filipino workers in Singapore and other receiving countries.

Democratization, EU Expansion and Migration

Democratization in eastern Europe and the subsequent expansion of the European Union has led to large-scale migration within the EU and to the entry of workers from countries outside the EU.

About two million Romanians (8 percent of the population) have migrated across Europe in recent years, primarily to Spain and southern Italy. At the same time, 800,000 Poles and 600,000 Belgians have left to work in other countries.[17] Indeed, so many people have left Romania and Poland that local labor shortages have developed and the government has allowed the entry of workers from outside the EU to meet demand. The Polish government has permitted workers from the Ukraine and former Soviet republics to enter; the Romanian government has permitted the entry of workers from as far away as China.[18]

As we have seen, receiving countries have benefited from the influx of low-wage workers; and sending countries from remittances and foreign exchange earnings; remittances from Romanian workers amounted to US$12 billion in 2006.[19] But a number of problems have also emerged. First, although migrant workers may be EU citizens, they could find themselves treated differently from those citizens in destination countries, since EU member states can adopt separate policies toward migrants. The Scandinavian states, the Netherlands, the United Kingdom and Ireland have relatively "open" policies, while Germany, France and Belgium have fairly "restrictive" policies. The differential treatment of migrants can create problems in diplomatic relations between sending and receiving countries. Furthermore, there is a fair amount of "illegal" entry by EU migrants, so states must manage and police migrant populations from EU countries as well as migrants from outside the EU who have been resident for a long period (e.g. Turks in Germany) or who have recently arrived.

Second, European states have granted rights to "new" immigrants, who came from states that were recently admitted to the EU, while withholding rights from "old" immigrants who came from countries outside the EU – i.e., from Turkey and former European colonies – and have been residents for a long time. For example, 20 percent of the foreign population of Germany – mostly Turkish – has lived in Germany for more than 30 years. This has created antagonism between "new" and "old" migrants. Recent migrations have also created antagonism between migrants (both old and new) and domestic populations, contributing to the rise of anti-immigrant and racist sentiment in many countries. These problems tend to become more acute when economic growth slows and unemployment rises.

Large-Scale Migration in Large States:
the United States and China

In recent years, developments associated with globalization have prompted large-scale migrations in the United States and China. Although both countries have relatively "closed" or restrictive migration policies, the demand for low-wage labor has encouraged migration *despite* policies that would prevent it.

In the United States, the adoption of the North America Free Trade Agreement (NAFTA) in 1992 resulted in a series of developments that contributed to a surge in cross-border migration and illegal entry from Mexico and other Central and South American countries.[20] This increased the foreign-born population in the United States, which had been created by earlier waves of both legal and illegal immigration. The United States has more than 38 million foreign-born immigrants, and perhaps one-third of them are "illegal aliens."[21] Although workers who enter the United States illegally are subject to arrest and deportation, they can also obtain some benefits – send their children to school, pay taxes, receive pensions, obtain medical care, obtain driver's licenses – despite their legal status.

Migration into the United States is driven both by the demand for low-wage workers in the United States and by high rates of unemployment and poverty in Mexico and Central America. For Mexico, remittances from migrant workers amount to about US$6.5 billion annually, providing hard currency to the state and capital to the people.[22]

Large-scale, legal and illegal migration into the United States poses several problems. First, migration and the growing Hispanic population have contributed to anti-immigrant sentiment. In some cases, private citizen's groups and militias have been organized to patrol the border, prevent illegal entry, and report people suspected of immigration violations to the authorities. Second, the influx of low-wage workers has kept wages low for other indigenous workers in some industries and contributed to poverty, which the government has tried to address through its anti-poverty programs. Third, in the wake of 9/11, the government has spent heavily on border security, in part to prevent the entry of "terrorists," and has increased spending on bureaucracies responsible for policing borders and immigrants.

These developments pose several, familiar problems for sending states. Mexico is concerned about the treatment of Mexican workers and nationals in the United States and the effect on remittance income and domestic unemployment if large numbers of Mexican workers are deported from the United States or denied entry.

Globalization has also spurred large-scale migration in China, which is unusual because the current number of migrants in China – 114 million – is so large.[23] It is also unusual because it is Chinese workers who migrate, not foreigners. But while these migrants are Chinese citizens, they are treated as "illegal aliens" by their own government, and can be arrested and deported to rural areas if they violate the government's residential permit system (*hukou*), which requires citizens to apply for government permission to change their place of employment or residence.[24] While migrants are closely monitored by the 65 million members of the Communist Party, they are allowed to migrate illegally because they provide a vast supply of low-wage labor that drives down wages for "legal" Chinese workers.

The Chinese system, which encourages large-scale migration but treats migrants as illegal workers, creates problems for other states because it suppresses wages for low-paid workers in other countries and diverts foreign investment from other low-wage economies, such as India and Mexico, to China. By capturing a global, comparative advantage in low-wage labor, Chinese economic development has come at the expense of economic development in countries that have recently democratized.[25] This system is also a problem for foreign investors because they are required to hire legal Chinese workers, while Chinese firms can hire lower-paid illegal workers, which gives them a competitive advantage over foreign firms doing business in China.

Citizens, Denizens and Subjects

States assign different legal statuses to cross-border migrants.[26] Historically, states have divided resident populations into three groups. The first group is treated as "citizens," which means they can vote, bear arms, hold property and access the government's legal system. In the past, states granted these rights only to adult males who were born or naturalized in the country. In the second group, states treat some people as "denizens," which means they have some but not all of the rights given to citizens. In the past, states granted restricted rights as denizens to women, minors and immigrants. In the third group, states treat some people as "subjects," which means they possess few, if any, legal rights. In the past, slaves, debtors, indentured servants, convicted criminals, illegal aliens, indigenous peoples, the mentally ill and people with tuberculosis were assigned this status.

Over the last 200 years, states have generally extended the status of citizenship to a wider group of people and narrowed the definition of denizen and subject, though they still remain as status categories, even in the most "democratic" states. It is important to note, however, that these categories have been challenged and contested by people assigned them, and many have objected to the unequal rights that these legal assignments confer. Over the last 200 years, women, slaves and immigrants have objected to their positions as denizens and/or subjects and in many states have demanded and even achieved equal rights. Because migrants are among those who have objected to their unequal legal status, and because domestic populations often object to their demands, migration has created legal challenges to states that send and receive migrants. Migration can test a state's legal system and the particular definitions of citizen, denizen and subject that it employs. In the end, this may be the most important challenge that migration poses to states.

4

Immigration and Outsourcing: The Growing Fault Lines and Aftershocks of Globalization

John Mahon

Prime Minister Tony Blair of the United Kingdom and Jose Maria Aznar Aznar of Spain proposed at last year's (2002) European Council meeting meeting in Seville that the European Union withdraw aid from countries that did not take effective steps to stem the flow of illegal emigrants to the EU.

... Australia received severe condemnation worldwide last summer (2002) when a special envoy of the UN High Commissioner for Human Rights exposed the deplorable conditions in detention camps that held Afghan, Iranian, Iraqi, and Palestinian asylum seekers who had landed in Australia.[1]

Immigration has the potential to cause a variety of problems, as is evident in the opening quotes above. Immigration, migration and outsourcing are the products of globalization and the internationalization of commerce. Catastrophes (both human and natural), personal choice, and organizational economic decisions fuel these actions. They pose problems for individuals and families, for businesses, for governmental authorities and for societies and culture. The pace of immigration, emigration and outsourcing has accelerated in the last few years and shows absolutely no sign of slowing in the foreseeable future. As a consequence, they can no longer be seen or treated as aberrations or as problems that will resolve themselves in the short run.

In this analysis, we shall examine globalization as an "earthquake" affecting the world community and, as we shall see below, will discuss a specific aspect of globalization that is not always recognized. As with any earthquake, there are fault lines where pressure is increased or decreased, and often the aftershocks of a quake are equally damaging, or at the very least, surprising. Immigration, migration and outsourcing are new fault lines, encouraged and enhanced by the accelerating pace of globalization, that continue to create "aftershocks" to this very day. Governments are now faced with the erosion of national culture and identity. How will the nature of citizenship, politics and religion change and what responses will be required of government, business and society? What are the ramifications of continued increases in immigration, migration and outsourcing on domestic economies, politics, society and social responsibility/ethics?

In the past, such questions were unimportant, as the ability for individuals to move across borders permanently was quite limited (owing to distance, language, cultural issues and the like). However we are moving toward a world without borders where commerce can be conducted electronically on a continuous basis. There are three interesting examples of how nations deal with such issues in the United States, the United Arab Emirates (UAE), Sudan and adjacent nations. In this presentation we shall look at how these nations are – or indeed are not – dealing with challenges related to immigration, migration and outsourcing. From this brief analysis we may then develop some suggestions for policy makers and business executives.

Immigration and Migration

Immigration patterns have changed significantly as we have moved from the twentieth to the twenty-first century.[2] People have always migrated from one area to another for a variety of reasons, which we shall discuss below, and new reasons and causes for migration continue to emerge in the 21st century.[3] It is clear, however, that reduced travel restrictions and citizenship requirements, as well as the globalization of business and society are having an impact. Adding to this mix as a "counter balance" is the growth of outsourcing. As will be discussed below, outsourcing of jobs can serve both to entice a population to stay in its current location and attract immigrants seeking employment.[4]

As a simple indicator of the significance of these changes, consider the following: in 1969, approximately 70 million individuals migrated worldwide. This is the equivalent of the entire populations of Denmark and France packing up their personal effects and moving elsewhere—try to imagine the impact on the nations receiving these immigrants and on the nations losing this precious human resource. In 2007 it was estimated that more than 270 million individuals migrated—an increase of nearly 286 percent. The scale of this migration is the equivalent of the entire populations of France, Germany, Greece, Iran, Saudi Arabia, Syria and Yemen moving elsewhere. The United Nations in 2000 estimated that 140 million people (2 percent of the entire world's population) resided in a nation other than that in which they were born—in other words these are people who have immigrated.[5] According to the International Migration Institute, over 200 million people today reside in a nation where they were not born and in excess of 14 million are refugees.[6] There are observers who have noted that if we considered the number of people migrating and immigrating as one collective mass, this would be the equivalent of the third largest nation in the world on the basis of population. The amount of money that migrants and immigrants send back to their prior home nation exceeds the total of worldwide foreign aid. By any measure, be it population size or economic impact, migration and immigration have profound impacts.

It is important at the outset of this analysis to distinguish between migration and immigration. Migration is the movement of people as a result of problems and challenges in their home nation. Usually migration is of short-term duration, with individuals not planning to establish residency in the host nation but hoping to return home as quickly as possible. Migration can be seen as either forced or encouraged. Forced migration is often a result of natural disasters (e.g. earthquake, famine or flood), but human catastrophes can also drive relocation (e.g. civil war, genocide or persecution). The demands on the host country of such migrants can be sudden and expensive. Governmental social agencies and non-governmental organizations can be overwhelmed by demands to satisfy food, shelter, education and health care needs. Such demands can disrupt the economy and stability of the host nation, cause resentment toward the migrant population and in some cases even alter the political leadership of the host nation. One only has to look at the challenges facing the Syrian government as it deals with the influx of Iraqi citizens and how the Iraqi's themselves attempt to adapt to a much longer than anticipated stay in Syria.

Encouraged migration is where a nation seeks temporary workers to work in specific sectors (e.g. in construction, agriculture, hospitality) as the economy expands[7] and/or the local resident population either does not desire to do the necessary work or is of insufficient size to perform the task. When the economy contracts or the need for the workers ends (e.g. construction is completed, the harvest is over or the tourist season closes) they are sent back to their home countries. The United Arab Emirates, as we shall see below, is an exemplar of encouraged migration.

Table 4.1 provides some comparative data on (im)migration patterns. If we focus more narrowly on a specific region, we obtain the results shown in Table 4.2 for nations in the Middle East.

Table 4.1
(Im)migration Patterns (est. 2007)

Nation	per 1,000 pop.
European Union	1.6
India	-0.05
Liberia	26.86
United States	3.05
United Arab Emirates	26.04

[90]

These are net migration figures (those entering and leaving in a given year). Thus, a negative number means that the nation is losing more individuals than it is gaining. High levels of migration can cause problems (increased unemployment and potential ethnic strife [if people are entering the country]) or a reduction in the labor force, perhaps in certain key sectors (if people are leaving the country).Note the very high levels of net migration into Liberia and the UAE.

Table 4.2 shows some interesting patterns. Only Bahrain, Jordan and the UAE are gaining population as a result of migration and immigration patterns. The UAE is a unique case as it is experiencing enormous economic growth and extensive construction projects. As a result, workers from other countries are literally pouring into the UAE to provide the necessary work force for economic growth—but the nation is not affording these migrant workers citizenship. It is easy to imagine, as time unfolds, the pressure that will build from these migrant workers for political representation.

Table 4.2
(Im)migration Patterns (est. 2007)

Nation	per 1,000 pop.
Bahrain	0.6
Egypt	-0.21
Iran	-4.29
Jordan	6.11
Saudi Arabia	-5.95
United Arab Emirates	26.04

Immigration is where individuals move from one country to another for the explicit goal of establishing citizenship and permanent residence in the host country. Individuals immigrating are leaving their home country for another. There are numerous reasons for such immigration—e.g. improved standard of living, educational opportunities and the like.

Recent data suggests, for example, that 66 percent of individuals who leave China for education do not return. Immigration and migration can have impacts on the ethnic makeup of a host nation as shown in Table 4.3. Note the differences in the ethnic makeup of the population across the nations shown. The UAE, with its explosive growth, small native population and demand for workers, has a significant level of diversity. In fact, some observers suggest that the percentage of native Emiratis in the population of the UAE will drop below 1 percent by 2025 if current trends continue.

Table 4.3
Impact of Immigration/Migration

India	China	Egypt	Saudi Arabia	United Arab Emirates
72% Indo-Aryan	91.9% Han-Chinese	98% Egyptian	90% Arab	19% Emirati
25% Dravidian	8.1 %Other	2% Other	10% Afro-Asian	23% Arab and Iranian
3% Other				50% South Asian
				8% Other

What will it mean to a nation when the indigenous population of citizens who rule that nation come to represent an increasingly smaller portion of the overall population? Furthermore, what does this mean for the culture of the nation, its politics, economics and religious and business practices? A revered former ruler of the United Arab Emirates, Sheikh Zayed Bin Sultan Al Nahyan, once observed that "A nation with no past has neither a present nor a future." How does a nation dealing with rapid migration and huge numbers of migrant workers maintain/remember its past as it moves forward into the future?

Cross-border immigration is usually subject to regulations, legal procedures and safeguards. In many cases, immigration from one area or nation to another is limited (to a specific number or quota), and individuals may have to wait several years to obtain an immigration visa.[8]

As a consequence there are numerous examples of illegal immigration—where an individual seeks to establish permanent residency in the host country but cannot under quotas or because immigration laws ban their specific skills (the skills might be in abundance in the host country or the host country may not need certain skills/abilities in immigrant populations).

According to John Slocum, in the developed world there has been an "unprecedented increase" in undocumented (illegal) immigration.[9] In the United States, numerous sources estimate the undocumented population to be between 10 and 12 million; in Europe it is estimated to be in the range of 6 to 15 million. The range of these estimates reflects the difficulties inherent in obtaining reliable data and statistics on illegal populations.

Curiously, the movement of people from one nation to another can take on unexpected characteristics based on perceptions. As individuals move to a new nation and acquire a job, the perception is that jobs are plentiful. The ability of a nation to deliver on this perception is, as noted earlier, driven by its absorptive capacity to generate jobs and to employ those entering the nation. The problem is that the ability (or absorptive capacity) of a nation to employ (im)migrants is far from unlimited.

The Aftershock/Fault Model

Imagine a nation that experiences a sudden large influx of people as a result of migration/immigration (also consider the impact of such a loss of people on the nation from which they are migrating). The United Arab Emirates is experiencing just such an unfolding situation.

Clearly the economic and political strength and stability of any nation receiving an influx of people is important here in terms of its absorptive capacity, but let us consider two additional examples that will clarify some of the material discussed thus far.

Migration from Mexico to the United States

The United States has had to deal with migration from its southern neighbor, Mexico, for some time. This migration occurs both legally and illegally, but the impacts on the states bordering Mexico (including the United States) are quite profound. The migration of Mexican citizens to the United States is often driven by the opportunity for an improved standard of living, and since we are using the term migration very specifically here, the individuals are not seeking to become permanent residents.

Interestingly enough, this improved standard of living is not achieved in the United States but in Mexico, as a result of the migrant population sending US dollars back home. They are in the United States in order to earn a better living than they could in Mexico, and when they retire or achieve a certain economic status they seek to return home. As such, they have no intention of assimilating into the culture and society of the host country (i.e. to become immigrants).

Let us explore, briefly, what the impacts of migration are on both countries. The migration of Mexican citizens to the United States has impacts on the economy, on politics, on culture/society, and on social responsibility/ethics that are both subtle and direct. The subtle impacts are the alteration on the "micro-culture" of the towns and cities experiencing this explosive migration.

When individuals migrate from Mexico to the United States they are often willing to work for lower wages, for cash and/or for less – or no – benefits (such as health care, retirement benefits, social security, etc.). US employers are tempted to hire these individuals as they provide organizations with clear cost savings compared to employing US citizens. This could afford such organizations short-term strategic advantages in terms of their competition with other firms in their industry, and lead to unemployment among citizens of the United States.

Immigrants in the United States are also having an impact on the political debate regarding how to tackle illegal immigration, and on the historical alignment of the democratic and republican parties not only in the states bordering Mexico, but throughout the entire country. The rhetoric and political debate on how to combat illegal immigration have become quite heated and intense and are of particular importance now, considering that this paper is being written in the midst of a US presidential campaign.

Immigrants from Mexico are having an impact on the culture and society in the areas in which they are located. Cuisine choices in these areas change, teaching in public schools is altered, internal materials published in organizations have changed (much of which is now produced in both Spanish and English), and social services and welfare programs are affected by migrant patterns. Finally, considerations of social responsibility and ethics change as the demands of migrants on NGOs and other societal organizations differ from those stemming from US citizens. Several NGOs have been established to aid these migrants and to protect them from deportation. The employers who hire these migrants are breaking the law, or at the very least are exhibiting poor ethical choices.

Fortunately, the United States is a wealthy country and has been able to absorb this influx of migrants and the associated costs, but there is increasing concern over the nation's ability to continue to absorb such costs in the future.

As these individuals live and work in the United States they send their earnings home to families in Mexico. Thus, Mexico benefits from an influx of foreign currency and if the workers stay in the United States long enough they become eligible for health care and retirement benefits. To the extent this occurs, the Mexican government is relieved of the costs of health care and retirement benefits for these workers. In short, this is a win-win situation for Mexico.

One final observation; Mexico has very tight border restrictions with its neighboring countries and is aggressive in deporting illegal migrants. Yet when the United States attempts to tighten its borders with Mexico, the Mexican government protests such actions as "inhumane."

[95]

Migration from Sudan and Iraq

The recent tragedy in the Sudan – involving famine, civil war and genocide – has led to the migration of Sudanese to neighboring countries including Chad, Congo, Egypt and Ethiopia.

There are major differences between this example and that of Mexicans migrating to the United States. The motivations for migration are quite different. In the Mexico–US example, the primary reason for migration is to achieve a higher standard of living. In this example, however, the primary reason is not economic but is inspired by simple survival. As such, these migrants are not seeking (immediate) employment but are looking for food, shelter, clothing and protection. As the dangerous situation in Sudan continues to prevail, migrants will remain in their host countries—and if it exists for long enough, these migrants may seek permanent residency. Finally, the surrounding nations do not have the same degree of absorptive capacity as that of the United States. That is, Chad does not have the same level of resources that Egypt has to deal with these migrants—and both countries do not have the same level of resources as the United States to deal with the influx of migrants. As such, these migrants place a greater strain on host countries' resources, and the longer they remain in these countries, the greater the potential impacts.

According to Sudarsan Raghavan, nearly 2 million Iraqis – approximately 8 percent of the pre-war population – have migrated to Jordan, Syria and Lebanon.[10] Another 1.7 million have moved inside Iraq from one area to another seeking safety. According to the United Nations, 50,000 Iraqis a month flee the country. Initially only the wealthy fled Iraq, but as the strife has continued, the poor have begun to leave in large numbers. This migration is particularly problematic for Jordan, which is already home to nearly 2 million Palestinian refugees (about one third of the entire population of the nation) and the nearly 1 million Iraqi migrants have further strained the resources of the nation. Iraqis are blamed for rising fuel, food and housing problems in Jordan, for taking scarce jobs and for bringing a different culture to their new host nation. There is also growing concern that the sectarian strife in Iraq might also spread to the refugees in the neighboring host countries. Jordan views these individuals as temporary visitors and is making it increasingly difficult for Iraqis to establish legal residency in the nation.[11]

These examples demonstrate the enormous implications for governments, non-governmental organizations (NGOs), business organizations and for the individuals involved. Figure 4.1 is a very brief attempt to capture the impacts of (im)migration – as addressed by the previous examples – on major elements of modern society. It is by no means exhaustive of the impacts, but illustrative of the possible alternative dynamics as a consequence of (im)migration.

Figure 4.1
The Aftershock/Fault Model

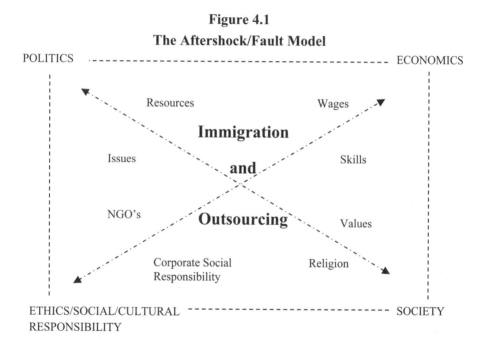

Clearly, politics in a nation are impacted by how the economy performs, and politics have an impact on the performance of the economy. Likewise, economic performance has an impact on and is impacted by the overall cultural and societal context. The cultural/societal context is impacted by and impacts the practice of corporate social responsibility and ethics, and thus we arrive back at the politics of a nation. Across what is termed the "fault lines" are examples of how changes will be transmitted and impacted throughout nations—so, for example, as the economy is impacted by (im)migration, changes can occur in wages and salaries and in terms of the new skills needed in the future as well as the decline and alteration in the need for existing skills. Our discussion of the United States, Mexico, Sudan and Iraq provide a clear set of examples of the argument contained in graphic form in Figure 4.1. These "shocks" will continue in both the host and home countries for some time to come. It is the rippling impacts of migration and immigration that, as we have attempted to present herein, provide challenges for the host nation, which are not always predictable in advance.

The Absorptive Capacity of a Nation

In this analysis, reference has been made to the absorptive capacity of a given nation. This refers to the ability of a nation to absorb an influx of people (whether by migration or immigration).

In order to address this phenomenon we must first understand the layers of employment found in every economy/nation, as are shown in Figure 4.2.

Figure 4.2

Layers of Employment in an Economy

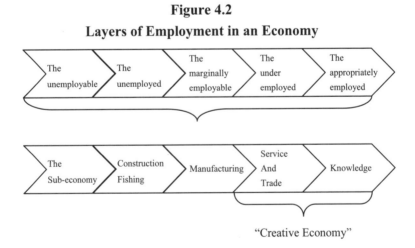

"Creative Economy"

[98]

In both the host nation and the home nation, the labor market can be segmented as shown in Figure 4.2. In any society there are those who are simply unemployable. The reasons for this are varied—babies are unemployable, the elderly and those with major health issues are likely to be unemployable. Those in prison are not employable and those whose skills are no longer necessary or in demand are unemployable.

At the next level are the unemployed. Individuals can be unemployed for a variety of reasons—personal choice (e.g. receiving education/retraining, choosing to remain at home to raise a family) being between jobs (e.g. firm closed, seasonal work or a layoff of employees). This is a stock of people who could potentially be employed, are often eager to be employed and may simply be in transition. This layer of employment is simultaneously most likely to migrate and to see their job taken away by migrants. These are the most at risk if they remain at home.

The next layer is the marginally employable. These are individuals with limited skills and abilities who often have jobs on the fringes of society and business. They can certainly work a job with dignity and earn a living (although the standard of the living might be low) but they are at risk from technological advancement and changes in the skill requirement for jobs. It is difficult for the marginally employable to migrate as they often do not have the skills, ability or education to secure employment in another country.

The next layer consists of the underemployed. These individuals have more skills, ability and education than is required for the job they currently hold. This could be a result of conscious choice (the individual chooses to be under-employed) or of changing economic circumstances (e.g. the economy is contracting, or a particular industry is being subjected to contraction and consolidation).These individuals are on the lookout to improve their economic status by using their skills that are currently not being used. This group also can easily migrate as they have the ability to obtain better jobs in other locales.

[99]

The final layer is what I term the "appropriately employed." An engineer working in an engineering firm or on engineering projects is appropriately employed. A sales person working in sales, doctors working in a hospital, a bricklayer working in construction are all examples of appropriately employed persons. In general these individuals have achieved a match between their education, skills and abilities and the job or position they hold. These are unlikely candidates for migration or immigration as they hold secure and financially secure positions. However they can also be encouraged to migrate/immigrate by multinational employers or by offers from other firms for their services.

In terms of the host country that is receiving individuals, the preferred order of migrants/immigrants would be: appropriately employed, underemployed and then unemployed, as the talents and skills within these layers are desirable. The marginally employed, the unemployable and some elements of the unemployed are less attractive. However, no matter what the "layer" there are often opportunities for employment in the lower paying segments of societies.

Further complicating this relationship is the fact that each of these layers exists within each sector of the economy (for example in fishing, construction, manufacturing, service and trade, and in knowledge industries).The demand for employees in each of those sectors varies over time and by nation. It is therefore possible for a nation to have migration occur across different sectors of the economy and across different layers of employment as discussed above. It is necessary therefore, for a host nation to assess the employability of migrants and the needs for each sector within the economy. In the United Arab Emirates, for example, there is extraordinary demand for construction workers because of the explosion in building nationwide.

Often, the restrictions on immigration reflect the layers of employment noted earlier and the need for such skills in the various sectors. In more developed countries, for example, appropriately employed individuals in the knowledge sector are greatly sought after and often find it easier to obtain a visa and permanent residency status.

Recall, however, that migrants often do not arrive seeking employment—or at least not in the more skilled sectors and layers. Migrants are quite willing in many cases to work on the fringes of society as the wages they earn are often in excess of what they could earn at home.

Outsourcing

Let's turn our attention to outsourcing and assess how this fits into the overall pattern of migration and immigration (and aftershocks).

We have already defined outsourcing (see note 4). Examples of outsourcing include: manufacturing (electronics [games, radios, televisions], clothing, shoes, etc.); financial services (including accounting and tax services); technical writing/architecture/legal research (a relatively new area of out-sourcing growth); information services and backroom operations; call centers of all types; newspapers and local economic development committees. Outsourcing opportunities used to be confined to manufacturing (the goal being cheap labor) and information technology work. As can be easily seen, the nature of work being outsourced has greatly expanded and diversified. Also, restricting outsourcing to low paid, low skilled jobs is becoming less and less likely. This means that the marginally employable and some segments of the unemployed might find it increasingly difficult to find jobs and to migrate or immigrate in search of jobs.

This interacts with our concept of employment layers. For example, imagine a firm that employs individuals in high salary/wage jobs. If this firm outsourced its work, it leaves behind well-trained individuals. If the employment market cannot absorb these individuals, they can: (1) become underemployed; (2) become unemployed; or (3) migrate in search of a new job. In the nation receiving the outsourced jobs, however, it creates new opportunities for their citizens and/or serves to attract migrants/immigrants.

Conclusion

The ongoing globalization of international economies will continue to place pressure on firms to pursue strategic outsourcing. Such outsourcing will move job opportunities to other nations—and that movement can inadvertently encourage migration both within and across borders.

Continuing civil and military tensions, catastrophes, etc. also contribute to migration. In short, migration and outsourcing are issues that will continue to challenge nations in the future. The following suggestions can be made to deal with these unfolding problems:

• *Recognize that immigration and outsourcing are related problems and opportunities.* Unless we are willing to close off borders and take aggressive steps to prevent migration and even illegal immigration, governments and NGOs will still need to deal with these dislocations and the challenges they pose for the host country. The first step is to begin with thoughtful consideration of the impact of migration on the fault lines discussed in this paper. Aldous Huxley once observed that "facts do not cease to exist because they are ignored." The issue of a political and social voice for migrants is not going to go away because we choose not to address it. To be clear, the problem is twofold: first, some migrants do not wish to be assimilated into the host country as citizens but might nonetheless remain for lengthy periods of time—this is the challenge facing the UAE; second is the absorption (not just culturally, socially and politically) of immigrants who wish to have legal residence in the economic and employment life of their new host nation. As we have noted earlier, there are multiple layers of employment and the exact make up of both the immigrant population and the host nation must be considered. As outsourcing of jobs continues and moves up the employment ladder in terms of skills and abilities, newly outsourced jobs will be an attraction for the local population to remain as well as a positive inducement for (im)migration.

- *Reconsider what constitutes citizenship over time or develop alternative visa status or perhaps different citizen status.* Today an individual can be a citizen of a nation, but there are other alternatives—a non-citizen with a work permit; a non-citizen in the process of applying for citizenship; or an illegal immigrant not eligible for citizenship and not pursuing such status. The question is, what is the proper role (if any) of non-citizens in terms of representation in the political arena and in influencing governmental policy—not only as it pertains to them, but also policy on the range of issues that plague governments? Finally, as we consider civil society, what is the appropriate citizenship status for individuals who are living in a country for extended periods of time? Specifically, what voting and political (as well as civil) rights should they enjoy?

- *Make painful choices regarding the 'how' of inclusion.* Co-existence? Separation? What is a host nation to do with a large influx of migrants (for example Jordan and the influx of Iraqis)?What is a host nation to do with an increase in illegal immigration and/or a jump in requests for legal immigration? How will these individuals be socialized and absorbed into the host nation in such a way that encourages them to consider themselves citizens? This assimilation process is not easy, as James Fallows notes:" The median income of Muslims in France, Germany and Britain is lower than that of people in those countries as a whole. The median income of Arab Americans (many of whom are Christians originally from Lebanon) is actually higher than the overall American one, as are their business-ownership rates and their possession of college and graduate degrees. The same is true of most other groups who have been in the United States for several generations, a fact that in turn underscores the normality of the Arab and Muslim experience. The difference between the European and American assimilation of Muslims becomes most apparent in the second generation, when American Muslims become culturally and economically Americanized while many European Muslims develop a sharper sense of alienation. "If you ask a

[103]

second-generation American Muslim," says Robert Leiken, author of *Bearers of Global Jihad: Immigration and National Security After 9/11*, "he will say, 'I'm an American and a Muslim.' A second-generation Turk in Germany is a Turk, and a French Moroccan doesn't know what he is."[12] This is not to argue that America is better than Europe but that the assimilation of immigrants in America seems to be different to that in Europe. What can we learn from these experiences as a nation tries to assimilate diverse cultures? What can immigrants learn from those who have gone before them?

- *Continue the dialogue as more creative alternatives may emerge.* The issues surrounding migration and immigration used to be centered on what relief efforts were necessary to provide for the migrants, what necessary *temporary* support and aid were required to assist refugees (who would be returning home soon) and what regulations and border security measures were needed to prevent illegal immigration. The debate is now shifting to the issue of the political and social engagement of immigrants and migrants and how to ensure that they eventually feel a part of their new culture. The riots of young disenfranchised and jobless Muslims in France are ample demonstrations of the consequences of failure in this regard.

- *Earthquakes are difficult to predict—but so too are the aftershocks and the development of new fault lines.* We cannot predict where the next large migration is likely to occur, nor can we predict those nations in the future that will become attractive as potential permanent homes for immigrants. We can predict, however, that there will be continued large migrations and that people will move to other countries to improve their lives and that of their families. As such, strategies to deal with migration, immigration and possible fault lines should be considered immediately and constantly reviewed as circumstances change. We should also be prepared to learn from experiences with different nations and cultures and adapt accordingly.

- *The law of unintended consequences is always at work—we engage in actions to achieve a specific result but we also experience unintended/unanticipated results as well.* Restrictions on individuals and denial of citizenship can have consequences that we are as yet unaware of and impose unexpected costs on host and home nations. Again, we must consider the implications of changing patterns of migration and immigration as we proceed.

- *Finally, how we manage migration, immigration and outsourcing reflects our national and international leadership, sensitivity and flexibility as individuals and as societies.* People live in hope, and one hope is to improve their own lives—mechanisms such as migration, immigration and outsourcing offer such hope.

SOCIAL IMPLICATIONS OF GLOBALIZATION

5

Social Implications of Corporate Responsibility: Demands on Global Organizations

Steven L. Wartick

The purpose of this paper is to examine the interconnectedness of corporate social responsibility (CSR) in a globalized business world. Unlike most of the other papers presented at the 2007 conference titled "Globalization in the 21st Century: How Interconnected is the World?" globalization of the business world in this paper is taken as given, and therefore it will focus more on interconnectedness.[1]

This paper begins with a brief historical review of the development of the CSR concept from an international perspective. Based on this review, an international CSR conceptual framework is developed, beginning with CSR for US companies based within the US business environment and ultimately reaching the topic of CSR for non-US companies operating within the US business environment. The changing American business environment during the post-9/11 years is then explored, and an examination of three distinctions which are useful for understanding the CSR of non-US based companies operating within this environment is presented. The paper concludes by extending these three distinctions for use in other parts of the world in order to consider the question of the interconnectedness of CSR in a globalized business world.

A Brief History of International Corporate Social Responsibility Concerns

Although the history of concerns relating to the role of business in society can be traced back to the beginnings of business as a socially accepted activity,[2] a direct focus on CSR is more of a post-World War II topic. More specifically, the most formative discussions of the CSR concept in the first few decades of the post-World War II period seem to have taken place primarily within the context of the United States. In the 1950s, for example, H.R. Bowen stated that companies in the United States had responsibilities that reached well beyond mere profit-making.[3] Countering Bowen's argument, Theodore Levitt expressed his concern that the United States should not only be wary of the development and encouragement of a military–industrial complex, but of a *social*–industrial complex as well.[4] Milton Friedman also contributed to the early CSR debate by positing that the only social responsibility of business was to make a profit within the "rules of the game," everything else being mere theft of shareholder resources.[5] By the mid-1970s (after the tumultuous 1960s when US business issues had been raised with regard to environmentalism, equal employment opportunities, women's rights, product safety, workplace safety, etc.) more serious efforts were being made in both the academic and business communities of the United States in order to understand better and analyze more thoroughly the concept of CSR.

It could be argued from an international perspective that during much of the three decades following the war it was only the United States that had the luxury of considering whether business had responsibilities beyond profitability—western Europe and Japan were consumed during this period with the rebuilding process following the war; eastern Europe had fallen under Soviet communist rule; Mao had closed China; African nations grappled with de-colonization; and South American countries seemed focused more on issues of social inequality than of business practices.

As CSR analysis gained momentum in the United States, discussions relating to the role of business in society began to occur throughout the rest of the world, but CSR had yet to become a consuming focus of these discussions. China, for example, subordinated the role of business to the role of government as it began the long process of opening up to the rest of the world. Japan had by the mid-1970s only just begun to establish a presence in the world business community, and the concept of *keiretsu* (i.e., industry councils made up of interlocking directorates among manufacturers, suppliers and bankers) was serving its purposes well. Europe was mostly focused on the development of the European Common Market, but the key issue relating to business activity within the context of European re-development was the extent of American global power, spread through US-based multinational corporations (MNCs). Works like J.J. Servan Schreiber's *The American Challenge*[6] advanced these concerns, and then others such as Richard Barnet and Ronald Muller in *Global Reach*[7] extended the argument beyond Europe and to all parts of the world. Thus, while Europeans and others were examining their own issues relating to "business in society," by the mid-1970s the most formative discussions of the CSR concept remained rooted in the United States.

From this predominantly American concern in the mid-1970s, both interest in the concept of CSR and its actual development spread in tandem with the globalization of business throughout the 1980s, 1990s and early 2000s. First, interest grew surrounding the question of the CSR of US-based MNCs operating outside the United States. Issues such as Lockheed's "questionable" payments to Japanese government officials in 1976, the Amoco Cadiz oil spill off of the coast of France in 1978, Union Carbide's chemical plant explosion in Bhopal, India, and Nike's labor practices in Asia fueled this concern. This first major extension of CSR thinking therefore revolved around applying the concept of CSR to US companies in non-US business environments.

Soon after, questions arose regarding non-US based MNCs, and their practices both within as well as outside their home countries. For example, Nestlé may have been operating in a perfectly responsible manner within Europe, the United States and other developed regions, but how responsible were their marketing practices for infant formula in developing countries where literacy and sanitation were far below the levels of developed countries? Did Shell Oil act appropriately with regard to the assassination of Ken Saro-Wiwa in Nigeria?[8] If US-based MNCs refused to make questionable payments in countries outside the United States would they simply lose out economically to non-US based MNCs that had greater tolerance for payoffs and bribes? As a result of such concerns, CSR issues of non-US based MNCs, both inside and outside their home countries,[9] became layered onto the CSR concerns regarding US companies both in the United States and abroad.

The development of a comprehensive international CSR perspective therefore requires increased consideration and analysis of the concept of CSR for non-US based companies within the US business environment. Figure 5.1 attempts to illustrate this progression.

Some might argue that taking this last step in coming full circle in the development of an international CSR framework is not really necessary because – after more than thirty years – the CSR concept within the US business environment is well established and non-US based companies need only to plug in to existing frameworks or systems (economic, legal and social) in order to avert major problems. Others might contend that attention given to the CSR of non-US based companies operating within the US business environment is not necessary because the negative consequences of resulting problems or issues pale in comparison to the negative consequences of CSR "violations" elsewhere in the world. To both of these views, one might respond that Dubai Ports World should be asked whether the CSR of non-US based companies in the United States is either clearly articulated or relatively unimportant; or Toyota Motors, which in a recent *Business*

[112]

Week article was described as being "afraid of the backlash" which it anticipates as it closes in on General Motors in terms of market share within the enormous US automobile market.[10] Furthermore, ask British Petroleum or Shell Oil whether the CSR of non-US based companies within the US business environment is either clearly articulated or relatively unimportant when it comes to current expectations about alternative energy sources (e.g. ethanol, solar power or wind power). Finally, ask the Brazilian meat processing company, J&F Participacoes, S.A., what concerns it has about CSR in the US business environment as it takes over the assets and operations of Swift & Co., the third largest processor of beef and pork in the United States.[11] All of the above would likely posit that the current US business environment is significantly different from that of earlier times in terms of CSR expectations, and that to ignore or downplay this aspect of the international CSR model, especially within a globalized business world, is a foolish move indeed.

Figure 5.1
International Corporate Social
Responsibility (CSR) Development

		Non-US Business Environments	
	US Business Environment	Developed Countries	Developing Countries
US-Based Companies	(1st)	(2nd)	
Non-US Based Companies	(4th)	(3rd)	

Notes: To adapt this framework to current situations as opposed to an historical perspective, any country or region can replace the "US" in the 2x2 matrix. So, for example, if the focal country is the United Arab Emirates (UAE), the four factors subject to cross-comparison would be "UAE based companies," "non-UAE based companies," "UAE business environment," "non-UAE business environment," and so forth.

A Look at the Current American Business Environment

So, what does the current US business environment look like for the companies mentioned above and other non-US based MNCs, and how has it changed during the past decade? In a macro sense, the US business environment during the past decade has become more restrictive and the attendant CSR expectations have become more demanding. In a micro sense, four major factors have led to this more restrictive and demanding US business environment that has emerged in the last decade. These four factors are: the terrorist attacks of September 11, 2001; increasing US experience with the North America Free Trade Area (NAFTA); the incredible expansion of information technology through the Internet; and changing expectations relating to energy sources and uses.

Post-9/11 Impacts

There can be no reasoned dissenting view to the proposition that the "post-9/11" US business environment is substantially and substantively different from that of the previous decade. For example, organizational security and foreign ownership of US assets are just two of many business-related issues that have been dramatically and quite obviously affected by 9/11.

In terms of organizational security, most businesses operating within the United States see travel limitations due to security as the most visible change in the US business environment. Yet organizational security extends well beyond just travel. For example, recently it was announced that even though Google CEO Eric Schmidt was paid a salary of just US$1 last year, the company paid $532,755 for his personal security.[12]

In addition to business responsibilities like organizational security that incur direct costs, the costs of government fines and penalties can be both substantive and a major source of motivation for both responsible and irresponsible business actions. A recent newspaper article reported that a 250-page US Treasury Department "Watch List" is "being used by credit bureaus, health insurers and car dealerships as well as employers and landlords" [13] to deny services to innocent people. The list includes some of the world's most common names such as Gonzalez, Lopez, Ali, Hussein, Abdul, Lucas and Gibson, and the companies using this list feel compelled to turn people with these names away rather than risk penalties of up to $10 million and 30 years in prison for doing business with members on the Watch List.[14] In terms of organizational security responsibilities in the post-9/11 US business environment, some might argue that the United States has merely caught up with the rest of the world with regard to concerns over terrorism, but business responsibilities related to organizational security have certainly added a new dimension to CSR within the United States

With regard to the foreign ownership of US assets, the American business environment for non-US based MNCs has also become more restrictive. For example, in the spring of 2007, the US House of Representatives passed legislation that would "change the composition and procedures of the interagency panel (the Committee on Foreign Investment in the United States, or CFIUS) which scrutinizes foreign purchases of US businesses for national security threats."[15] This structural change was a direct response to the Dubai Ports World issue (a topic discussed in more depth later in this paper) and represents the increased concern about non-US ownership of assets or companies in strategically important industries. However, it is not only the US federal government that is being pressured to act on this issue; state government action is yet another focus of concerned interest groups. For example, in Iowa, the President of the Farmers Union has called for a ban on foreign ownership of ethanol plants (another topic to be discussed later in this paper) that are popping up all over the state.[16] The point is that like organizational security, changing public policy relating to foreign ownership of American assets is creating a more restrictive US business environment as these changes raise compliance issues within CSR discussions.

[115]

The list of 9/11 business-related issues goes on and on, including concerns relating to information provision, banking, transport, etc. The point is that the post-9/11 US business responsibilities have been altered to reflect the threats of terrorism which were previously only nominally considered within the United States.

NAFTA Impacts

Besides the "post-9/11" impacts on the US business environment, another major source of change has been more than a decade of experience within the North American Free Trade Area (NAFTA). Although not necessarily directly related, dramatic shifts in the US position within the international macroeconomy during NAFTA's existence have resulted in major new CSR issues for both US-based and non-US based companies. As the United States moved from having the largest trade surpluses in the world to having the largest trade deficits in the world (as well as being the world's largest debtor nation), changing expectations regarding CSR were triggered. Trade and investment relations with the BRIC countries (Brazil, Russia, India and China) make for important "new" issues as US investment dollars flow to these countries while imports from the BRIC increase. Still, the American consumer market continues to be the largest in the world and the relative political stability within the United States continues to make foreign direct investment (FDI) attractive. A look at a couple of the issues related to NAFTA therefore seems warranted.

Obviously, the issue of moving jobs outside the United States (particularly to Mexico and BRIC) has implications for CSR that rest heavily on employee relations (a more extensive look at the outsourcing of jobs will be offered in the next section). One could argue that one of the responsibilities of companies in the United States is to offer retraining for displaced workers and to be sure that suppliers from outside the country maintain quality standards and appropriate employee policies, but these are not really "new" changes. These concerns have been around since the 1980s and are merely being redefined and redeveloped as a result of NAFTA.

A more divisive and pervasive NAFTA-related CSR issue in the current US business environment is illegal immigration. The US Congress has provided funds for building a 700-mile long fence along the southern border of the US, and "crack-downs" on illegal immigrants (less so, "crack-downs" on businesses that employ illegal immigrants) are occurring all over the country. At the same time, and in somewhat of an opposite direction, the federal government is providing funding for the construction of a NAFTA Super Highway which extends from Mexico City, Lazaro Cardenas, and other major sites in Mexico, through the middle of the United States and on to Vancouver and Quebec in Canada.[17] More to the point, "according to the National Conference of State Legislatures, more than 80 immigration-related laws were enacted in 32 states in 2006; most of these measures were attempts to crack down on illegal immigrants."[18] The most restrictive action therefore appears to be taking place more at the state and local level than at the federal level, where consensus on illegal immigration policy (besides building a fence) appears distant. So businesses are left with competing "responsibility" conflicts: abiding by the law which prohibits the hiring of illegal immigrants, but losing a source of cheap labor; ignoring the costs of stringent citizenship and visa checks, but failing to comply with state government mandates; paying higher wages to attract US workers, but adding to costs and reducing international competitiveness, etc. The "responsible corporation" might simply argue that compliance with the law is all that is required, but the laws are not clearly articulated nor are they evenly enforced (e.g., the type of industry involved is critical). The ultimate resolution which should guide management decisions is, at this point, excessively ambiguous and managements are left to accept the risk and consequences of whatever decision they reach.

The US experience with NAFTA has generated a host of other CSR-related issues as well. One of these which is of particular interest for businesses operating in the United States relates to how the NAFTA experience will influence further free trade agreements beyond NAFTA. Just prior to 9/11, President Bush was in Mexico City to discuss with other heads of state the further development of a Free Trade Area of the Americas; however, this economic integration has been on hold ever since. In early 2007, the US government completed negotiations on a free trade pact with South Korea, the harbinger, perhaps, of more Pacific Rim free trade activity.[19] So, the question remains as to whether the NAFTA experience will have positive or negative impacts on the CSR implications of these and other economic integrations.

Information Technology Impacts

In terms of all matters related to business, including CSR, no single development has led to more change than the increasing use of the Internet and related technologies (e.g., cell phones). The communication, information, interaction and processes of business throughout the world are simply not the same as they were a mere decade ago. In 1998, for example, PricewaterhouseCoopers (PwC) found that less than one-third of CEO's had "logged on" to the Internet for 10 days or more in the previous month.[20] Now, business activities relating to any sort of information process are being performed anywhere in the world where quality can be maintained with lower costs. This impact on business is what underlies Thomas Friedman's popular notion that the "world is flat,"[21] but what does this mean for CSR in the US business environment? At an abstract level, Friedman argues that technology and the resulting "flatism" are vehicles for the moral development of corporations:

> In the flat world, with lengthy supply chains, the balance of power between global companies and the individual communities in which they operate are tilting more and more in favor of the companies, many of them American-based. As such, these companies are going to command more power, not only to create value but also to transmit values, than any transnational institution on the planet. Social and environmental activists and progressive companies can now collaborate in ways that can make both the companies more profitable and the flat earth more livable.[22]

Friedman's optimism is appealing. Yet cynics might wonder whether the Westernization implied by and underlying this value transmission will be embraced in social activism throughout the world. Conversely, the CSR practices of the non-US based company operating within or planning to operate within the United States may help to temper or adapt the Western values that are part of this transmission. So, the role of the Internet and related technology in this diffusion of values may go beyond its central role as a vehicle for exchange, since the Internet allows for the challenge of CSR propositions by providing increased transparency and disclosure as well as a forum for debate and discussion.[23]

On a less abstract level, the increased use of the Internet and related technologies has led to CSR issues stemming from increased offshoring of not just manufacturing jobs but also those in areas such as information systems, legal and medical services, and customer service activities. To illustrate, *Business Week* reported the following 2005 financial levels of offshoring by US based companies[24]: $179 billion for logistics and procurement (just-in-time shipping, parts purchasing, and after-sales repairs); $170 billion for manufacturing (contract production of everything from electronics to medical devices); $90 billion for information technology (software development, Web site design, IT infrastructure); $41 billion for customer care (call centers for tech support, air bookings, bill collection, etc.); $27 billion for engineering (testing and design of electronics, chips, machinery, car parts, etc.); $13 billion for human resources (payroll administration, benefits, and training programs); and $12 billion for analytics (market research, financial analysis and risk calculation). Beyond these 2005 levels, there is no real reason to believe that offshoring is going to stop. With infrastructure development such as the NAFTA Superhighway (mentioned above) and the results of offshoring producing the lower prices that US consumers demand, offshoring appears to be a fact of business life that is spreading even more so into professional areas such as legal services, architecture, medical services, accounting, etc.[25] In short, the offshorers have won and the CSR question is how will businesses operating within the United States respond? More specifically for the CSR implications of non-US based companies operating within the United States, the central issue is likely to be to what extent their activities within the United States are viewed as bringing new jobs and resources back to the United States. In other words, will non-US based companies be seen as offshoring to the United States, and thus counterbalancing the outflow of jobs and resources by US-based companies?

Impacts of Energy Sources / Uses

Energy-related matters have been on the table in the United States for decades, and it is reasonable to question whether changing the expectations and demands that have emerged in the past decade is any more likely to lead to real change than earlier movements. If more recent changes do reflect a tangible change in expectations and demands, CSR expectations for US-based as well as non-US based companies are certain to be affected. A few recent actions on the part of government at different levels within the United States suggest that this round of energy-related concerns may in fact lead to real change.

Consider for a moment the changes that took place in the energy arena at the federal level of government within the United States. In the Spring of 2007, the US Supreme Court ruled that carbon monoxide and other greenhouse gases are air pollutants under the Clean Air Act and that the Environmental Protection Agency (EPA) has the authority to regulate those emissions from new trucks and cars.[26] The Court rejected auto industry-influenced government reasons for not doing so and in the process business has been told that increased governmental regulation relating to global warming is on the horizon.

However, state and local governments may be jumping far ahead of federal actions when it comes to energy sources and uses issues. For example, consider the US Mayors Climate Protection Agreement which is designed to reduce a city's "carbon footprint." Currently, there are 442 US cities which have signed on; these cities include not just the mega-cities but also smaller towns like Decorah, Iowa (population, 8,000).[27] Also in Iowa, its newly elected governor has declared that it is the policy of the state to be free of dependence on foreign oil by the year 2025 (wind power already accounts for nearly 20 percent of Iowa's electricity needs) and that $100 million over the next four years is being budgeted toward this effort.[28] Some argue that this move is largely motivated by the fact that Iowa is producing about 25 percent of total US ethanol production (about 1.1 billion gallons per year) and that the United States appears to be making a commitment now to this corn-based alternative energy source. For example, President Bush during a recent trip to South America refused to eliminate the $0.54 per gallon tariff on imported sugar-based ethanol from Brazil (there was, however, an agreement reached on common standards for the product).[29] Yet, the commitment is not without its downside. For example, the price of corn this year doubled from $2 to $4 per bushel, and critics of ethanol are posing questions about the impacts of using corn for ethanol as opposed to contributing corn to world food supplies; about the amount of energy necessary to create ethanol; and about the negative consequences of, or need for, expansion of oil refinery capacity in the United States if ethanol is deemed to be the fuel of the future.

Beyond governmental actions, other indicators of changing expectations and demands relating to energy sources and uses include the introduction of new fuel-efficient hybrid automobiles by Toyota, Honda, Ford and other auto producers, and Discovery Communications' recent announcement that it is launching *PlanetGreen*, a new 24-hour environmental lifestyle cable TV channel.[30] Optimism for positive change may seem warranted, but the main point relating to this paper is that non-US based companies operating within or planning to operate within the United States need to be aware of these heightened energy-related concerns and their attendant impacts on CSR within the US business environment.

[121]

Three Distinctions for the Analysis of CSR in the United States

As noted above, 9/11, NAFTA, advances in communications technology, and energy issues have all contributed to a noticeably different US business environment into which non-US based companies venture with their products and investments. To complete the full circle of CSR outlined in the first section above (see Figure 5.1), a more in-depth reconsideration of the CSR expectations and demands for non-US based companies within the current American business environment is necessary.

To lay the groundwork, a quick look at CSR issues in the United States during the mid-1990s is helpful. Selection of this period as a comparative point is intended to describe the US CSR environment before the major impacts of 9/11, NAFTA, communications advances, and changing attitudes toward energy sources and uses. PricewaterhouseCoopers, for example, conducted their first survey of MNC executives in 1998 and described the mid-1990s era as "let the good times roll."[31] More specifically related to CSR issues, a business group called the Social Venture Network published a 1995 book describing the "75 best practices for socially responsible companies."[32] Actions included in this collection came from big and small business, retailers and manufacturers, well known (e.g., Dupont, 3M, and J.C. Penney) and less well-known companies (e.g., White Dog Café, Tabra, Southwire), and service and goods companies. Interestingly, only one non-US based company, Anita Roddick's Body Shop, appeared in this collection. Even more to the point, in terms of CSR in the mid-1990s US business environment, consider Table 5.1 which lists the topics offered as CSR "best practices."

Table 5.1

Social Venture Network

Best Practices for Socially Responsible Companies (1995)

Employees:	Empowerment	Egalitarianism, and Sharing Wealth
	Job Security	Pay and Evaluation
	Benefits	Support for Working Parents
	Workstyle and Fun	Diversity
	Promotion from Within	Support for Retirees
	Health Care and Safety	Training, Education, and Personal Growth
Customers & Suppliers:	Social Criteria Purchasing	Social Mission Purchasing
	Overseas Suppliers	Exceptional Customer Service
Community & Society	Social Leadership	Cash and In-Kind Philanthropy
	Activism	Advertising and Marketing
At Large:	Social Entrepreneurship and Community Development	Socially Acceptable Products / Services
Planet:	Energy Efficiency	Packaging and Facility Design
	Transportation	International Standards
	Landscaping	
Organization:	Social Auditing	Governance

Source: Reder, A. *75 Best Business Practices for Socially Responsible Companies* (New York, NY: G.P. Putnam's Sons, 1995).

Of the more recent issues attendant to the changes noted in the preceding section of this paper, only the offshoring of jobs (which might be generally considered as part of the "job security" issue within "employee" relations) and "energy efficiency" (part of "planet" section of issues) are mentioned. Issues such as organizational security, foreign ownership of US assets, illegal immigration, economic integration extensions, and alternative energy sources do not show up as part of this

CSR compilation. Although this Social Venture Network catalogue of CSR practices may not be totally exhaustive of all CSR considerations in the mid-1990s, it does help to provide a baseline to reflect both the change that has occurred during the past decade and the importance of thinking beyond older conceptualizations of what should be included in CSR activities.

So, for the non-US based MNC operating within or planning to operate within this newer US business environment, how can the CSR changes resulting from the post-9/11, post-NAFTA, Internet-based, energy sensitive global business environment of present and future United States be more effectively detected and addressed? The following three distinctions relating to the analysis of CSR are instructive in this regard: (1) motivations versus outcomes; (2) shareholders versus stakeholders; and (3) idealists versus pragmatists. Focusing extensively on only one part of any of these three distinctions while largely ignoring the other (e.g., focusing on motivations more than outcomes or outcomes more than motivations, focusing on shareholders more than stakeholders or stakeholders more than shareholders) is a formula for missing important changes in CSR expectations and demands.

Motivations versus Outcomes

During three decades of CSR development, no conceptual distinction seems more important than that between motivations and outcomes. Without getting too deeply into the academic details, this distinction suggests a fundamental difference in the relevant unit of analysis.[33] Within academic discussions, motivations have come to rest upon inputs, i.e., perceived economic, legal, ethical and discretionary obligations that underlie business actions.[34] Outcomes, on the other hand, rest mostly upon actions, i.e., observable programs and behavior leading to measurable changes in identifiable societal variables. Thus, the motivations side of the equation is most frequently related to ethics and the rhetoric of right and wrong while the outcomes side focuses on outputs and the assessment of positive and negative actions.

[124]

For the non-US based MNC operating in the current and/or future US business environment, understanding the distinction between – as well as the connection among – motivations and outcomes is critical. The Dubai Ports World issue mentioned earlier offers an excellent example to illustrate this point.[35] The March 2006 acquisition of the British-owned Peninsular and Oriental Steam Navigation Company (P&O) by the UAE-based Dubai Ports (DP) World seemed on the surface to be just another business transaction in a global economy which met both economic and political legitimacy for both home and host country concerns. DP World believed that for most observers, changes in port operations (including six ports in the United States) would not be noticeable with the change from British to Arab ownership. Thus, from an outcomes perspective, no major concerns existed. However, from a motivations perspective the sale of P&O to DP World became a major domestic and international incident. As the debate shifted quickly from outcomes to motivations, arguments were raised about: (1) US port security interests in 9/11 United States; (2) a double standard being applied to British versus Arab interests; (3) the process of approving foreign investment and ownership in the United States; and (4) the reconciliation of the issue within such cultural conflict. All of these points were input-oriented and related to future arguments about what is right and wrong, because at the time there were no real output or performance-related arguments to evaluate; DP World was not given the chance to show that performance would outweigh speculative motivations. The transaction was met almost immediately with criticism from indignant US politicians and social commentators, and the result was that DP World ended up agreeing to sell P&O to US interests.

From a CSR perspective, this issue formed and was debated around the notion of what *could be* (motivations) rather than what *was* actual performance (outcomes). The issue centered on possibilities not actualities, proaction not reaction, inputs not outputs. The issue became politicized as the discussion of the past gave way to debate about the future, and the economics of the acquisition were subordinated to political interests and social criteria. This is typical of the organizational security and foreign ownership of US assets issues discussed earlier as relevant to CSR in the post-9/11 US business environment.

Thus, the lesson of this first distinction is that non-US based MNCs operating within the United States should take heed of the "gotcha" factor, i.e., assuming that the company will be assessed on performance (outcomes) when ethics or some other input (motivations) end up being the evaluative framework or, indeed, assuming the converse to be likely. Both parts of the motivations versus outcomes distinction must therefore be considered in order to create effective CSR.

Shareholders versus Stakeholders

The second distinction relevant to CSR analysis needs little explanation because almost everyone now understands the relationship between shareholders and stakeholders. During the past twenty years, stakeholder analysis has advanced considerably from the old debate of "who should management serve, shareholders or stakeholders"? Most executives and academics now recognize the positive sum nature of stakeholder management that posits that the goal of decision makers should be efforts to serve all stakeholders (including shareholders as one important group of stakeholders), thus allowing the organization to thrive. When conflicts arise between stakeholder interests, the work of Mitchell, Agle and Wood has clearly suggested that pertinent to a given issue, stakeholder power, legitimacy and urgency are the factors which lead to the effective resolution of such conflicts.[36]

To illustrate these points in more detail, a good example is the concern mentioned previously that Toyota is about to experience a "backlash" ("Buy American," boycott Toyota) as it positions itself to overtake General Motors in US automobile market share.[37] First of all, the economics are clear; Toyota sales (along with profits) are rising while GM continues to lose sales. For this development, Toyota shareholders should be pleased.

[126]

However, according to Harris Interactive one third of US car buyers (consumers as a stakeholder group) are biased against imports, and even with five manufacturing plants within the United States (employees and communities as stakeholder groups), Toyota believes that they are still viewed as a foreign company. Furthermore, with so much information (true and false) available through the Internet from "watchdogs" of all types (both bloggers and more traditional critics/evaluators like *Consumer Digest* or J.D. Power) providing assessments of company performance, managing one's reputation has become a responsibility that only the most naive of companies would ignore.[38] Toyota of course is not one of these naive companies, so to avoid being seen as the one that pushed GM over the edge, Toyota (using solid stakeholder management) is "launching literacy programs in San Antonio, vowing to share technology with Ford, and pouring money into lobbying ..."[39] These efforts are in addition to Toyota providing funding to the National Center for Family Literacy, dispatching their efficiency gurus to companies like Viking Range Corporation and Boeing, providing $1 million to the Blanchette Neurosciences Institute at West Virginia University and partnering with the Sierra Club to sponsor "green" events and to promote hybrid automobiles.[40] Additionally, in the American Midwest, where Toyota is believed to face the most resistance, they are sponsoring livestock shows, bass fishing tournaments, and NASCAR vehicles.[41] Stakeholder analysis/management makes all of this activity commonly acceptable as good business practice.

Whether these philanthropic, public relations and government relations activities taken by Toyota will succeed in averting a backlash remains to be seen, but it should be noted that Toyota may have less to be concerned about than they think. In the most recent *Fortune* "Most Admired Companies" survey, Toyota ranked third overall, they were the only non-US based company in the top twenty, and they ranked second behind General Electric in terms of positive global reputation.[42] Toyota's efforts illustrate the point that the role of CSR perceptions attendant to managing reputation is one of the "new" responsibilities in the current US business environment.

So, in addition to the distinction between motivations and outcomes, the distinction between shareholders and stakeholders and efforts to serve both as part of solid stakeholder management is ignored only at the peril of non-US based companies operating within the US business environment. In fact, by coupling the two distinctions together, it is easy to see that within each stakeholder relationship there are both motivation and outcome dimensions, and progressively managed non-US based companies operating in the United States will recognize and respond to this reality.

Idealists versus Pragmatists

A third important distinction that is useful when analyzing the CSR practices of non-US based companies operating within the US business environment is the differences between the recommendations and insights offered by idealists and pragmatists. The important point when considering this contrast is to position the recommendations and insights of those who want to define CSR (i.e., the idealists) in parallel with those who study the process of implementing CSR (i.e., the pragmatists). This contrast is closely related to the first distinction noted above – motivations versus outcomes – and it extends nicely from the second consideration, stakeholders versus shareholders. The central point of this third distinction is that both idealism and pragmatism are revealing for companies seeking to understand and implement the motivations and outcomes of CSR through effective management of stakeholders and shareholders.

An excellent illustration of the distinction between idealists and pragmatists can be found in the current conditions within the US automobile industry. As noted earlier, the increasing emphasis on energy conservation within the United States (spurred largely by $3 per gallon gasoline) has led both US-based and Japan-based producers to develop more fuel-efficient hybrid (electric and gasoline combination) automobiles. For decades, the environmentalists (the idealists in this case) have advocated increasing automobile fuel efficiency to conserve energy and to decrease pollution. Governments have passed fuel efficiency standards for company production and tax breaks for fuel-efficient auto purchases. Thus, competitors are carefully watching each other for movements in the production of more fuel-efficient autos. In addition, the development of alternative bio-fuels is adding to what some see as the "greening" of the auto industry. With this "greening" of the industry, sympathetic consumers do the best they can given the automobile company model offerings, suppliers provide whatever requested, employees produce whatever instructed, and shareholders evaluate auto company financial performance. As a result, tax breaks and subsidies save customers hundreds of dollars, new suppliers (e.g., ethanol producers) are appearing, and different types of jobs are being created. Oil companies have even begun to speak the language of alternative fuels more frequently; BP, for example has launched a $200-million image campaign that says that "BP" stands for "Beyond Petroleum."[43] Environmentalists are happier—not *happy*, but *happier*.

In terms of CSR, whatever improvements these idealistic efforts motivate are laudable. However, the pragmatist would argue that the "greening" of the automobile industry is much more complex than is suggested above. For example, government standards without accurate mechanisms for measurement and "teeth" for enforcement make adherence to these "greening" efforts more like form over substance (i.e., "feel good" PR) and compliance more like a luxury that is subject to good times—while back-pedaling occurs during difficult times. Pragmatists will suggest that even though in the United States alone, more than $2 trillion is currently invested in so-called CSR funds (e.g., the KLD index[44] and the Dow Jones sustainability indices[45]), owners must be convinced of the financial opportunities of these efforts in order for change to really occur. Pragmatists will point out that customer purchases of automobiles occur in a longer time cycle than most consumer products, and as a result the long waiting lists for hybrid autos have now been eliminated and auto makers have already had to start discounting the price for hybrid models and finding newer marketing techniques to sell them.[46] The pragmatists will also note that alternative fuels create consequences that cannot be ignored; the doubling of the price of corn last year, using corn for fuel not food, and the energy costs of producing bio-fuels have led some to speculate that the alternative fuel movement in the United States has merely produced a "dot-corn" bubble.[47] As a supplement or complement to idealism, solid CSR analysis must therefore turn to the insights of the pragmatists. Pragmatists may tend to accept the general propositions of the idealists, but they look more closely at actual conditions and at what appears to be working.[48]

So, in addition to understanding and analyzing both the motivations and outcomes of corporate actions as well as the importance of stakeholders versus shareholders, the third important distinction for non-US based MNCs operating within the US business environment is reconciling the advocacy of the idealist and the reality of the pragmatist. With this third distinction elaborated, attention can now be turned to the final topic of this paper, the interconnectedness of CSR expectations and demands.

Interconnectedness of CSR Expectations and Demands

Thus far, this paper has examined important principles and changes in CSR that should be considered by non-US based companies operating in the US business environment. More generally, however, the intent is to come full circle in forming more of an international framework for considering CSR. With these points in mind, the final section of this paper turns to the broader concern of how interconnected CSR expectations and demands are within the global business system. Using the same three distinctions discussed in the preceding section, the question becomes one of the extent of the commonalities and differences related to CSR in view of the impact of globalization on the business world. This focus on interconnectedness also provides an opportunity to review major CSR lessons that MNCs must consider as they operate in an increasingly globalized business system.

Motivations versus Outcomes

One point which seems clear within the current global situation is that there are several variations of acceptable CSR motivations and outcomes. For example, based on the idea that business CSR motivations are comprised of perceived economic, legal, ethical and discretionary responsibilities, the *economic* dimension of CSR seems to be the area where the greatest amount of interconnectedness can be found. As the principles of market economics become more accepted and prevalent than the principles of socialist economics, the interconnectedness resulting from such values as profit making, market determination and competitiveness pull global businesses together. Yet, the same cannot be said for legal, ethical and discretionary dimensions of CSR. Substantive governmental and cultural variations still exist throughout the world and lead to substantive limitations on global business practices.[49] Recent PwC surveys of global business executives have found that "nearly 70 percent of CEOs said that CSR is 'vital' to profitability,"[50] but that "cultural issues and conflicting regulatory requirements top the list of obstacles encountered or anticipated by CEOs when going global."[51] As noted earlier, this is the arena within which DP World was caught (DP World thought that economic responsibilities would dominate when in actual fact the political and social dimensions prevailed), and it is also where Toyota seems to be working hard to avert a US backlash as it overtakes General Motors in US market share (Toyota is focusing observably on the political and social dimensions of their "American citizenship" in order to counterbalance the perception of the company as "foreign" and its products as "imports"). Any MNC operating within a different national or regional arena than that of their home country must beware of this lack of interconnectedness of the political, ethical and discretionary dimensions of CSR motivations.

[131]

On the outcomes side, however, there appears to be more consistency within the global business community. For example, based on a 2001 survey of consumers by Environics International (now Globescan), the five most important things a company can do (in order of importance) in order to be seen as socially responsible are to: (1) treat employees fairly; (2) protect the environment; (3) create jobs and support the economy; (4) provide social services and give back to the community; and (5) provide safe, high-quality products and services.[52] CEOs of global companies have similar views when suggesting that the five factors which most influence their companies' social reputations are (in order of the percentage of those responding and with percentage scores of at least 70 percent) are: (1) providing a healthy and safe working environment [86 percent]; (2) acting responsibly towards all company stakeholders regardless of whether this is legally required [84 percent]; (3) creating value for the company's shareholders [74 percent]; (4) fostering good environmental performance [71 percent]; and (5) supporting community projects [71 percent].[53] The consistency in these views from both consumers and CEOs is striking, as far as intended CSR outcomes are concerned. Similar findings can also be found in efforts like the Business in the Community 2005 Corporate Responsibility Index for Great Britain.[54] With such consistency relating to CSR outcomes, the major concerns leading to increased interconnectedness are measurement and strategy communication. As suggested by the International Institute for Sustainable Development (IISD):

> [I]n order to move from theory to concrete action, many obstacles need to be overcome. A key challenge facing business is the need for more reliable indicators of progress in the field of CSR along with the dissemination of CSR strategies. Transparency and dialogue can help to make a business appear more trustworthy, and push up the standards of other organizations at the same time.[55]

Measurement, in particular, seems critical for both nations and the businesses that operate within their borders. The IISD goes on to contend that the following positive outcomes are associated with various CSR demands and expectations:

Company benefits: improved financial performance; lower operating costs; enhanced brand image and reputation; increased sales and customer loyalty; greater productivity and quality; more ability to attract and retain employees; reduced regulatory oversight; access to capital; workforce diversity; product safety and decreased liability.

Benefits to the community and the general public: charitable contributions; employee volunteer programs; corporate involvement in community education, employment and homelessness programs; product safety and quality.

Environmental benefits: greater material recyclability; better product durability and functionality; greater use of renewable resources; integration of environmental management tools into business plans, including life-cycle assessment and costing, environmental management standards and eco-labeling.[56]

"Balanced scorecards" and social audits of different types (e.g., the "three P's" approach that emphasizes people, planet and profit) are reporting efforts designed to quantify and operationalize CSR outcomes, and to the extent that these activities result in factors that are measured accurately and reliably, companies should be motivated to advance their levels of CSR and interconnectedness should increase.

So, from the point of view of the motivations versus outcomes distinction, CSR interconnectedness within the global business system seems to rest more (in actuality and in potentiality) with actions rather than words. However, for the MNC operating within several different CSR environments, the key lesson is that ignoring outcomes and emphasizing motivations (rhetoric over actions) or ignoring motivations and emphasizing outcomes (actions without supporting logic) are both formulae for vulnerability in CSR assessments. To see this point in even more detail, a look at interconnectedness using the second distinction, stakeholders versus shareholders, is instructive.

Stakeholders versus Shareholders

Earlier in this paper it was noted that there is now general agreement among most executives and academics that the positive sum nature of solid stakeholder management, where the goals of business decision makers should be to serve all stakeholders (including shareholders as one important stakeholder), leads to an organization's success. The overall proposition is that serving the interests of multiple stakeholders ultimately serves the interests of all stakeholders including shareholders or owners.

In terms of the interconnectedness of stakeholder interests in the broader global business system, employee interests were shown in the preceding section to be at the top of the list for two important stakeholder groups—consumers and business executives. This high priority given to employees is most likely the foundation for the PwC findings that: (1) successfully dealing with employee issues and social goals are the top two legacies that CEOs would like to leave their successors;[57] and (2) when "discussing how best to attract and retain talent ... 65 percent (of CEOs) agree or strongly agree that active engagement in social issues will be a key success factor in this regard."[58] However, the CSR importance of stakeholders besides employees should not be overlooked. IISD is again helpful in this regard by identifying six key external stakeholder pressures that are driving the international development of CSR: (1) the shrinking role of government; (2) demands for greater disclosure; (3) increased customer interest; (4) growing investor pressure; (5) competitive labor markets; and (6) supplier relations.[59] Exactly where these pressures will lead in the future is not at all certain, but they do suggest that both the future importance of stakeholder management and the interconnectedness of stakeholder management influences on CSR outcomes are likely to be enhanced.

To illustrate this point in more detail, the lessons for MNCs from enhanced stakeholder pressures and their perceived importance can be sketched by examining attendant implications for each stakeholder group noted in the preceding paragraph. For example, given that CEOs see conflicting regulatory requirements as one of the major obstacles to globalization, the interconnectedness of CSR principles via solid stakeholder management may serve as a strong motivating factor for companies to pursue enhanced CSR and offer it as an effective substitute for government regulation. As demands for increased disclosure from many different stakeholders are met[60], interconnectedness is likely to be enhanced proportionately and MNCs that lead in this disclosure effort will be capable of exerting the greatest influence on the principles of CSR. The Environics International study found that one in five consumers in their G20 survey admitted to "punishing" a company that they viewed as irresponsible;[61] thus, creating more effective reputation management and the costs attendant to ignoring the importance of reputation[62] can only be viewed as further sources of increased CSR activity and expanded interconnectedness. Beyond the growth of social investment funds, the Environics International survey found that more than one in five investors in Italy (33 percent), the United States (28 percent), Canada (26 percent), Japan (22 percent) and Britain (21 percent) bought or sold shares based on a company's CSR[63]; the implications of this development for CSR and its interconnectedness can only be positive if this circumstance grows at all. Labor market competition has now expanded beyond just developing versus developed country competition and on to developing versus developing country competition, and further, even within many developing countries that are considered to be sources of low cost labor, industry by industry competition is beginning to take hold[64]. The CSR focus on employees and working conditions and any resulting interconnectedness is again likely to be mostly positive. Finally, both the diffusion of CSR and its interconnectedness are likely to be enhanced as the Nikes, BPs, Mittal Steels, and Walmarts of the world become the arbiters and enforcers of more responsible actions among their suppliers[65]; the "when in Rome, do as the Romans do" approach to CSR has largely failed in the eyes of home country stakeholders and more broadly based principles of company behavior appear to be the growing norm.

Thus, from the point of view of the second distinction – shareholders versus stakeholders – the evidence seems to indicate that through the interconnectedness of businesses, governments and non-governmental organizations (NGO's) the foundations are being laid for improvements in

CSR. Neither the speed of the change in CSR nor the eventual level of attainment of CSR is entirely clear, but the interconnectedness provides a strong potential for optimism. Yet, as CSR and its interconnectedness change, they are sure to be influenced significantly by both idealists and pragmatists—the third distinction used to analyze and understand CSR.

Idealists versus Pragmatists

After considering the first two distinctions for effective CSR analysis, it seems clear that the impacts of outcomes (somewhat more than motivations) and stakeholders (encompassing more than just shareholders) seem to be the directions of interconnectedness in the future. The third distinction, idealists versus pragmatists, adds even more substance to this observation.

To illustrate, first consider such idealist efforts as the United Nations' Global Compact,[66] or ISO 26000.[67] Although some might be critical of particular elements of these efforts, it is hard to argue against such idealistic global goals as upholding human rights, respecting reasonable labor standards, preserving the environment, and combating corruption. In the same way that the rhetoric of motivations provides CSR goals for MNCs, the idealists preach the macro-principles of international CSR for business in general. However, like the ethicists and others who offer principles underlying the motivation of CSR, the idealists have little compliance authority. For example, the Global Compact is merely described as follows:

> The Global Compact is not a regulatory instrument; it does not "police," enforce or measure the behavior or actions of companies. Rather, the Global Compact relies on public accountability, transparency and the enlightened self-interest of companies, labor and civil society to initiate and share substantive action in pursuing the principles upon which the Global Compact is based.[68]

But even though the idealists lack the authority for across-the-board enforcement and the tools for forcing compliance, they do provide the foundations for moral persuasion regarding what international businesses should be doing. In this manner, the idealists provide a valuable overarching CSR contribution to interconnectedness.

Conversely, more substance comes from the pragmatists as they examine CSR within a system of increased business globalization. Without pretending to know all of the findings of analysts worldwide, one good example of the pragmatists contribution comes from the previously noted 2001 Environics International study.[69] When developing a CSR Index for the G20 countries, this group focused on consumer behavior and whether consumers: (1) had punished a company for being irresponsible; (2) think that companies should go beyond their traditional economic role; (3) are influenced by CSR factors in forming opinions about companies; and (4) are capable of naming an irresponsible company.[70] From these criteria, Environics International offered the survey results (beyond those already mentioned above) shown in Table 5.2.

To the extent that these findings have held true over the past few years, the variability with which consumers in different parts of the world view CSR is striking. Levels of CSR expectations, major topics of concern, variables included in CSR reputations, and actions taken against companies viewed as "irresponsible" all vary significantly. These types of findings are the lessons which the pragmatists provide to MNCs as opposed to the directives provided by the idealists.

Of particular importance from the Environics International study as it relates to interconnectedness in a globalized business world is the pragmatist's perspective of a developing global system of CSR. The findings suggest that in the current situation, the United States, Canada, Mexico and Great Britain could be seen as comprising a "Maturing" level of CSR, while most other European countries along with Argentina comprise a "Developing" level of CSR and Brazil, Chile, Turkey and Asian countries make up an "Emerging" level of CSR. Nigeria, Russia and India comprise the lowest level of CSR expectations for individual countries.

[137]

Table 5.2
Environics International CSR Findings (2001)

[C]onsumers in the **US, Canada, the U.K. and Mexico** demand the most from companies in terms of being socially responsible. Most **European countries, as well as Argentina**, are ranked as second-tier countries … Companies can expect only modest demands...in **France, Brazil, Chile, Turkey, and Asian countries** … **India, Russia, and Nigeria** represent markets where there is the least demand for companies to be socially responsible.

Generally, **fair employee treatment** is regarded as the most important descriptor of social responsibility in many countries including the United States, France, Switzerland, Italy, the Philippines, and all Latin American countries surveyed. **Environmental protection** is the top mention for Canada, Great Britain, Australia, and Indonesia. Turks think that **charitable donations** are most important, while South Africans and South Koreans most often say companies should **give back to the communities** in which they operate.

Citizens in wealthier countries are particularly critical of industry performance and are highly expectant of good performance around responsibilities such as **product safety and environmental protection**.

Consumers, especially those in North America, are likely to **vote with their wallets** against companies whose social and environmental performance is perceived to be poor. **Forty-two percent of North American** consumers reported having punished socially irresponsible companies by not buying their products. **In Asia, by contrast, … only eight percent** of consumers said they had boycotted companies with low standards of corporate behavior.

When forming an impression of a company, **45 percent is based on non-CSR related factors** such as brand quality reputation and economic contribution whereas **49 percent is based on CSR related factors** such as environmental impacts, labor practices / business ethics, and demonstrated responsibility to broader society.

Source: Environics International, *The Corporate Social Responsibility Index*, July 2001, (www.globescan.com/csrm_research_findings.htm).

Within each of these levels there seem to be different topical emphases (e.g., fair employee treatment is regarded as the most important descriptor of CSR for the United States and Mexico, but environmental protection is at the top of the list for Canada and Great Britain), as well as different process emphases. (Citizens in wealthier countries are particularly critical of industry performance and are highly expectant of good performance in terms of responsibilities such as product safety and environmental protection; consumers, especially those in North America, are more likely to vote with their wallets against companies whose social and environmental performance is perceived to be poor.) Overall, CSR-related factors appear to balance non-CSR related factors when consumers form an impression of the quality of company performance. Thus, there is a vertical interconnectedness suggested by this implied four level typology of CSR as companies within countries move from one level to another (hopefully all towards "Maturing" CSR) that appears to be stronger at this point than the horizontal interconnectedness suggested within each level. Again, the future direction of change within this implied CSR system is not at all clear, but the fact remains that the pragmatists' ability to ascertain such a system speaks well for the future development of CSR and its interconnectedness.

So, after looking more carefully at the distinction of the idealists versus the pragmatists from an international perspective, it seems safe to conclude that the efforts of the pragmatists (e.g., the Environics International surveys as well as the frequently noted PwC surveys and other assessments like those from the FTSE4GOOD index[71]) add considerably more detail to the understanding of the interconnectedness of CSR. Also, the pragmatists' efforts are even more instructive when they are coupled with the advocacy principles of the idealist approach offered by groups like the Global Compact or ISO 26000 creators. Along with the other two distinctions discussed above, the distinction of idealists versus pragmatists adds even more understanding to the question of the development of CSR within an increasing globalized business system.

[139]

Final Comments and Conclusions

The overall purpose of this paper was to examine the interconnectedness of CSR in a globalized business world. After examining the history of CSR in an international context and reviewing the changing US business environment, three distinctions were used to reconsider the CSR of non-US based MNCs operating within the US business environment as well as the CSR of MNCs more generally operating in a broader globalized business system. The general conclusion that can be offered from this review and analysis is captured appropriately by using the three-part title of the PwC 2007 survey of global executives.[72] This three part title consisted of three observations about global business in general: (1) WAS: within borders, (2) IS: across borders, and (3) WILL BE: without borders? In terms of the implications of CSR and its interconnectedness in the global business system, it seems fair to conclude that CSR still exists very much within the constraints of national borders, that it is starting perhaps to move more across borders, but it is still a long way from being without borders.

6

Globalization and Religion

Bahman Baktiari

The phenomenon of globalization has attracted more significant global attention than perhaps any other issue in recent memory. From the slogans of corporate moguls and trade ministers to television documentaries and academic books, globalization has captured the imagination of people the world over. For a term that was used for the first time in 1962, it is amazing how much literature exists on this subject. However, there remains little consensus on its extent, evolution, causation, consequences or responses.

Today, globalization reflects the development of structural forces in world affairs which are far stronger than at any previous time. This means that a single explanation of what causes globalization is not possible. What is clear is that globalization occurs in a number of ways via processes of interaction, emulation and norm-building that affect our identity and perspective of what it means to be "global" today.

The term "globalization" describes a process of intensification of relationships between societies in terms of their economic, social, political and cultural practices and ideas. It is relevant to religion because it touches on every aspect of religious belief, ethics and cultural authenticity.

The debate about globalization and its impact has often overlooked the place of religion in the global age.[1] Millions of people today, regardless of their nationality, perceive global conflicts in terms of competing revelations, dogmatic purity and divine duty. For many scholars of globalization and international relations, it is assumed that greater economic and political interdependence will ultimately weaken the hold of traditional religions, and that human beings have learned to separate religious issues from political ones. This assumption has shaped the way scholars of globalization view religion—often either as a force that succumbs to the pressures of globalization and becomes pluralistic or one which remains an atavistic ideology requiring sociological analysis but not serious intellectual engagement.

This chapter examines the relationship between religion and globalization in a world that is subject to both political fragmentation and powerful forces of global integration. A standard assertion about globalization's impact on religion and cultural values claims that globalization leads to cultural homogeneity, increases integration and diminishes difference, and inculcates global norms, ideas or practices that overtake local mores.[2] In other words, globalization itself is a form of religion with universalistic objectives.

A counter-argument maintains that increased interaction is leading to new mixtures of cultures and that integration is provoking a defense of tradition,[3] while yet another group claims that globalization has increased religious fundamentalism because it has led not only to uneven economic growth and greater disparity between rich and poor, but also to increased secularization.

There is no question that globalization poses important challenges for traditional monotheistic religions, but this does not mean that it has altered the status of religion and its appeal. For millennia, religion was the only construct human beings used for expressing their thoughts about politics and human relations. What is clear is that globalization has led to new discourses about religion and religious values, but also concerning the meaning of global citizenship, ethical stands on important global issues, and the role of the individual. Aptly characterized as the "new fault line" on the world's ideological map, globalization will continue to be a topic of much debate and discussion for some time.

Prior to the emergence of what we know today as globalization, for more than two centuries advocates of modernization in the Middle East took it for granted that science, technology, urbanization and education would eventually change the religious identity of people, and that with time people would either abandon their traditional faiths or transform them politically, as was the case in Europe. However, this has not happened. These views stretched across a varied spectrum of scholarly approaches to the Middle East: at one pole stood the *optimists* predicting sure success for modernization in the Middle East; at the other stood the *pessimists* who saw the region as doomed to remain traditional and "primitive." They shared two assumptions: one was that non-Western societies – particularly Muslim societies – stood to benefit from Westernization. The second was that a society's ability to become fully Westernized (i.e., "modernized") depended to a large extent on doing away with religious and traditional values.[4]

What is Globalization?

Let us now turn to the challenge of definition. The word "globalization" was used for the first time in 1962, in an article in *The Spectator* magazine (UK). In this article, titled "The US Eyes Greater Europe," it occurs in the following sentence: "After so long privately chiding the French for their fear of *mondialisation*, the Americans are struck by the thought that globalization is, indeed, a staggering concept."[5] The vocabulary has spread in other languages over the past several decades. Examples include: *lil 'alam* in Arabic; *Jahaneeshodan* in Persian; *quanqiuhua* in Chinese; *mondialisation* in French; *gorobaruka* in Japanese; *globalizatsia* in Russian; and *kuresellesme* in Turkish, and forty years on, it remains "a staggering concept."

Does globalization refer to a condition, an end-state, or a process? Is it mostly a state of mind, or does it consist of objective circumstances? What are the arrangements from which globalization is a departure? Few topics invoke as much passion among present-day social researchers as the issue of globalization. Political scientists, economists, management scholars, marketers and sociologists have been scrutinizing the globalization phenomenon for more than two decades. Like any sweeping trend with widespread, profound effects, globalization is highly complex. The term describes a bewildering number of relationships and arrangements that are inevitably subject to strategic, political, social and cultural – as well as purely economic – influences.

In contemplating the profound impact of globalization, Joseph Prabhu observed, "Globalization might formally be conceived as a set of processes that enacts a radical transformation in the spatial and temporal organization of social relations and activities, resulting in a palpable sense of worldwide interconnectedness."[6] In a major work entitled *Why Globalization Works*, Martin Wolf offers an array of statistical evidence to support how market economies and capitalism have improved global conditions.[7] He focuses on China and India, maintaining that China achieved an increase in real income of over 400 percent between 1980 and 2000 as a result of liberalizing its economy.[8] Countries that have opted for market economies have become richer, healthier, more democratic and more egalitarian. Wolf argues that the principles that make capitalism a force for social development within national borders are the same ones that make it a force for good across borders.[9]

Even though market forces have linked people globally, it does not follow that they connect people everywhere to the same degree. As Jan A. Scholte has pointed out, "globalization is not universalization. On the contrary, the incidence of contemporary trans-planetary connectivity has varied considerably in relation to territorial location and social status. Some people continue to live lives that are relatively untouched by globality."[10] This paradoxical nature of globalization was captured by Roland Robertson: "We may best consider contemporary globalization in its most general sense as a form of institutionalization of [a] two-fold process involving the universalization of particularlism and the particularization of universalism."[11] As will be demonstrated, globalization has come to mean more than just how capitalism and market forces are expanding, "the term reveals most about social relations when it is understood as the spread of trans-planetary (and in contemporary times also increasing supra-territorial) connections between people."[12]

Andre Frank and Barry Gills have argued that the process of globalization is not new: "The existence of the same world system in which we live stretches back at least 5,000 years."[13] The argument regarding the long history of globalization has been more recently supported by Amartya Sen, the economics Nobel laureate. Sen attested that the process of globalization is at least a few thousand years old but that the West had a minor role to play in its early phases. Until about 1,000 AD, Sen observed, globalization was triggered by countries in the East, not the West. Then, as now, the process was accelerated with the aid of technology. At that time, the technology of the day comprised the likes of paper and printing, the crossbow and gunpowder, the clock and iron-chain suspension bridge, and the wheelbarrow and rotary fan.[14]

Discussing religion and globalization forces us to decide when we first find the latter process in human history. The four main drivers of globalization across time have been: religion, technology, economy and empire. These have not necessarily acted separately, but have often reinforced each other. For example, the globalization of Christianity started with the conversion of Emperor Constantine I of Rome in 313 AD. The religious conversion of the head of the empire started the process under which Christianity became the dominant religion not only of Europe but also of many other societies thousands of miles away. In this regard, Göran Therborn's schema for the phases of globalization dating back to the era of the expansion of the world religions makes perfect sense.[15] The expansion of the world religions by missionaries among nations and across the frontiers of empires can clearly be considered the prototype or at least the earliest instance of the process of globalization.

The phenomenon of a religious expansion without ties to a specific nation, society or ethnic group is not, in itself, new. Religion is fundamentally endowed with the power to expand. When it comes to the concept of globalization, it is important to emphasize the fact that the monotheistic religions of Judaism, Christianity and Islam established religio-cultural spheres throughout the world. Across the globe one can observe the deep connection between religion and states or ethnic groups, and religious structures – together with the characteristics originally held by the religion or sect – have often undergone great transformations in the process of developing within specific nations or ethnic groups.

In this context, the globalization of religion can be understood as a process of realignment, a process which involves the following three facets: First, it implies the inevitable transformation of individual religious organizations; second, it can be expected that new characteristics will be produced in the contents of doctrines, rituals, and practices; and third, globalization will be accompanied by changes in the populations supporting religions, particularly in their intellectual perspectives. In this context, the primary effect of globalization is "the relativization of particularistic identities along with the relativization and marginalization of religion as a mode of social communication."[16]

Globalization, Modernity and Religion

In the twentieth century, most Western politicians and intellectuals (and even some clerics) assumed religion was becoming marginal in public life; faith was largely treated as an irrelevance in global politics. In the 21st century, by contrast, religion is playing a central role. From Nigeria to Sri Lanka, Chechnya to Baghdad, people have been killed in God's name, and money and volunteers have poured into these regions. Once again, one of the world's great religions is experiencing a bloody divide (this time it is Sunnis and Shias, rather than Catholics and Protestants). Meanwhile, the power of governments to control religious politics has declined, and we are witnessing an increase in interdenominational violence, as well as religion-linked terrorist attacks.

[146]

Figure 6.1

Interdenominational Violence and Religion-linked Terrorist Attacks

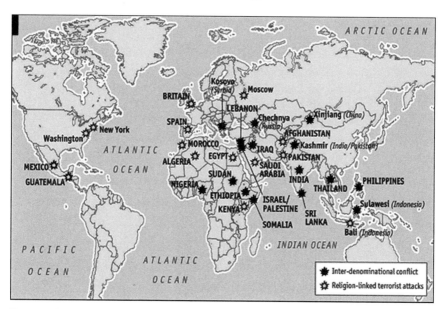

Source: *The Economist*, November 3, 2007.

As global current events demonstrate, religion is essential to the fabric of individual and community identities. In the modern world, religions face two major challenges. The first is the emergence of a global, scientific–technological culture stemming from a scientific view of the world. One of the effects of this development has been the re-definition of the role of religion, in which the place of science and technology is recognized but in which religion is seen as focusing on the "ends" of life and of well-being while science focuses on the "means." At the same time, there has been a tendency for religion to withdraw into personal areas of life, leading to a secularization of public life, allowing people from many different religious faiths to share a common social life.

Anthony Giddens describes one of the fundamental tensions resulting from this aspect of globalization:

[147]

> The battleground of the twenty-first century will pit fundamentalism
> against cosmopolitan tolerance. In a globalizing world where information
> and images are routinely transmitted across the globe, we are all regularly
> in contact with others who think differently, and live differently, from
> ourselves. Cosmopolitans welcome and embrace this cultural [and
> religious] complexity. Fundamentalists find it disturbing and dangerous.
> Whether in the areas of religion, ethnic identity or nationalism, they take
> refuge in a renewed and purified tradition—and quite often, violence.[17]

Lester Kurtz, in his book *Gods in the Global Village*, describes the
emergence of this global, scientific–technological culture related to a
scientific view of the world. One of the results of this development has
been the challenge to re-define the role of religion in a world where the
more rational a society, the less that society draws on religious
interpretations to structure the social order.

However, Lester Kurtz overlooks the notion that the social structures
and cultural categories used in his book – and by a majority of
globalization theorists – are derived from the Western model of a liberal
social order. The transformations that take place through the process of
globalization are largely features of a world system first institutionalized
by Western societies. Since both the liberal model and the emerging world
system are characterized above all by their movement away from
Christianity and have relegated religious symbols and institutions to
subordinate roles, globalization is partly a process of secularization.

As we have witnessed in the past two decades, however, the rise of
fundamentalism in the United States, Israel, the Middle East and Asia
demonstrates that globalization has had the opposite effect. Instead of
religion disappearing, we are witnessing a religious revival. This means that
although the process of secularization and globalization can place limits on
religion's sphere of action, it does not erase it as a social phenomenon.

Understood this way, the debate over whether globalization will bring
about the disappearance of religious universes is inconsequential. It is enough
to remember that Emile Durkheim, in discussing the supremacy of science
over religion, said that from an explanatory point of view religion lost ground

to scientific thought; nevertheless, since science for him was a "morality without ethics," – that is, an interpretative universe incapable of giving sense to collective action – the potential of religion to be an ethical basis for action in the world, a way of orienting behavior, remained completely valid. In fact, modernity does not eliminate but, rather, dislocates the place religion occupied in past societies. Consequently, the end of the religious monopoly does not imply the decline of religion *tout court*; instead, it is a sign of religious plurality and diversity, either from an individual or a collective standpoint. In logical terms, then, there is no reason for us to imagine the "return" of something that never went away in the first place.[18]

People's religious habits do not change quickly. Cultural traditions, including religious ones, maintain themselves through families and other interaction-based social networks without the assistance of overarching systems, organizations or social movements. Indeed, the increasing availability of religious alternatives can just as easily lead to the reassertion of one's traditional religious identity. History teaches us that, contrary to conventional wisdom, human beings are much more willing to die for ideas than for interests; interests can be bargained for, but ideas are the foundation of identity, and no one wants to compromise their identity.

Globalization and Religious Pluralism

Some proponents of globalization maintain that increased economic, political and social interaction among nations and states will undermine religious authoritarianism. They maintain that global migration patterns and modern communications technologies have spawned more active transnational religious communities, forming a new religious pluralism. On the one hand, global religious identities have encouraged inter-religious dialogue and greater religious engagement around issues including international development, conflict resolution and transitional justice. On the other hand, however, more intense inter-religious competition has contributed to controversy over the meaning and scope of religious freedom.

[149]

Furthermore, globalization has intensified nationalistic tendencies, and instead of bringing religious pluralism, has allowed radical religious leaders to use religion as a powerful ideology to advance political goals. For example, Europe saw a *de facto* religious conflict in the early 1990s between Croats, Serbs and Bosnian Muslims in Bosnia-Herzegovina. Each combatant identified religious and cultural (not ideological) allies, for example in Germany, Russia and the Arab–Muslim world. This was a surprise—not least because it occurred in the former Yugoslavia, a country whose people were long thought to be inexorably secularized under the Communist regime which had taken power after World War II. Later in the 1990s, a further conflict erupted: civil war in Kosovo between Muslim ethnic Albanians and Christian Serbs, with the former aided by co-religionists from the Middle East.

The influential World Council of Churches held its 50th anniversary meeting in 1998 in Zimbabwe. Globalization was a key item on its agenda. The meeting's official report, *Together on the Way*, regards globalization as a threat; "The vision behind globalization," it says, "includes a competing vision to the Christian commitment."[19] With a similar position to that taken by the Vatican, the World Council of Churches describes globalization as a vision that creates conflicts among religious communities by attempting to inculcate a "neo-liberal" faith in competitive markets and individual consumption that is bound to produce a "graceless system that abandons the disenfranchised and the poor because they cannot compete with the powerful few."[20]

The intensification of the relationships between societies in terms of economic, social, political and cultural practices and ideas creates the impression that "the world is a single place."[21] In his book on religion and globalization, Peter Beyer argues that globalization has created contradictory processes of homogenization and distinctiveness. On one level, more religions are coming into contact with each other more than at any time in their history; yet at the same time, there is an increase in a fundamentalism that claims distinctiveness from global trends towards homogeny. Beyer notes, however, that most emerging fundamentalist groups are associated with world religions. Most are basing themselves on claims that they represent "orthodoxy" of those major traditions. In a sense, the problem of religious fundamentalism has come to light in part as a consequence of globalization. Whether or not fundamentalism is a global category is a matter of some contention, but no one denies the link between globalization and fundamentalism. In a sense, "fundamentalism is a rational response of traditionally religious peoples to social, political and economic changes that downgrade and constrain the role of religion in the public world."

This does not simply mean that religion views itself as the antithesis of globalization; it signifies that across the world, various individuals have consciously chosen to evince religious identities in their personal, micro-political struggles in order to make sense of what has occurred in and around their lives. This perspective goes some way towards explaining the Islamic revival and the place of radical Islam within it. It is important to note that radical Islam constitutes just one part of a wider renaissance that has been taking place over the last several decades. The renaissance that is occurring in all sectors of Muslim societies – from culture and political life to private beliefs and civic networks of faith – is part of a wider global religious response to globalization.

By the late 1960s, Muslim societies faced a profound crisis with cultural, political, social, economic, psychological and spiritual dimensions. Secular ideologies and models of development had failed to produce prosperous societies that could match those of the West, allowing Islamic revivalist movements to surge into the public sphere, promising a return to Islamic greatness and dispelling the "hopelessness and pessimism" that pervaded Muslim societies.[22] The *raison d'être* of Muslim revivalists can be succinctly articulated: "the very integrity of the Islamic culture and way of life is threatened by non-Islamic forces of secularism and modernity, encouraged by Muslim governments." Significantly, they not only opposed external actors and concepts, such as

[151]

the West or globalization, but also their own governments, which had failed to solve the inherent problems in their societies. In this context and by these actors, globalization is viewed as an aggrandizing influence that heralds patently non-Islamic ideas and practices, such as secularism, liberal democracy, consumerism, etc.—essentially the products of the West.

Few observers are willing to defend the hypothesis that, globally speaking, we live today in a truly secularized society. It may be that globally, at the level of individual involvement and orientation, religion is as strong or as weak as it has ever been. Yet that idea does not address the question of the social forms of religion and their broader societal influence and significance.[23]

Globalization and the "Clash of Civilizations"

Tensions, entanglements and violence are themes that are emphasized by proponents of theories that predict a clash of civilizations – or, indeed, of religions – such as Samuel Huntington. In essence, Huntington's thesis depends on orientalist understandings of Islam, in which Islam – the "other" – is perceived as culturally inferior to the religion of West and identified as a threat and even an enemy.[24] Surprisingly, the Library of Congress has classified the *Clash of Civilizations and the Remaking of World Order* as "history," which it assuredly is not, either in scope or in method.[25] Although Huntington lists five or possibly six non-Western civilizations that could come into conflict with the West, it is Islam that appears to pose the most serious "threat." Huntington's understanding ignores the diversity, plurality and various dynamics of Islam and the Muslim World as well as that of "Islamism" and "Islamic fundamentalism."

Almost sixty states exist today whose majority populations adhere to Islam; nearly 1.2 billion people across the globe call themselves Muslims. To assume that they will all contest globalization and engage in some epic "clash of civilizations" or participate in a "coming anarchy" erases much of the discursive and ideological map of possibilities that awaits the Muslim world. Moreover, the revival of Islamic identities and the

[152]

emergence of new Muslim movements, including radical fundamentalist networks, account for only one element of a broader magnanimous trend: the resurgence of religion as a salient dynamic that reshapes identities, behavior and orientations in the late stages of globalization.[26]

Huntington's thesis has been widely criticized for its pessimistic, if not paranoid conclusions.[27] It is certainly simplistic and highly problematic, both in its use of evidence and in its understanding of the cause and effect of modernity. Nonetheless, his work offers an example of how those promoting globalization perceive Middle Eastern and Islamic culture. In this way, it is easy to portray the Middle East as an unchanging and dangerous barrier to globalization.[28]

Is Globalization a form of Religion?

The most popular proponent of this school is Thomas Friedman who in a recent book has argued that the world is becoming "flat." He states the following:

> In today's world, having an Indian company led by a Hungarian–Uruguayan, servicing American banks with engineers from Brazil managed by Indian supervisors who have learned to eat Uruguayan vegetables and food is just the new normal.[29]

In a sense, what Friedman is telling us is that globalization is like a religion advancing a social order, and that one measures worth in terms of to what extent one's taste has become global. However, Friedman fails to mention why the Indian company was established in the first place. The reasons had nothing to do with the intention of creating a global religion; if you ask any CEO of such a company, they would say that their reasons have more to do with language, the need to be close to clients, and the tyranny of time zones.

When it comes to religion and globalization, Friedman pays particular attention to Islam and Muslim communities living in societies with a secular tradition. This quote illustrates his view of Islam and globalization:

[153]

> A south Asian Muslim friend of mine once told me this story. His Indian Muslim family split in 1948, with half going to Pakistan and half staying in Mumbai. When he got older he asked his father why the Indian half of the family seemed to be doing better than the Pakistani half. His father said to him, "Son, when a Muslim grows up in India and he sees a man living in a big mansion high on a hill, he says, 'Father, one day I will be that man.' And when a Muslim grows up in Pakistan and sees a man living in a big mansion high on the hill, he says, 'Father, one day I will kill that man.'"[30]

Friedman treats the Arab and Muslim world as an aberration. While Wolf placed the blame on the inability of Middle Eastern governments to develop the legal structures that nurture globalization, Friedman sees it as a cultural issue: "For complicated cultural and historical reasons, many Muslim countries are not able to manage the pressures of globalization that require both openness to the outside world and an ability to assimilate transformation."[31]

Conclusion

As stated by Scholte, globalization has not homogenized the world, nor has its universalization affected everyone in the same fashion. Religious responses to globalization have varied depending on regional location and the extent of global interaction.

It is important to note that in the struggle over globalization, religious voices have been more articulate and less deterministic than the proponents of globalization who advocate uniformity. Jonathan Sacks asks "Can we make space for difference?" His answer is that we must; for humanity to continue with integrity and dignity, "we need not only a theology of commonality [globalization], but also a theology of difference."[32] In fact, religious leaders like Sacks have acknowledged that the 21st century world is a place of interdependence and affinity; today the challenge is to learn about and acknowledge new kinds of recognition through diversity of needs, nationalities and experiences. We must be willing to push against the constraints of our own self-imposed structures and barriers to communication:

[154]

God has spoken to mankind in many languages: through Judaism to Jews, Christianity to Christians and Islam to Muslims. No one creed has a monopoly on spiritual truth. Judaism is a particularist, not universalist, monotheism. It believes in one God but not in one religion, one culture, or one truth. The God of Abraham is the God of all mankind, but the faith of Abraham is not the faith of all mankind.[33]

Ultimately, there is a place for globalization in religious identity, as much as globalization has a place within religious perspective. The majority of religious people around the world will not mindlessly contest globalization; they derive meaning from it, which a minority of fundamentalists might interpret as threatening, while others derive more peaceful visions. Regardless of this diversity, religion will certainly not recede from globalization's horizons.

7

The World Economy
and the New Middle Ages

John Rapley

"Are we Rome?" This question has come to preoccupy American intellectuals of late.[1] Recent years have seen an explosion of American literature tracing parallels between the contemporary United States and the Roman Empire. Some of it is optimistic and calls for the United States to unabashedly assume the imperial role that Rome played in its day. More often, though, the literature is pessimistic or at least cautionary, warning that if the United States continues to operate in the same way, both internally and externally, it risks heading into a similar terminal decline to the great empire of antiquity.

However, as this paper will argue, while the lessons of Rome are instructive, the parallels which are pertinent to the present-day are of a different sort. Rome did not decay from within, nor need the United States. Instead, Rome was brought down from without, by the barbarian invasions. It is too early to predict the eventual end of the US as the world's sole superpower as a result of anything similar. Nevertheless, as will be shown, the same kind of inequality between empire and periphery which characterized the late imperial age prevails in the modern world. Furthermore, the imperial heartland in this case is not confined to the United States, since all the rich countries of the world are closely integrated and increasingly removed from the rest of the planet as a result of their aggregate wealth. The resulting tension between "empire" and periphery is giving rise in some parts of the developing world to what can be described as a new medievalism.

In recent years inequality has become an important object of study in the social sciences. In particular, there has been great debate involving two propositions; first, that inequality has worsened as a result of free-market reform programs, which have become ubiquitous; and, second, that this inequality is leading to rising social instability throughout the world. This paper will take a slightly different tack, though. It will argue that the significant question is not what is happening to income distribution *within* societies, but rather *between* them; and in particular, how this distribution is affected by an increasingly globalized world economy.

To understand what is happening, it is important to focus on the world's cities. For the first time in history, most of the planet's human population inhabits urban areas. Moreover, cities are ever more closely linked to one another, as nodes in an emergent global economy. Cities also stand at the vanguard of cultural globalization, with trends from around the world penetrating cities before they reach the countryside. The result is the emergence of an increasingly global community, linked by an emergent integrated economy, and growing ever more homogeneous.

At the same time, however, the world's national governments maintain immigration policies which limit the flow of populations from Third World to First World cities. This flow is increasing, no doubt, but the rate at which it is increasing has been constrained by policy regimes. What therefore results is economic and cultural integration in the midst of spatial segregation. The poor laborers of the South may work for firms closely integrated with their counterparts in the North; dressed in similar clothes, they may return at the end of the day to watch the same television programs and eat similar foods, but the economic space they inhabit remains radically different. It can be likened to the relationship between Johannesburg and Soweto in the era of apartheid.

The wealth of the "empire" is thus more visible than ever in the Third World's cities, and more and more people are there to see it. Yet it remains largely beyond their grasp. Only a relatively small share of the populations of developing countries ever has the opportunity to migrate to the rich world. Still, because fertility is declining in the rich countries, more people are migrating from the South. As they do so, they open up the vectors of communication along which illicit "raiders" – in particular, organized criminal networks – can move. Then, as they penetrate the industrial world and thereby increase their own resource bases, these non-state actors secure the resources they need to gain control over space back in the Third World cities whence they came. In the meantime, because free-market policies and globalization have constrained the activities of Third World governments, the latter are less able to contest the emergence of these new authorities. What results is an overlay of negotiated sovereignty, whereby states retain nominal authority over "turf" which, however, lies largely under the control of autonomous sub-state actors.

Sometimes these bodies are pernicious, like criminal or terrorist gangs; sometimes they are benign, like the Muslim brotherhoods of Senegal, but in all cases they are leading to the emergence of a new form of political organization. Because these are so similar to the political structures which emerged in much of Western Europe after the fall of Rome, this type of political organization has been called neo-medieval.[2]

While neo-medievalism has so far been largely confined to the developing world, that does not mean it could not spread into the developed world. As was the case in late antiquity, when the Roman Empire first began breaking up at its edges when nobles transferred their loyalty to raiding warlords, the advent of a new Middle Ages in developing countries could herald the shape of things to come. In particular, areas that lie increasingly outside the control of the state are beginning to emerge in cities in the industrial world, particularly those most integrated with the developed world.

Inequality and Instability

It has long been axiomatic in political science and sociology that economic inequality tends to produce political instability. Given that humans are social animals and thus compare themselves with one another in assessing their relative well-being – and also compete with one another on the basis of their control over resources – it follows that changes in income distribution will over time lead to increased social tensions as people attempt to redress the emergent imbalances. Over the last few decades the spread of free-market policy regimes across the world has given rise to an apparent increase in inequality. While labor markets have become more competitive and skill premiums have fetched higher returns, governments have been withdrawing the protection they once maintained to shelter citizens from the harsher effects of market economies.[3]

However, recent scholarship has questioned the claim that inequality has resulted from free-market policy changes and that this inequality, in turn, has prompted increased instability. There is considerable debate as to whether income distribution has worsened as a consequence of recent policy changes.[4] Nonetheless, a survey of the relevant literature would seem to suggest that, on balance, some worsening has occurred in recent decades, and that the effect has been particularly acute in developing countries[5]—a point that will be revealed as germane to this paper. Moreover, even in cases where inequality does not show up in standard measures like the Gini coefficient,[6] it does not mean it is not emerging. Frances Stewart's work on horizontal inequality has uncovered cases in which apparent inequality masks distributional imbalances that, because they occur not among classes but between ethnic groups, may not show up in standard measures: in short, there might not be more poor, but the poor may have an increasingly uniform hue, making social instability particularly likely since the inequalities are so visible.[7]

All the same, defenders of free-market policy reforms contend that even where inequality shows up, there is not a clear case that it is, in fact, leading in the aggregate to greater instability. Globally, the evidence of recent years suggests that the world is growing not more violent, but less so.[8] Meanwhile, some econometric work suggests that where it occurs, what drives violence is not rising inequality but rising poverty (since it reduces the opportunity-cost of violence).[9] Yet while there is some debate surrounding these econometric analyses, what this discussion may not adequately capture is that the significant feature of contemporary violence may not be its rising or falling quantity, but rather its changing quality. Many scholars now contend that the significant trend in violence has been not its increase or decrease, but rather its privatization.

The global decline in violence has essentially resulted from a decline in warfare, and in particular, interstate warfare. In the meantime, however, the growth of transnational criminal and terrorist networks; the increasing use of private security contractors by both governments and corporations; and the increasing employment of private security agents in many countries have all led to the emergence of a violence that is not immediately connected to states. Its volume may have diminished; but its greater unpredictability makes this from of violence particularly worrisome.

Moreover, its emergence may point towards the inequality that is perhaps most significant in assessing and predicting contemporary stability: that is the inequality not within, but rather between societies. Much privatized violence is in some way connected to defending or acquiring wealth by private means. Whether it be security contractors defending mining concessions or criminal gangs involved in human or drug smuggling, highly organized forms of violence are developing which appear to exploit the distributional divide that has emerged in the modern world.

Exacerbating this divide is the fact that the "one world" or "flat earth" scenario celebrated by the most ardent exponents of the current wave of globalization has to date been more of a cultural than an economic reality. As we shall go on to see, the evidence that globalization is leveling global incomes is – so far, at least – weak. Culturally, however, the planet's fare is converging at a considerable rate. Particularly in urban environments, the world's citizens are consuming an increasingly common diet of food,

[161]

music, film, fashion and television. Trends which emerge in the world's cultural capitals spread very quickly outwards. So while in rural areas traditional reference-points may persist and peer groups may remain local, in cities one increasingly determines whether or not one is "keeping up" not by comparison with one's immediate neighbors but with the images available on satellite television.

It becomes significant, therefore, that for the first time in history, a majority of the planet's human inhabitants live in cities, with the proportion growing ever greater. It is to be expected that changes in the organization of warfare may follow from this. The planet's urban land-space accounts for a tiny proportion of its total land mass—probably no more than one percent.[10] The nation-state was built upon the consolidation of the territories which provided governments their tax revenues. In a modern economy, with ever less of that revenue coming from land-intensive primary industries, control of urban space becomes ever more important. And yet, in these spaces, government control is becoming increasingly contested.

This is not necessarily a function of poverty. To cite an early instance of this development, in 1970s Tehran the oil boom attracted migrants from the countryside in such numbers that the government – despite its oil wealth – could not keep up with the added demands for public services and amenities. In this context, Islamic charities filled the breach, creating spaces within the city that lay increasingly beyond the state's control and hence gave the political opposition areas in which to implant itself. So it goes in many of the world's cities today: rapid population growth is straining the public sectors of even the wealthiest states, a trend exacerbated by the pressures governments everywhere feel to reduce the scope of government in order to maintain their bond ratings and standing in international financial markets. Where such vacuums emerge in urban spaces, there are almost always private agents with the capacity to fill them. Furthermore, whilst governments feel the pressure to keep government "lean," the tendency for state withdrawal appears to be most pronounced in developing countries, where it shows up in the form of reduced services.[11]

In the world's cities, moreover, citizens are far more likely to be exposed to a global cultural diet. The spread of things like shopping malls and supermarkets across the globe places cities on the vanguard of globalization. In fact, in cities which are more closely integrated with other cities than with their own traditional hinterlands, some scholars have detected the emergence of what they call the "global city."[12] The recent history of the growth of international commerce, shipping and travel is essentially a record of the growth in movement among the world's cities. Time-space compression has reduced the virtual distances separating these cities, whilst strengthening the vectors of communication joining them. Even though much of this communication is controlled or monitored by governments, much is not. This means that the possibilities for societies to interpenetrate increases commensurately.

So, even while the distances separating the cities of the developed world from those of the developing world have not changed, these cities are increasingly living side-by-side. Industrial societies, owing to their declining fertility, have grown increasingly dependent upon immigrant labor from developing societies. What results is economic integration in the midst of spatial segregation. In other words, economies are closely intertwined but immigration and security policies are geared towards keeping populations separate—the apparent motive being to keep the benefits of economic integration from leaving the wealthy countries. Some industries rely on immigrant labor, and the movement of peoples from Third World countries thus increases the volume of traffic along these vectors of communication. For many industries, however, the development of outsourcing means that a city's workshops can be located on the other side of the globe, but remain part of a highly integrated operation. Speaking proverbially, Johannesburg and Soweto may now be separated by huge distances, but their citizens – having worked to build the same global economy – may return home to watch the same television programs and eat the same food at the end of the day, only in different economic spaces.

[163]

The Global Divide

Whilst the citizens of Johannesburg and Soweto are more than ever aware of one another's conditions of existence, the inescapable fact is that the spaces they inhabit do remain, in fact, radically different. Neoclassical economic theory long assumed that in a globalized world – a liberal global trading environment – convergence between rich and poor countries would naturally occur. The logic is simple: when it is allowed to move freely, capital – be it financial, physical or human – will naturally move from capital-rich to capital-scarce regions, because declining marginal returns in developed regions force it outward in search of higher profits. Therefore, goes the logic, developing countries can move up the product life-cycle chain by applying factors of production in which they abound – namely, low-cost labor – to technologies which have already matured in their homelands.

Yet if the logic is disarmingly easy, the empirical evidence in fact does not support it. Since the dawn of the industrial age some two centuries ago, when the industrial countries shifted onto planes of sustained high growth, the gap between rich and poor countries has grown wider, from roughly 3:1 in 1800 to 60:1 at the turn of this millennium.[13] Various time-series and measures of income can be combined to produce different results, but in almost none of them does one find anything other than divergence.[14] Some scholars, arguing that convergence is a process which plays out over centuries and not decades, maintain that certain recent trends point toward the beginnings of a process of convergence. However, even they are forced to admit that this picture is skewed by the dramatic performance of China and, to a lesser degree, India in recent years (with respect to China, meanwhile, whatever aggregate convergence may be occurring needs to be set against a radical widening in intra-country distribution that has occurred over the same period).[15] Elsewhere, the picture remains one of divergence, not convergence.

Faced with this reality, a growing body of scholarship now argues that convergence is not likely to occur. Given the tendency for future demand

[164]

in the world economy to benefit knowledge-intensive goods, countries that rely on resource or labor-intensive development strategies – many if not most developing countries – are destined to under perform. All the while, the high capital costs involved in knowledge-intensive production create a bias in favor of developed countries that is likely to intensify over time. This bias is further reinforced by the economies of agglomeration that operate in human capital markets, which confer significant advantages on existing "knowledge poles" in the world economy. Human capital thus tends not to flow from capital-rich to capital-scarce regions, but in the opposite direction, with the resultant "brain-drain" inhibiting the growth prospects of poorer countries. Such an endogenous growth model confines convergence to a theoretical possibility, but not much more.[16]

Finally, it is even questionable that convergence would be a sustainable option for the future. Virtually all relevant models predict a global convergence that results from – to put it crudely – the enrichment of the poor countries, not the impoverishment of the poor ones. The typical vision is of a world in which Third World growth outpaces that of the First World, enabling the poor countries to catch up with the rich ones on higher planes of development, sometime near the end of the twenty-first century. However, for this to happen, at current rates of economic and demographic growth, the world economy would have to grow until it reached a level of output more than a hundred times greater than it is today. Given that most climate scientists reckon the world is already operating beyond its pollution-absorbing capacity, this goal seems to lie well beyond the realm of reason.[17]

Faced with this fact, developed countries have so far tended to gravitate towards policy solutions which "lock in" their existing wealth, whether by insisting that future rather than present polluters should bear the expense of adjustment to climate change – the current US position – or by adopting trade and immigration policies which protect the advantages of First World workers and firms. However, as this paper contends, such an attempt to prevent equalization is questionable. For by means fair or foul, citizens of poor regions and countries are finding ways to gain access to the rich markets of the world, and globalization both presents them with opportunities and challenges them to live like the top fifth.

Empires and Peripheries

An examination of history may help to give us an idea of what to expect of a world in which the rich try to keep their wealth from the poor, whilst seeking to further integrate their economies. While it has long been popular to attribute the fall of the Roman Empire to internal decay, recent scholarship has found that by most measures, Rome was relatively healthy on the verge of its collapse. What precipitated the fall of Rome was therefore not internal decay but rather the barbarian invasions, the repeated attacks on its frontier by the peoples on its periphery. A key motivation for this raiding was the considerable wealth which beckoned within the Empire, and which could not be accessed in any other way.

In the later imperial period, it appears that the outer areas of the empire augmented trade with peripheral regions, while simultaneously securing the imperial borders. This led to an increase in the wealth of elites on either side of the borders. Relative to the peasantry, the Roman aristocracy improved its position. Thus, this early process of economic integration had an effect similar to that of globalization today: increasing income inequalities whilst enriching the imperial heartland. However, in the periphery, raiding activity began, as marginalized peoples began trying to secure some of this wealth by violent means. In time, this activity spilled over into the imperial territory itself so that, by the end of the fourth century, some far-removed areas of the Empire were being drawn out of the Roman tax net.[18]

A vicious cycle then ensued. To reclaim the lost portion of its tax base, the Empire had to boost its military spending to take back the lands over which it was losing control. However, this necessitated increased spending, which in turn drove up taxes. As taxes rose, the aristocracy

[166]

which collected them began to gain an interest in cutting deals with the barbarian invaders, offering concessions on reduced taxes, or to transfer taxes collected to them in return for their protection. Gradually, therefore, the Empire was whittled away at the frontiers.[19] What replaced it was not a new Empire; the former imperial lands eventually shifted from being tax-based to land-based systems, with revenue coming not from taxes on production but from direct control of the land.[20] This new type of organization, which fused economic and political power ever more closely, appeared to reduce the burden of taxation for both the nobility and the peasantry.[21] The main loser was the imperial state.

In fact, while the period of warfare which followed the fall of the Empire worsened the lot of the peasantry, those who survived arguably ended up better off than their predecessors had been under the Empire. The glorious monuments and artistic achievements of the classical age were not conjured from thin air. Such ambitious public works, and the support of a leisured class able to devote itself to higher pursuits, depended on a state that was able to extract large surpluses from the populations it controlled. The relatively crude buildings and ceramics of the Early Middle Ages, and the large-scale disappearance of literary culture at the time, testify to the fact that the successor states were, if poorer, probably more egalitarian. While there is no clear evidence that the peasantry as a class saw an improvement in its condition in absolute terms – after all, the population declined after the Empire fell – the archaeological record indicates that land lost by the nobility continued to be used, suggesting that surviving peasants actually expanded their lands.[22] This situation persisted until the eleventh century, when the nobility succeeded in consolidating its hold over the peasantry, thereby acquiring a larger share of its output. It is no coincidence that this was the period when major monuments and a cultural elite – housed in the newly founded universities – reappeared on the European stage, while growth took off.[23] Thus, to use contemporary terminology, one might say that in the age-old choice between growth and development, the Early Middle Ages favored the latter.

The Early Middle Ages were characterized by instability, as warlords sought to secure their own small kingdoms. Economic decline, the erosion of the state, and chronic warfare changed the political culture of the successor kingdoms. Whereas literacy and a facility with high culture had been the hallmark of the Roman aristocracy, that of the medieval one was warfare.[24] The ubiquitous symbol of the European nobility in the Early Middle Ages was the castle, embodying as it did the security a lord could provide his subjects. A warrior culture thus emerged, celebrating heroism and triumph in the martial arts. For a time, literacy receded in significance.[25]

In sum, inequality – both within and without the Empire – lay behind both its triumphs and failings. The unequal distribution of wealth managed by the imperial state permitted the rise of the high civilization of which contemporary observers remain so enamored, but it also eventually prompted the raiding behavior that led to the Empire's downfall. What followed was a world that was more egalitarian, but also poorer and more violent. An Empire that had perhaps been more modest in its ambitions, a bit more egalitarian, and more concerned with the conditions of the states on is periphery, might have proved more durable, but in the event, what brought down Rome was not a rival empire; it was the impoverished peoples on its fringes. Imperial propagandists might have contrived all manner of intellectual justifications for the unequal world in which they lived – including depicting the speakers of "barbar" tongues as lesser beings (a prejudice which persists in the Western usage of the word barbarian to this day). These justifications carried little weight among marginal peoples. One could, therefore, say that ultimately, it was greed which brought down the Roman Empire.

The New Middle Ages

The new medievalism thus takes as its cue the new "empire." In comparing the present-day world to that of late antiquity, we must be clear that there is today no political entity quite like the Roman Empire of old.

Nor should we look for one: the comparison of the two periods does not depend on a repeat of political history. There is a great and growing body of literature which attempts to draw parallels between the present-day United States and the Roman Empire of old, whether to justify expansionism[26] or warn of its dangers.[27] Even if one could make a case that its degree of influence over much of the world approximates that of a Roman imperium which – owing to the great distances and primitive communications technology involved – had to rely on indirect rule, the United States is nevertheless not an empire with administrative control over colonies the way Rome was, or even for that matter as more recent European empires were.

The Rome analogy applies to this study in only one, limited respect: the wealth imbalance between the dominant economy and those on its periphery. Nor does it even have to imply an imperial or colonial economic relation between empire and periphery, as world systems theory, for instance, suggests. It may be that the world's chief economic poles enriched themselves at the expense of the poor regions of the planet, but it is immaterial to this particular discussion. The hypothesis of this paper is that human societies cannot easily abide extremes of wealth and income, and that doing so usually relies on a considerable amount of violence and oppression. Since globalization has increasingly created a global society in the cultural sphere – the very sphere in which expectations of abundance and just shares are shaped – the imbalances of the global economy have become ever more pertinent to the world's politics.

In speaking of these imbalances, therefore, the "empire" refers not merely to the world's dominant political power – which nobody contests is the United States – but indeed all those countries which have come to be known as "First World:" those countries which hold one fifth of humanity but four-fifths of its wealth (as measured by economic output). As it happens, a great many of these countries are either former European empires or their former colonies of settlement, like the United States, Canada or Australia. Some, like

Japan, are not, while still others – very rich but essentially underdeveloped, their wealth derived from a surfeit of oil – are neither empire nor periphery.

Most global trade and investment occur within this "imperial" bloc. By and large, the flow of populations among the countries concerned is relatively unhindered. Owing to the wealth of these societies, their states generally have consolidated control over their national territories, and are able to provide a full range of services to their peoples including, very importantly, security. As a rule, these societies, despite their diplomatic differences, are at peace with one another. They have also generally coalesced around a set of "Western" values.

However, the key point is that all of them, owing to their relative profusion of wealth, have an interest in preventing "seepage" of that wealth to poor regions. It is not that they oppose the development of poor countries as such. They simply – without exception – are committed to the rule that this development should not negatively affect their own prosperity. The rule is reasonable enough. However, in practice, it is leading to a variety of development that perpetuates the wealth of the rich countries.

Thus, in a global age, when the wealth of the empire is readily apparent to peoples all over the world, yet not readily accessible, illicit forms of raiding become likely options. In legal ways, too, opportunities to gain a share of the empire's wealth have been opening up—which have consequently facilitated the spread of illicit activities. A rule seems to prevail in developed societies, that as incomes rise, the opportunity cost of children also rises, leading to declines in fertility. As population growth slows – in a few rich societies, it has already begun to go into reverse – governments confront a dilemma: either they accept a slowing of or even a reversal of growth, since manpower remains the key input to the production process; or they maintain the prosperity of their societies by importing labor. If Rome's expansion necessitated recourse to mercenary armies, today's empire has come to depend not on imported soldiers but on imported workers.

However, as discussed, technological changes have made it possible for imported labor to sometimes remain offshore. Over the last few decades, a number of demographic, technological and economic developments have accelerated the changes taking place in the relationship between space and economic output. Included among these are: (a) the rapid urbanization of the planet; (b) the shift to knowledge-intensive production, which is reducing the "weight" of economic output and thereby diminishing the importance of market proximity in the location of manufacturing enterprises; (c) developments in communications technology, such as containerization and dramatic reductions in the cost of air travel, which have reduced the costs of transporting both goods and labor, thereby accentuating the trend identified in (b) above; (d) new managerial technologies, such as the "flattening" of administration, the elimination of middle management, the shift to flexible production and the use of networks and contracting; (e) rapid accelerations in the pace of change in information technology, and in particular the development of the Internet, which have made possible the exploitation of these new managerial technologies; and (f) new forms of migration from developing countries to developed countries, as declining fertility in the latter have necessitated the recourse to immigration to maintain industrial competitiveness.

The strategies of economic liberalization mentioned earlier have made it possible for firm managers to realize the new advantages that have arisen as a result of the changes outlined above. As a result, we appear to be standing on the cusp of an epochal change in the global economy. The possibilities of creating globally-integrated firms,[28] combined with urbanization and the new vectors of communication opened up by human migration, are giving shape to a global economy increasingly centered on the aforementioned global cities of the planet.

However, if the workshops of the world are increasingly being outsourced to poor regions of the planet, making it possible to bring the factory to the workers rather than the other way around, migration towards the industrial countries is nonetheless still rising. Many manufacturing and some service sub-sectors are susceptible to globalization, but others, such as retail trade or hospitality services, are not. This has necessitated the importation of labor to the First World. Two outcomes of relevance to this discussion result. One is that formal vectors of communication between rich and poor regions widen, making it possible for illicit forms of migration and trafficking to piggy-back on legitimate forms. The other is that financial flows – particularly in the form of remittances and, in the Muslim world, donations to charitable organizations – move from the First World to the Third World.

However, flows of illicit money also increase. The organized trafficking of humans, narcotics, weapons and money has been one of the fastest growing industries in the wake of the Cold War. Very often, these flows evade tax nets, going directly to households or, in many cases, to non-state organizations, be they drug gangs or Muslim charities.

The context into which these monies flow is equally significant. In the age of free-market reforms, governments in developing countries have faced pressure to pare back their spending. The greatest source of pressure has not been the traditional culprits of Western governments or multilateral bodies, but bond-rating agencies. This has to do with the fact that in the age of globalized financial markets, Third World governments have increasingly resorted to foreign bond markets to raise cash. Given that the bond-rating agencies have a considerable degree of influence over the interest rates governments must pay on their bond flotations, governments everywhere have been eager to curry their favor. This has created the universal tendency for governments to try to keep a lid on their spending, at the risk of incurring the wrath of financial markets. Only occasionally does this show up in the form of actual retrenchment. More frequently, governments continue to increase their spending, but at rates that are unable to match the growing demands for services on the part of an ever-more urbanized population.[29]

In the world's cities, exposed as they are to global currents, besieged by the "reality" programs and celebrity infomercials coming from the

[172]

West, citizens find their appetites for new resources stoked. The peer group by which one judges one's achievements is less and less one's physical neighbors, and increasingly people who live in other parts of the world—a tendency which appears to be particularly acute among younger people, who show a greater proclivity than their elders to forge communities in cyberspace. But these rising demands are occurring within states whose own resource-allocation powers have been constrained. As a consequence, private networks have emerged to provide a whole range of services in many Third World cities, from houses and schools to employment agencies and social services.

Examples of this abound. Hezbollah in southern Lebanon has drawn in large measure on the resources of the Lebanese diaspora to fund a state within a state, complete with schools, orphanages, public works[30] and a security apparatus sufficiently effective to have challenged Israel, the most powerful state in the region. In Pakistan, when deep budget cuts degraded the public education system, Islamists stepped into the breach and educated millions of students in their own academies and schools.[31] In the Indian city of Mumbai, the Hindu nationalist organization Shiv Sena has employed a not dissimilar model, and has built up an elaborate network of services which deals with everything from domestic quarrels to leaking pipes.[32] The list goes on. It extends past voluntary and essentially benign organizations to include drug gangs in cities like Kingston, Rio de Janeiro and many others which stand as trans-shipment nodes in the global narcotics trade. Across the developing world, where states are in retreat, non-state bodies have taken upon themselves the task of providing access to services which hitherto were claimed by the nation-state as its exclusive domain.[33]

However, perhaps the most significant service being offered is that which has been the *sine qua non* of states throughout history: security. In many of the world's cities, the police are poorly-trained, poorly-equipped and underpaid. Court systems, equally, may be under-resourced, inefficient or even compromised. In such circumstances, the opportunity-cost of corruption can be quite low. Corrupt police and ineffective courts, in turn, weaken citizen confidence in the state. Citizens then have a greater incentive to turn to other agents for security, contract enforcement and dispute settlement.

All this occurs in the midst of another significant development of the post-Cold War period, the so-called "privatization of violence." The proliferation of weaponry in private hands; the growth of criminal organizations; and the increasing use of private security firms by governments, private companies and even ordinary citizens; together create a situation in which the supply of security-provision agents has increased to meet the demand. The problem is that the supply is not coming from the state, particularly in much of the developing world. From vigilante (and often very effective) policing in Nigerian, South African or Senegalese cities to drug gangs in Kingston or Rio de Janeiro, non-state bodies are often assuming responsibility for the full range of security and justice-related services which a resource-constrained state is unable to provide.

Precisely because the state is unable to provide these resources, it finds itself in a weak position to challenge the emergent authority of these new rivals. Indeed, to the extent that these new players can plug gaps inadvertently vacated by the state, they can serve its purposes. Rather than repress them, state agents often face a considerable temptation to co-opt these agents. In Kingston, criminal gangs can cooperate with the police in order to improve security, in return for a blind eye to their own activities.[34] In Rio de Janeiro, criminal gangs not only perform this function but often underpin elected officials who count on them to deliver votes[35] (a function also performed by some Jamaican gangs). In the regions that straddle the Pakistan–Afghanistan border, and that lie beyond the control of either state, it has long been suggested that Pakistani security officials cooperate with the Islamist organizations on the ground.

It is not that states cannot eliminate these agents in the turf they control. In cases of so-called failed states, this is in fact so. Yet failed states are relatively rare.[36] More commonly, states could repress and eliminate some of these sub-state players, but they lack the ability to repress *all* of them. More tellingly, as a rule, they lack the incentive to repress them, because these organizations perform functions which are necessary to the stability of society, but which the state lacks the ability to perform. Accordingly, state agents will find ways to cooperate with these players in return for their delivering some tangible benefits to the state, whether providing resources or security to citizens in territory over which the state claims sovereignty, but which it is unable to govern fully.

The result is what can be called a negotiated sovereignty. The nation-state still claims exclusive control over the territory it governs; no foreign government contests that claim; and no associations within its territory challenge it. Thus, the formal requirements for sovereignty that are said to prevail under the Westphalian system remain fulfilled. Yet on the ground, the state's sovereignty is not contested juridically since it would not serve the interests of the new barons to do so. They, after all, still want passports to enable them to move about in the world economy in which they operate, and know that formal declarations of independence will only invite the opprobrium of the international community. In any event, they are unnecessary. Provided the gangs or brotherhoods serve the interests of the state, they enjoy considerable latitude to govern the territories under their sway as they see fit. They may not be kings, but they are now barons.

A Return to the Past?

This, incidentally, is much the sort of political organization which emerged in western Europe at the end of the Roman age. From the fifth century AD until the eleventh, with a brief "Carolingian renaissance" in the ninth century, Europe remained politically fragmented. Political authority was decentralized and most urban centers – having lost their functions as centers of bureaucratic and military control – went into decline, especially in northern Europe.[37] The common depiction of sovereignty as a modern notion – a product of the Peace of Westphalia – is somewhat misleading, because some concept of sovereignty existed throughout the Middle Ages. Nevertheless, the modern ideal of the nation-state, of a political body which had the ultimate say in all matters – both secular and spiritual – and which claimed unity of command and, as Max Weber famously put it, a "monopoly on legitimate sources of violence,"[38] was to all intents and purposes absent from western Europe. It survived in the Eastern Empire, and in the Arab empire then emerging. However, in medieval western Europe, authorities overlay, necessitating a great deal of cooperation. Kings depended upon the consent of their nobles, and nobles could not easily alienate their kings, if only because fragmented resource-bases gave each of them sufficient power to be able to press their interests. Thus, the medieval system was not one in which sovereignty was altogether absent, but rather one in which multiple and overlapping authorities, each equipped with autonomous resource bases (making it impossible for one authority to simply eliminate the other), coexisted in a complex system sanctioned by law.

Similarly, today's neo-medieval units of government – those extra-legal but more or less institutionalized entities operating below nation-states – are not wholly independent. Subordinate units are able to maintain themselves against central states because they render services to the latter. They provide access to basic services, they assist with schooling, and they provide access to housing, employment and minimal welfare needs. Very importantly, they create functioning – if often arbitrary – legal systems, complete with security and enforcement. In such ways, they provide the services citizens look to their states to provide. States unable to provide these services, at least fully, thus find that cooperation with the new barons enables them to retain legitimacy and the impression of sovereignty, however much this sovereignty is dependent upon the role played by the new barons. As for the barons, they are not operating as agents of the state. Their resources do not come from above. Rather, they control autonomous resource bases, whether from their control of international trade, their access to remittances, or their ability to "tax" economic agents on the turf they control. This autonomy gives them the ability to counter-balance the state; they cannot overthrow it, but nor can they be easily repressed by it. Out of this tenuous balance emerges a system strikingly similar to that which emerged upon the fall of Rome. Barring the element of legal sanction, and the peculiar role played by the medieval Catholic Church in sanctioning this law, these features characterize the political systems that are currently emerging in many developing countries. The state is not failing there. It is being reconfigured.

The discussion of early medievalism brings to mind another popular medieval trope—the notion of a Dark Age. Many contemporary critics argue that the West in general, and the United States in particular, is sliding towards another Dark Age owing to the sort of internal decay they purport to have seen in the late Roman Empire.[39] Yet there are many who dismiss this kind of pessimism, arguing that it is now all but impossible for another Dark Age to occur. They maintain that technological improvements and constant factor substitution have ushered in an age of endless growth, and that even if a nuclear holocaust destroyed civilization, the damage would be short-lived: the accumulation of knowledge in myriad easily-accessible nodes, thanks to the progress of the information revolution, would enable survivors to quickly restore the status quo.[40]

Both sides of the debate may be missing the point, because they are seeing the onset of a Dark Age as being the product of internal forces. The European Dark Ages – better yet, Europe's Early Middle Ages – were above all a prolonged period of political instability, state weakness and economic stagnation. The stock of technology accumulated in the Empire did not cease to exist. Roman roads, monuments and literature survived. Had they not done so, there would never have been a European Renaissance, but during the Dark Ages, the lack of demand for them meant that this knowledge ceased to be fungible. Amphitheatres were no longer used for public gatherings; their stones served the purpose of the time, which was to build rude habitations or to provide the outer walls for fortresses.

[177]

In the same way, to argue that the new age of endless growth cannot be reversed simply because the knowledge cannot be eliminated is somewhat of a non sequitur. If there is no demand for a particular stock of knowledge, the size of that stock is irrelevant. In today's global political economy, there is a huge supply of knowledge and technology which is not reaching the Third World for the simple reason that the demand there is insufficient to attract it. The question some adventurous theorists sometimes ponder is could this growing imbalance between rich and poor ultimately create a planet so unstable that the existence of the empire could itself one day be threatened? Could the empire's prosperity compel it to suck in resources – including human resources – from disaffected and marginalized regions that harbor populations hostile to the empire, who might then challenge it from within just as the mercenaries of the Roman empire gnawed away at its military capacity?

Answering this question is not the important point. Rather, the key thing to remember is that the presumption that supply alone governs prosperity is misguided. Demand is every bit as important. In a politically unstable world, such as that of the present day, an imbalance between demand and supply is conspiring to prevent the fruits of "progress" from reaching most of the planet's citizens. This reality, in turn, may threaten the stability of the political economy, particularly when it has become sufficiently globalized for want and plenty to coexist cheek-by-jowl, the very conditions which give rise to envy and anger.

Conclusion

If Rome offers one lesson to the modern world, it would be this: that trying to augment a state's wealth while perpetuating the marginality of the populations on its periphery – particularly when those populations are more numerous than those in the heartlands – is a recipe for tension and anti-systemic tendencies. It is perhaps tendentious to argue that "raiding" activity from the periphery is mere barbarism, and thus uncivilized. After all, one would be within one's rights to at least question the civility of an economic regime which more or less excludes four-fifths of the planet's population from the fruits of the economic boom of the last two centuries. The ability to fiddle while parts of the planet burn around it, was not a vice confined to ancient Rome.

As for the Gulf states, what does all this portend? Neither industrial nor developing, some of the oil-rich economies such as the United Arab Emirates are making great strides towards becoming service-intensive First-World economies. Yet given their own labor shortages, they have been compelled to do so using a supply of labor from some of the world's poorest regions. So far, tensions have been more or less contained. Nevertheless, the risks remain great when one is importing a labor supply whose conditions of existence – and perhaps more significantly, the conditions of existence of their loved ones' back home – are at variance with the environment in which they work.

That does not mean that one should look for outbreaks of tension within the recipient countries alone, and then express contentment if quietude prevails. For as this paper has argued, the resultant instability is more likely than not to manifest itself first in the peripheral region – that which is exporting the labor – and then, possibly, penetrate the importing region. In that light, it is perhaps noteworthy that some scholars have detected evidence that the intellectual and financial capital driving both Islamic and Hindu militancy in the Indian subcontinent has come from migrant workers in the Gulf states.[41] Able to carve out autonomous spaces in some of the countries whence these laborers come, sub-state networks – usually coexisting in some way with state authorities – have been able to create bases for their own operations that could, conceivably, be used to re-export their own struggles.

In the end, the cautionary tale that comes from this paper is that, whatever the intellectual justifications that have been crafted to explain a world of radical inequalities, globalization which fails to breach the divide between rich and poor is likely to harbor tendencies which are self-undermining. A more just world is thus probably not a moral imperative alone—it is probably a political one as well.

GLOBALIZATION AND SECURITY

8

Globalization and the International Order

Hassan Abu Nimah

In order to establish the basis for this article on globalization it is necessary to define this phenomenon and then review its development. This will facilitate an approach to globalization, not as a new phenomenon but as an advanced stage of a process of engagement that began with the very existence of human societies.

The belief that globalization has been so prominent in most aspects of our lives owes to the fact that it has reached such an advanced stage in removing barriers between the world's regions, countries and peoples that we have found ourselves exposed to influences that we are either not ready to comprehend, or instinctively reject for fear of their negative consequences. By the end of the twentieth century, globalization had led to the removal of barriers that had previously enabled a multitude of peoples, nations, countries and communities to retain their peculiar characteristics. Such barriers had preserved "national" character and the customs, traditions, beliefs, behavior patterns, history and aspirations that have bestowed on each human group its unique character.

Some, especially those in less developed states, have been caught unawares by the effects of globalization as the phenomenon has not developed within a man-made framework to regularize the process in a way that states and citizens are able to adapt to and comprehend. This served to suddenly unveil the realities of global imbalance, stressing the critical differences between those who had advanced and those who had been left behind.

Hence, in reacting to globalization there was little sober response or responsible desire to interact with the opportunities suddenly made available. Instead, many leaned towards rejection, fear, caution, and the projection of everything new as a hegemonic domination of the weak and the poor by the powerful and the rich.

Globalization: Definition and History

What is Globalization?

Put simply, globalization is increased engagement between different parts of the world; it is a movement towards integration and interdependence between the different countries of the world in the economic, social, technical, cultural and political fields as well as in security-sensitive areas such as environment conservation and the regulation of intricate and interrelated relations between peoples and states.[1]

Most definitions of globalization focus on the engagement aspect. The *Encyclopedia Britannica* defines globalization as "the process by which the [human] experience of everyday life ... can foster a standardization of cultural expressions around the world." Because human experience includes a limitless amount of action, activity, motion, development, knowledge, exploration and accomplishment, and because it is an experience that is constantly growing and developing, the same also applies to globalization. Yes, we are experiencing advanced stages of globalization, but we are quite far from reaching its end. Engagement continues, and when the Earth becomes a small village, the incentives for engagement will accelerate mankind's efforts to engage with the rest of the universe.

The term "globalization" began to be used in the second half of the twentieth century, but only became widely used in the 1980s.[2] In fact, globalization is as old as humanity. Man has tended, by nature, to be mobile, and such mobility is a requisite for survival—in searching for a living and securing the necessities of life. Man thus shifted from hunting to agriculture and later to trade that provided him with successive opportunities for communication. The "silk route" during the time of the Mongol Empire provides such evidence. Another human tendency is the desire for adventure and exploration. This has thrust mankind towards distant horizons and unknown worlds. It is also the very tendency that pushed humans towards space.

The silk route provided opportunities for communication and interaction. Subsequently, European trade expansion in the sixteenth and seventeenth centuries led to greater integration when both the Spanish and Portuguese empires were able to reach most parts of the world. The discovery of raw materials and precious metals necessary for industry – in greater quantities, at a lower cost or of a better quality than was available in the developed world – led to a process of reciprocal influence between regions. This provided developed states with the opportunity to invest in new discoveries abroad. Naturally, it was necessary to preserve these discoveries and gains, which required the protection of agricultural or mining investments or other sources of profit, and thus colonialism developed through expansion, increasing political hegemony and the establishment of military bases on foreign soil. Simultaneously, this process also preserved and enhanced means of communication. These developments were, and still are, among the positive and negative aspects of globalization.

At this stage, some of the core aspects of globalization began to emerge—the search for profit and business opportunities, the utilization of natural resources abroad, and the establishment of permanent bases or relations that ultimately afforded the strong more power over the weak.

More recently, the rapid advancement of technology in the post-World War II era led to the facilitation of communication and movement among

[185]

the world's different peoples and nations, providing greater opportunities for the transfer of individuals and goods, and the ability to cross greater distances in less time.[3]

The Beginning

Man began as a hunter. He then became a farmer and eventually a trader. All those activities required mobility as well as land ownership. With increased demand – especially for the most favorable lands with the most attractive resources – competition intensified, sowing the seeds of conflict and leading to contradicting interests and ultimately to war.

While the nature of the struggle has evolved with the advancement of mankind's capabilities in science and technology and in controlling the surrounding environment, the phenomenon remains. It sometimes takes the form of legitimate competition, regulated by the rules stipulated in agreements and laws; but often competition transgresses established boundaries and evolves into armed clashes and wars.

Man has thus far failed to create an effective political and social environment in which disagreements and conflicts are settled purely by civilized and peaceful means. That is why nations continue to require and develop armaments and defense capacities that become aggressive forces when warranted by certain circumstances.

In ancient times, simple distance would often provide partial protection from aggression, as would rough terrain and natural coastal boundaries. Thus, communities tended to be built on elevated areas which overlooked the surrounding terrain and facilitated the detection of hostile enemies. Natural barriers such as vast valleys, high mountains, rivers or even exposed plains all formed layers of protection. In the absence of such barriers, people would build trenches, walls and sand barriers. This led to the separation of human communities from one another except when contact was required—be it voluntarily in peace-time, or by necessity during war.

The golden rule was to maintain a balance between isolation and separation—to preserve one's survival, but also to communicate and interact with others when necessary. The nature of this balance was determined by the prevailing circumstances, with greater isolation in times of war and conflict, and more engagement during times of peace. Nations and human communities tended to favor more isolation when self-dependence was possible, and vice versa. Nevertheless, these factors did not eliminate the tendency to communicate in order to discover and learn, which existed in varying degrees depending on circumstances.

While people were initially forced by necessity to move, communicate and discover new environments and different communities, engagement resulted in an accelerated process of cultural intermingling, exchange of experiences, learning, teaching and imitation. Yet, this in turn invigorated the spirit of competition and sometimes led to conflicting interests or disagreements over the possession of riches or territory, resulting in conflicts and wars which necessitated the development of fighting capabilities, be they defensive or offensive.

At subsequent advanced stages, these circumstances created the need to organize relations between various human communities in the form of treaties or bilateral agreements that eventually culminated in the contemporary international order that includes: international law, bilateral and multilateral treaties, and covenants and regulations that generally organize the way man deals with the surrounding environment, both human and physical.

The Globalization Shock

The Time of Bipolarity

Before globalization had developed into the well-known, controversial phenomenon it is today, the world was divided into two major camps – or what I refer to as two 'poles' – that preserved the world balance: a pole led by the Soviet Union comprising states under its direct influence; and another led by the United States and the Western world. The latter pole also included countries which chose to be members of what was known as the "Free World" as opposed to the Communist or Socialist world with its totalitarian regimes governed by inward-looking ideologies behind the Iron Curtain.

The theory of the Iron Curtain, which placed strict constraints on the movement of people across it, was based on complete isolation. Isolation entailed ideological, intellectual and military conflict, accelerated arms races and the development of weapons of unprecedented lethality. It also brought about an economic conflict – both in terms of theory and practice – which rendered interaction between the economies of both poles impossible. This resulted in a rapid widening of the gap between the lifestyles of the two poles which regressed on the Soviet-controlled side but advanced rapidly on the other, further accentuating the discrepancies between them.

In the West, freedom flourished, rights were defined, and people were presented with the opportunity to increase their knowledge and develop their skills via the use of all means afforded by material, spiritual, intellectual and social progress. However, such values and opportunities simultaneously diminished on the other side of the Iron Curtain.

With the growth of democratic institutions in the Western world, individuals' characters evolved within frameworks that guaranteed full rights and complete freedom, they built a relationship with the state and government institutions, and developed security measures such as independent judicial institutions to protect those rights from any aggression or attempt by the state to diminish them. This was enhanced by a focus on freedom of expression which in turn led to the proliferation and development of intellectual thought, science, research, dialogue, criticism and the revision of axioms. It also contributed to the creation of the press and its role in monitoring the behavior of rulers and governments, mobilizing public opinion, spreading awareness and helping the legislature set the necessary balance between the government and the governed. Combined, these developments led to today's widely accepted rules of good governance.

Such progress was absent at the Socialist pole composed of totalitarian regimes and one-party rule where the ruling authority had the final say on all matters and the individual was merely a passive recipient rather than a meaningful actor, with no power or right to discuss, object, express or think. In other words, the states in the Socialist camp monopolized the rights of individuals and confiscated their humanity, transforming them into cogs in a larger machine that performed pre-programmed duties to maintain the absolute minimum work necessary for its survival, like a machine which requires only fuel and basic maintenance.

In the Free World, the state also undertook a range of vital functions on behalf of its people. However it was also a body, elected for a specific period, that acted on their behalf within the framework of regulations and laws set by peer assemblies. Ultimately, the people had the right to withdraw their confidence from the state if it failed to adequately carry out those duties, violated its mandate or lost the capacity to act according to sound practices and good governance. Ironically, these democratic characteristics were the same as those advocated by the Socialist pole, only they did not occur in practice.

Before making further comparisons between these poles, two points should be raised: first, democracy may be the best framework of governance that the human intellect has managed to devise so far, but it is not ideal. It is still undergoing growth and development to iron out its defects and shortcomings. Secondly, while the individual within a true democracy enjoys a great deal of freedom of thought, expression, innovation and practice within legal limits compared to his counterpart under a totalitarian regime, democracy has not provided societies with a foolproof system of rights—indeed, we continue to witness violations under the strongest of democracies. Prosperous societies under democratic regimes also still suffer from peculiar shortcomings and problems sometimes created by material luxury, undisciplined intellectual openness and excess practice of liberties that at times contradict beliefs, traditions and customs and even moral ideals and established values.

The division of the states of the world into two poles – either side of the Iron Curtain – and the difficulty of bringing each side together to form some kind of homogeneous package highlighted the basic lack of homogeneity between each side. The countless differences between these sides served to prolong this separation. However, the states one each side of the divide were not identical to one another. On both sides of the curtain there were numerous differences that were to gradually diminish thanks to the growth in modern methods of communication.

Nonetheless, there were – and are – still many differences between parts of the Western world and among the West and Asian, African or Latin American countries. The principal difference, however, was the psychological barrier between the Socialist and capitalist poles. These remained until the Iron Curtain disappeared with the rapid and abrupt fall of the Soviet Union, when people from both sides found themselves exposed to their opposite counterparts.

The Great Transformation

The fall of the Iron Curtain resulted in societies which had for decades been accustomed to different patterns of life and practice suddenly meeting face to face. As the rules governing relations between these societies at the time of their division were different from those required for the new conditions, and because no amendment to those rules was made, confusion surrounding the new environment led to globalization being viewed as a phenomenon which would aggravate and worsen the unjust differences between peoples and societies.

The new openness prompted by globalization revealed substantial gaps between advanced and less-advanced states. It was normal for the latter to fear the dangers of hegemony. That is because the strong – not necessarily only militarily – will automatically dominate the weak; a strong economy will dominate weaker ones, invade markets and prosper at the expense of growth opportunities in these economies. Yet that is the nature of competition in a world without constraints. The solution cannot be to ask the advanced to slow their advance for the sake of the weak since logic dictates that advancement should continue in every field possible. Nor can the solution be to ask underdeveloped nations to make a sudden leap to modernity to equal advanced nations. This process can only progress gradually with sound planning and under favorable domestic and international circumstances. It is important here to emphasize the existence of "favorable circumstances" since they indicate a suitable environment for the less-developed to catch up. However, how will they ever catch up when the gap is forever widening between advanced and less-advanced nations? That is the most important dilemma to face in attempting to achieve balance and equity among states.

What applies to the economy also applies to education and progress in the fields of culture, politics, contemporary institution-building, technological development, and modernization of utilities that satisfy people's needs. However, supremacy in those fields facilitates hegemony, which is one of the natural shortcomings of globalization. Likewise, rejection and fear of hegemony are also natural reactions to globalization that must be tolerated and understood within an objective framework.

For instance, in the marketplace a desirable product will often dominate the market, attract the interest of the consumer, diminish the chances of a similar product being sold and may even expel rival products from the market altogether. This empowers the owner of the successful product and bolsters his supremacy over his competitors. This scenario can be applied to aspects of education, technology, administration, science, art, literature, culture, invention, and other countless human and societal activities.

The Arab World

In the Arab world, we have felt, perhaps more than others, the pressure of globalization both for the reasons mentioned above and for other reasons peculiar to the region and its people. Globalization abolished the previous division of the world into two camps. Bi-polarity prevented either pole, regardless of the degree of its prosperity, power or progress, from dominating less-developed nations and societies in the other pole's zone of influence because the leadership of each side provided protection to its followers. The hegemony of one pole over the nations and societies in its orbit did not constitute a dilemma in itself, yet no hegemony was able to cross the barrier between the two camps as a result of complete isolation, polarization and separation.

What made the Arab world more sensitive to the invasion of globalization is the way the features of the new age affected vital political issues whose roots go back to the start of liberalization and independence after the downfall of the Ottoman Empire. Specifically, owing to the fact that the United States is the superpower that has taken the lead in a globalized world after the demise of the Soviet "adversary," completely controls developments – not just of a political nature – in the region and is staunchly committed to Israel, concern, and even fear, has increased that globalization could become a means to arrange the region's affairs in a final way that does not reflect rights, justice or the aspirations of the people. This issue has become more complicated and intermingled with the growth of prevailing security risks, increased violence and terror, and the failure of efforts to redress the negative impacts of globalization.

Laila Sharaf attributes the Arab reactions of fear and suspicion of globalization to the fact that the phenomenon has "started to destroy the balance of power to which we used to resort from time to time [sic]. It is as if globalization has opened the doors wide for the hegemony of the remaining super power that has not in turn failed to parade before us its military, economic, and more dangerously, social and cultural strength."[4] She adds:

> I also claim that globalization has taken the Arabs by surprise, whilst we were not ready. This is because the first tool of globalization is knowledge and knowledge production; we have been behind in such production for centuries. It adopts advanced technology to enhance its capacities; we are still incapable either of producing it or maximizing our benefit from it in development processes. Globalization resorts to proactive media; we

depend on constrained media. It seeks to widen its spaces by setting up economic, and sometimes political, blocs; we are scattered, fragmented and, at times even, conflicting. It indicates moving beyond the borders of the nation-state; we still dream of the state of the unified Arab nation. Last but not least, it adopts the vitality of cultural interaction and freedom to create; we adopt educational systems that limit such interaction and do not encourage initiative and innovation.[5]

International Order in the Age of Globalization

Vicious Circles

Unfortunately, a vicious circle has developed around the issue of hegemony. While it is vital that new rules be developed to regularize international and human relations to limit hegemonic influence, the domination of hegemony has itself prevented the establishment and growth of such rules. It has even hampered existing rules such as international law and the role of the United Nations. As a result, our world has found itself without appropriate laws at a time when openness and the removal of barriers necessitate more legislation. Thus, the face of globalization has changed, as has its message, from one of participation, spreading experience and enabling those with less capacity, knowledge, money and opportunity to benefit from the capacities and potential of others, into one which restricts success and privilege and prevents others from benefiting from them. In other words, the message of globalization has changed into a message of hegemony and the exploitation of new circumstances and opportunities in the absence of justice, equity or sound rules of interaction.

Because this has also affected political situations and relations, yet another vicious circle has developed: hegemony has facilitated the control of powerful countries over less powerful ones. This has intensified the injustice felt by the latter, which has often been expressed through violence or "terrorism," as it is widely known. In turn, this violence has encouraged countermeasures in the form of more control, constraints and

[193]

violation of fundamental rights which, in turn, has produced even greater feelings of injustice. This action–reaction cycle has continued to escalate in a negative and dangerous manner.

These are some of the direct outcomes of globalization. There are other deeper and broader impacts, i.e. those related to the re-formulation of the international order, the definitions of the nation-state, sovereignty and borders in the political and sovereign sense, rather than in the geographical and regional one. All these concepts have been shaken and have, at times, been on the verge of collapse.

The issue of sovereignty has grown and become entrenched with the foundation of independent states that have established relations with other states on the basis of reciprocity either in terms of interests or even in competition, conflict and contradicting tendencies. The principle of reciprocity is not confined to diplomatic interaction; it is in fact much broader than this. Sovereign states reciprocate every action, if not to protect their perceived interests then at least to maintain their dignity and status and avoid being seen as weak.

Before the foundation of the first international organization, states resorted to force or effective political pressure to resolve their disputes. This approach has changed since states have realized that wars are neither the best nor the only option in settling disputes. The first international formation, the League of Nations, was set up after World War I in response to the "idealism" of Woodrow Wilson, the then US President. Yet the foundations of the existing international order date back centuries earlier to the Peace of Westphalia in 1648. This was the outcome of the Treaties of Münster and Osnabrück which were signed in the same year and which brought an end to the Eighty Years' War and the Thirty Years' War. The peace which led to the two treaties was agreed by the Holy Roman Emperor, Ferdinand III Habsburg, German princes, Spain, France and Sweden, along with representatives of the Dutch Empire. Eleven years later, in 1659, the Treaty of Pyrenees ended the war between France and Spain and was considered part of the overall Peace of Westphalia.

Historians refer to those conciliations as the foundations of the contemporary international order (although some historians disagree with such generalized deductions).

Getting into the details of this ancient period is beyond our present scope. Yet, for the purposes of this paper, it should be emphasized that the Peace of Westphalia gave birth to major principles, particularly the principle of state sovereignty, the right of self-determination, legal equality between states and, most importantly, non-interference in the affairs of other states. This last principle, which was affirmed by all subsequent international agreements over four centuries, and which became part and parcel of the system of international law, is one of the main principles that has been threatened as a result of the shortcomings of globalization.

Following World War I, the most dangerous and most atrocious of all wars, President Wilson tried hard to establish an international order. He put forward his program which has become known ever since as the "Fourteen Points," the last of which stipulated that "a general association of nations must be formed under specific covenants for the purpose of affording mutual guarantees of political independence and territorial integrity to great and small states alike."

Although Wilson's "idealism" was met by stiff opposition in the United States and other countries, it managed, eventually, to secure the foundation of the League of Nations and the reconciliation of European states in Versailles. Immediately after the fall of the League of Nations following World War II, the United Nations (UN) was born and continues to act as the international umbrella to protect the rights of states and regulate international relations among them according to defined and specific covenants, rules and regimes. That was how things were supposed to continue, but the reality has been completely different. The UN does not play that effective role and is incapable of imposing the will of the international community, maintaining the rights of member states, enforcing the UN Charter in a fair and equitable manner, putting an end to wars, or settling disputes in accordance with the law. Globalization has indeed had a major role in much of this, but it was not solely responsible.[6] As was the case with the rules upon which the League of Nations was founded, the UN Charter also was not without its weaknesses. Foremost among these is the inequality between member states, in spite of the Charter's assertion to the contrary.

A New Concept of Sovereignty

While states of the world were discussing the Charter of the League of Nations, they encountered a significant obstacle, namely the fact that commitment to any collective charter or rules that were to be applied equally to all member states entailed an implicit surrender of a certain degree of sovereignty. Sovereignty, in absolute terms, denotes the right of the state to act independently in all conditions and under all circumstances. Compliance to collective rules or covenants, however, meant that a state must succumb to the will of the majority, even if this were to contradict its own desire or interests. This places a part – although not of course the whole – of the absolute right of sovereignty in the hands of the majority.

This situation was not to the liking of the "great" powers; neither those who triumphed after World War I nor those who came out of World War II as victors. They did not like the idea that their decisions would be subject to the will of the majority, which is normally made up of small, weak or insignificant states that become more influential when they join forces. This dilemma continued to constitute one of the main shortcomings of the international order, and was officially recognized in the form of the veto. This is, in essence, a privilege that the great powers conferred upon themselves in stark violation of both the letter and spirit of the Charter which stresses equality between member states. It also contradicts the principle of international democracy required as a basis for justice, and to guarantee the power of law. The veto, which is largely responsible for the paralysis of the contemporary international order, is merely a guarantee for the great, or super powers to exempt themselves from the decisions of the majority. It is true that this only applies within the framework of the Security Council, yet General Assembly resolutions, which no member is allowed to veto, are non-binding, as is widely accepted. Furthermore, the Security Council represents the effective executive body within the structure of the international organization.

This imbalance existed even before the full effects of globalization upon our contemporary world were felt. That is why the damage has intensified and the imbalance become more serious with the downfall of the Soviet pole and the overall control by a single pole of the world's destiny.

I referred earlier to the interconnectedness of political and security developments and the acceleration of globalization. This has magnified the shortcomings of globalization while covering up some of its advantages.

Iraq's Invasion of Kuwait

The most significant event in the Arab world after the collapse of the Soviet Union was the invasion by Iraq under Saddam Hussein of the State of Kuwait. This provided the single super power in the international arena with a rare opportunity to adopt a strategy over which there could be no disagreement: to counter the Iraqi aggression, liberate Kuwait from occupation and diffuse the danger posed by Iraq to the region. This was welcomed by both the international community and the Arab world (with some exceptions), and provided the United States with an opportunity to prove its world leadership. The nature of the mission enabled the construction of an international alliance at the political and military levels, giving it legitimacy through the United Nations, and ensuring the success of the war to liberate Iraq and destroy the Iraqi army. It also enabled the United States to impose greater political and military hegemony in addition to reinforcing its technological and economic hegemony. This significant historical event was an opportunity as well as a test: an opportunity for the United States to assert its leadership and a test that it passed. As a result, its unrivalled leadership was established.

Although intervention in this case gained international legitimacy in the form of successive UN Security Council resolutions, the precedent of intervention for this legitimate purpose – as well for other purposes at other times – was established.

Humanitarian Intervention

With the collapse of the Soviet Union and the disappearance of its protective umbrella over affiliated states, a process of settlement of ancient ethnic and religious issues began to take place in eastern Europe and the Balkans. Civil wars broke out and ethnic cleansing began. Africa witnessed brutal massacres, and peoples in other areas were subjected to oppression by the ruling authorities. This invoked widespread condemnation that accused the international order of negligence and failure to protect victims of violence, oppression and torture. What was known as "humanitarian intervention" now became a desirable option.

At this stage, political borders began to lose their solidity, as did sovereignty. The debate intensified over whether states capable of intervention had the right to use their power to intervene on behalf of minorities oppressed by repressive and tyrannical regimes or whether they should ignore the stark abuse of the innocent without coming to their aid on the pretext of respect for sovereignty and compliance with the principle of non-intervention in the internal affairs of states in accordance with the requisites of international law and the UN Charter. That dilemma persists today. Nevertheless, with the loss of sovereignty the strong allowed themselves to usurp the weak either by threat, inflicting direct damage or imposing positions that are met by agreement or, otherwise, force.

Humanitarian – or indeed "non-humanitarian" – intervention has become a significant issue in current international relations. This pretext has provided some states with the opportunity to settle scores with their adversaries and is still utilized without consideration for international law. Serious and negative consequences have resulted when international law and the international order have become tools in the hands of the strong to

[198]

serve their political interests and desires. The UN Security Council has acted swiftly, decisively and strongly only when it has suited the interests of influential powers. In other words, international law has become selective, temperamental and devoid of justice and impartiality.

At the non-political, non-military level, interdependence between states in trade and economic affairs, protection of the environment, securing transfer routes, communication, protecting the world's common resources and regulating their exploitation (such as fishing regulations) have led to the development of new relations that have melted rigid borders and decreased the importance of independent national personality. Communities have come together to share numerous mutual and coordinated features, common interests and convergent desires to serve collective interests. These are advantages, the importance of which must be stressed since they are, in the long run, the more long-standing, positive results of globalization.

A Major Turning Point: Pre-emptive Strikes

After the events of September 11, 2001, another important factor emerged on the road to political and military hegemony, namely the right of states to carry out pre-emptive strikes against those who constitute, or are thought to constitute, a danger to them. Although this phenomenon clearly contradicts international law and the covenants that organize relations between states, it has not prevented recourse to it as a new right of self-defense by states that feel under threat. This has dealt a new, and perhaps fatal, blow to international law.

Following Israel, the United States was the next country to adopt this new pattern of international policy. In fact, the use of pre-emptive measures by states to protect themselves from a certain danger is explicable and perhaps justifiable. It is inconceivable that a state would refrain from carrying out its duty when it observes that an evil act is being planned against it or its citizens without attempting to foil it. Would not this be part of the right of self-defense, albeit pre-emptive? Would it be better for the state to wait until the danger takes place, at which time any response would be too late?

The problem here lies in the necessity to prove the danger, which is an extremely difficult task. In the absence of decisive evidence that a pre-emptive strike is fully justifiable based on irrefutable events, any pre-emptive measure would be an unjustifiable aggression. The right of nations to carry out pre-emptive strikes based on their own estimations of danger would then turn into a weapon in the hands of any state to attack another on this pretext. That is what happened in the case of Iraq after the events of September 11. Just as the invasion of Kuwait by Iraq gave the United States the opportunity to lead an alliance to respond to the aggression and liberate Kuwait and thus prove its leadership, so the events of September 11 provided the Bush administration with the opportunity to settle old scores with Iraq in the name of combating terror and "pre-emptive" self-defense. It has now become clear that Iraq had no relations whatsoever with the terrorist organization that planned and carried out the attacks on New York and Washington, and that Iraq was not manufacturing weapons of mass destruction (WMD) to put at the disposal of terrorists, as was claimed by the Bush administration in the run-up to the war on Iraq. It has also become clear that the decision to launch the war on Iraq was taken even before the occurrence of those events which were used to justify it.

Gordon Prather quotes Former Treasury Secretary Paul O'Neil as saying: "going after Saddam was topic 'A,' ten days after the inauguration [of George W. Bush] – eight months before Sept. 11." He mentions this in his article "Enabling Bush's Wars of Aggression"[7] to prove that President Bush and his Vice-President Dick Cheney came to power looking for an excuse to depose Saddam Hussein and that the events of September 11 provided that excuse. The article describes in detail how the administration based the justification for the war on Iraq on the pretext of preempting the transfer of Iraqi nuclear weapons to terrorists, and how the media cooperated in promoting the arguments for that purpose.

In spite of the catastrophic outcomes of the war and the exposure of its deceptive and false justifications, the imbalance of power still favors the strong at the expense of international law, justice and logic. All this has encouraged the continuing adoption of double standards.

Having become a hallmark of international behavior, double standards have, in practice although not legally, given this right to the strong alone. Among the outcomes of the quest to acquire ever-greater capabilities of force is the ability of the strong to impose rules that allow them to achieve what they desire whereas the weak essentially lose the right and ability to defend themselves. This simply means that the winning argument is always that of the stronger party regardless of how erroneous it may be, and that the argument of the weak will be dismissed regardless of how valid or just it may be.

No single actor has the power to deter the United States from launching pre-emptive strikes to put down any threat it claims to face. In spite of the concerns of states that this could prompt a global regression to the "law of the jungle" and lead to the collapse of the whole international order, and regardless of the fear that this "right" may become a weapon of aggression (in the name of combating potential threats even if no such threats exist) in the hands of any state wishing to settle old scores, no action – international or regional – was taken to prevent the development of this phenomenon.

The war on Iraq was a flagrant example of misuse of the principle of pre-emptive strikes. The whole world now bears witness to the serious consequences of this illegal, unjustified and irrational war. The region now faces similar threats of pre-emptive strikes against other states such as Iran, Syria and, probably once again, Hezbollah in Lebanon.

If strong states continue to insist on imposing their political, economic and military hegemony in the name of self-defense or combating terror in spite of the law, the world will indeed continue to move rapidly towards a return to the law of the jungle. This spells a future full of violence, regional and international chaos, and degeneration.

[201]

Consequences of a Globalized International Order

To What Extent is Globalization Responsible?

Is globalization responsible for all this? The answer is both yes and no. Globalization has indeed increased the exposure of the world's various regions and states to one another. This has given violators of international law an opportunity to make use of the absence of protective measures to seek to satisfy their desires and promote their interests. They began to resort to force, aggression, threats and tyranny regardless of any common benefit, international law or the world's security and safety. He who has the power is capable of imposing all forms of hegemony. That actually is the case. In the absence of the law or sufficient respect for it, the majority comes under threat, and the positive sides of globalization disappear. In the world economy, the rich become richer, and the poor become poorer. Those who are prosperous become more so, while the underdeveloped lag further behind, and their feelings of disappointment, outrage, and despair mount. Things may even spiral out of control, leading to violence and desperate action, especially when there are other causes as well, and the afore-mentioned vicious circle continues to grow.

As the Brazilian politician and academic Cristovam Buarque states in his book, *Golden Curtain – The Shocks of the End of the Twentieth Century and a Dream of the Twenty-First*, "while the rapid integration of the world is a pleasant surprise for mankind, the fragmentation of the human society within the world village is terrifying." He states that the past century has witnessed widespread inequalities and created unprecedented social disintegration.[8]

Shall we continue on the road of disintegration and social chaos as a result of the collapse of the international order and lack of respect for the rules, albeit far from ideal, that used to run relations in a way that preserved the organization of this world's affairs? or will our world wake up to what has befallen it and thus stop the deterioration? but how?

The Present Situation

Globalization is a continuous process, and there is no way to stop it. Actually, we should not consider stopping it since this would disrupt the development of humanity and obstruct the course of history. What is required, instead, is for us to adapt to the requirements of globalization so that we are able to control its shortcomings and capitalize on its benefits. This has not happened; in fact, the complete opposite is happening.

The world is like a pair of families that were once separated by immovable barriers, much like the walls between different rooms in a building. In one room lived a rich, strong and influential family. In the other room, there lived a poor, destitute and powerless family. Since there was a wall between the two families, none of them was aware of the others' conditions and was not, therefore, affected by them. All of a sudden, the wall came down, and both families found themselves exposed to each other. The poor family witnessed the luxury, wealth, comfort, prosperity, abundance, warmth and happiness of the richer family. The rich family, on the other hand, witnessed the misery, destitution, deprivation, hunger, cold and wretchedness of the poor family. However, faced with this new situation, the rich family did not rush to help the poor one, alleviate its misery or narrow the gap between them as befitted the new situation which requires consideration for the feelings and interests of others, sharing their woes and seeking to ease them in the name of friendly, cooperative and respectful relations. Instead, it boasted about its luxury only to aggravate the poor family's predicament and deepen its sense of injustice. In addition, the rich family used its privileges to deplorably exploit and underpay members of the poor family to increase its luxury at the expense of its neighbors. While the wall was in place, the poor family used to find the little it had sufficient, but compared to what the new neighbor had, it was not sufficient anymore. You can now imagine the new situation with all the animosity and hatred it has created.

This simple metaphor understates the complicated status of our contemporary world, but provides a miniaturized picture of what is

[203]

happening in our world. In this contemporary world, borders are collapsing. Europe is finally on its way to real union. The European Union (EU), which is an ideal example to us in the Arab world, has been based on the gradual removal of variation and difference, not on preserving and spreading them. The greatest challenge for western Europe was the collapse of the Berlin Wall separating it from eastern Europe. It was not easy for western Europe to open the gates of integration without addressing the vast social, economic and living discrepancies between the two sides. Nonetheless, that was the path it chose from the very beginning, and it put in place comprehensive plans to dissolve differences after barriers were removed. The European experience has succeeded in all its stages, although it still has a long way to go. Europe handles its resources on the basis that they belong to all. In our countries, however, borders are strengthened; people in each country hide behind barriers for fear of integration and unity. This of course is the exception rather than the rule; and globalization will conquer us while we are still unprepared to adapt to it, which will make the necessary period of adaptation last even longer.

Over and above the variations and differences has come hegemony, only to make things worse. In the absence of international order, we entered into a phase of political disintegration and chaos.

What are the New Rules?

If we are to accept gradual integration and the removal of barriers between us as states and peoples, the first and simplest prerequisite would be an equitable distribution of wealth, opportunity and privilege that treats the world as a village, as long as we accept it as such, and interacts with the destinies of the world as a whole. Living together in one village necessitates fairness and equality. There is enough to make sharing possible without the need for great sacrifices on the part of those who have more than others.

If this requires sacrificing rigid national identity and sovereignty, it should be for the sake of an effective and equitable international order that is capable of protecting the rights and interests of all, without bias, injustice, selection or double standards. Only the establishment of such an international order will mend international relations, eliminate the specter of continuous threat to, and blackmail of, the small and less powerful countries and enable them to pursue their life and growth in a legitimate climate of security and safety.

This world will not be able to overcome its weakness and imbalance unless it reverts to applying the law, administering justice, fighting injustice and dissuading aggression. It is only then that the world and its peoples may be liberated from the evil of terror and violence; there would be no need for the new arms race which we are witnessing; the relations between peoples would be purged of the impurities of hatred, rage, rejection and condemnation; we would overcome social, economic, moral and environmental pitfalls; development would be promoted; the structure of the most sublime features of civilization would be erected; science and knowledge would prosper; humankind's innovative capabilities would bloom; we would move towards more integration, voluntary participation; and bring wars under control and avoid their consequences and woes.

The amount of money so far spent on the Iraq War and on other absurd conflicts is enough to achieve the greater portion of development aspirations and overcome many of the world's problems. However, the money was spent establishing evil and destruction and spreading injustice, violence and instability. It is in fact a combined loss that we chose as an alternative to a certain and increasing profit. It is a waste of money and life and of man's capabilities and energies. The war has achieved nothing and nobody has won.

In fact, the war has sown the seeds of sectarianism, deepened hatred, enhanced terrorism, spread instability and set back the process of progress years, if not whole decades. It is not globalization itself that is responsible for this. It is our way of dealing with it, and the way mankind has used it in the most horrible manner.

[205]

9

Religious Fundamentalism and Terrorism

Sebestyén L. v. Gorka

Religious fundamentalism and terrorism have both existed since the dawn of time. Unlike terrorism, however, fundamentalism is not an inherently bad thing. The fundamentalist is not by necessity a terrorist, but can become one. Before discussing the current situation we find ourselves in, we must identify exactly what we are to discuss. Fundamentalism is relatively easy to define; terrorism, however, is not. The increasingly popular online encyclopedia Wikipedia's multi-page entry for fundamentalism starts by linking this English word to a movement within North American Protestantism that arose in the early part of the twentieth century in reaction to modernism. However, it goes on the state, correctly, that:

> The term [fundamentalism] is now used much more widely, indeed often simply as just an emotive, pejorative term.
>
> ... In its broadest usage in general terms, it denotes strict adherence to any set of basic ideas or principles; or, in the words of the American Heritage Dictionary: "a usually religious movement or point of view characterized by a return to fundamental principles, by rigid adherence to those principles, and often by intolerance of other views and opposition to secularism."

Terrorism, on the other hand, is more difficult to define—at least in a way that is objective and widely accepted. In fact, the United Nations has been trying for over 30 years to decide upon a definition that might win unanimous approval from the members of the General Assembly. In this it has repeatedly failed, due predominantly to political factors, most of these being summarized by the hoary adage: "one man's freedom-fighter is another man's terrorist." Unfortunately this cliché is in fact a lie, and a most immoral one, that has been used to justify some of the most heinous acts of violence. We must be able to draw a line between the non-violent fundamentalist – or even the non-believer activist – and the terrorist. Quite simply, that line is crossed when the former decides to harm an unarmed target in the name of some cause. As a result I posit the following working definition of terrorism: "the use of violence (or threat thereof) by a non-state actor against those who cannot defend themselves, in the name of a political, ideological or religious end-state."

As a result we should be clear that there is nothing intrinsically 'wrong' with being a fundamentalist, be it an Islamic, Jewish or Christian fundamentalist. The line is crossed when an individual uses faith to justify harm to another who cannot defend themselves.

As with the famous phrase regarding death and taxes, there is another element of human existence that we can count upon to always be with us and which is linked to this discussion: the phenomenon of general armed conflict. Any discussion of the significance of fundamentalism and terrorism in today's globalized world must begin with an understanding of the broader context of conflict. However much we may have faith in multilateral institutions such as the UN, or in the spread of fundamental human rights across the globe, the fact remains that the history of mankind is more a series of war stories than a recounting of centuries of peace followed by more centuries of peace. This is true even today and even in the so-called civilized, or developed world. The twentieth century saw two global conflicts, each one emanating from Europe and each one meant to be the last of its kind. Yet even after the menace of the Third Reich was vanquished and Western Europe began to build what Robert Kagan famously called a "Kantian world of perpetual peace," the fact remains that for the next four decades the threat of thermonuclear war between East and West loomed large. Once that apocalyptic threat eventually dissipated, on the very doorstep of Europe people began killing each other in vast numbers simply because the 'enemy' spoke the wrong language or belonged to another religious community. It took the so-called "civilized" and "developed" West four years to finally put an end to the mass-killings in the former Yugoslavia, by which time at least 400,000 people had died. This was in the heart of Europe and only 12 years ago.

While man's proclivity to kill his fellow man – or woman or child – has not abated (as Algeria, Somalia, Rwanda and Darfur have of late clearly demonstrated), the 1990s did at least seem to present a respite for the West from the bloodiness of previous centuries, at least in terms of scenarios for conventional war. While the less developed parts of the world were still held hostage to atavistic tribal violence employing the most ancient and crudest of methods, with the demise of the Soviet Union and following the first Gulf War, strategic thinkers within the first world planned for a new reality. With the threat of mutually assured destruction (MAD) alleviated, it was argued that we were now in a post-modern threat environment.

Numerous theories were posited as to what kind of new world order was developing, the two most famous being Samuel Huntington's *Clash of Civilizations* and Francis Fukuyama's *The End of History and the Last Man*. Although very popular in their own right – Huntington's theory would a decade later be said to have had a great influence on the neoconservative administration of the United States – not even these grandmasters of political science and international relations succeeded in composing a handbook for the post-Cold War world, a manual for the new age that would convince the majority of Western decision-makers.

During the previous forty years, from the Berlin Blockade onwards, there was a "glue,"[1] as Phillip Gordon has referred it, that kept the West in agreement and which meant that Portugal, for instance, had the same threat perception as the United States, and France the same as the United Kingdom. It was the overarching agreement as to the universality of the

[209]

challenge posed by the USSR and its colonized satellites that would allow one telegram, written by a Moscow-based US diplomat, to eventually shape the foreign and security policies of all the future NATO nations. George Kennan's classified cable, later parsed into the anonymous *Foreign Affairs* article, "The Sources of Soviet Conduct,"[2] would be translated by the "wise men" of the post-war US administration into a very simple doctrine. That doctrine, named after President Truman, was containment of the Communist threat and the prevention of a domino-like collapse of other nations into the sphere of influence of the USSR. The doctrine's strength was its simplicity. Every soldier, every intelligence operative, even the average citizens of the free world could understand this grand-strategy. It was not some complicated, secret arrangement resulting from a machtpolitik negotiation concerning balance-of-power. The enemy was known, his intentions were clear and due to their global nature posed a threat to all the free peoples of the world. The task for all could be simplified even further: the West must prevent World War III if possible, if not, the West must win World War III.

But then the West received the greatest Christmas present in modern history. On December 25, 1991, without one shot being fired across the Iron Curtain, the Evil Empire ceased to exist. It was divided up into 14 newly independent states, some of which had existed before, and the new, much smaller, Russia Federation. Although the new Federation was not in a position to turn itself from a dictatorship into a functioning liberal democracy overnight, under the leadership of its new president, Boris Yeltsin, the Kremlin formally stated that it no longer considered the USA or its NATO allies to be its enemies (with Yeltsin even toying at one point with a Russian entry into the Alliance!). Subsequently the question was: to what end do we maintain our advanced defense assets? Who or what is the enemy in the post-Cold War world?

On the eve of the first Gulf War, at a point when it was clear not only from the events occurring in Moscow, but from the series of regime-changes and velvet revolutions in Central Europe that European

Communism had drawn its last breath, George Bush senior was already preparing to address a joint session of Congress with a speech entitled: "Toward a New World Order." Despite the phrase having been previously associated with the likes of President Woodrow Wilson and even the former Soviet premier Mikhail Gorbachev (who had used the same phrase when addressing the UN General Assembly just two years previously in December of 1988) the idea would become irrevocably associated with the elder Bush.

At the time, the concept was criticized by both left and right, with the President and his Secretary of State, James Baker, being accused of policy vagueness. There was some meat to the idea, however, as the speech did detail the seminal role of the United States as a leader of the international community; the potential for a partnership between Washington and Moscow aimed at energizing the UN and securing democracy globally; the rise of economic sources of conflict as opposed to ideological ones; and the need for countries such as Germany and Japan to be strategically emancipated. Nevertheless, as unveiled by President Bush, this was definitely not a doctrine that could even come close to the simplicity and neatness of containment policy. In fact, it could not rightly be called a doctrine.

As a result, the fundamental issues of national interest and national security would have to be approached in a different way by the nations of the West. Without a global menace, threats would be dealt with as and when they materialized. The first was, of course, posed by Saddam Hussein and his invasion of Kuwait. In response to this act of aggression the United States gathered an ad-hoc coalition of forces, both NATO and non-NATO (and even Warsaw Pact nations, since the WP was not dissolved until several months later in the summer of 1991) to face the amassed Iraqi forces. After having rehearsed for decades a grim scenario of war in Europe, on the territory of the two Germanys and involving extended fighting in a theater of operations laid waste by nuclear, chemical and biological weapons, this coalition of Western, Eastern

European, Arab, South American and even African nations routed the huge Iraqi forces occupying Kuwait and threatening Saudi Arabia, in a land campaign that lasted less than 100 hours and which saw no use of the arsenal of Weapons of Mass Destruction (WMD) which Saddam Hussein had manufactured.

While the generals and military planners were happy to conclude that the future of conventional warfare was safe and the utility of the Main Battle Tank was confirmed, the truth was that Operation Desert Shield represented the anomaly of the 1990s. The list of security challenges was destined to grow and would soon include new threats as well as revived challenges. The decade saw Western armies and national security agencies trying to cope with such diverse challenges as ethnic cleansing, mass migration, proliferation of WMD technology and know-how, organized crime and rouge states. Together, these and the other threats that emerged proved too diverse and unpredictable for any one Kennan-like thinker to create a singular new post-Cold War doctrine that was as useful and as beautifully simple as containment had been.

Then came the dramatic events of September 11, 2001. On that Tuesday morning the United States suffered the greatest terrorist attack ever recorded. In the space of less than two hours Osama bin Laden's al Qaeda operatives managed to murder more people than the IRA or the Baader Meinhof gang had managed to kill in the space of thirty years, and simultaneously brought the world's financial hub to a standstill.

While Nikita Khrushchev may have once promised to "bury" the United States, he never did act on the threat. Osama bin Laden had managed something that neither the mighty USSR nor even the Third Reich had achieved: the mass murder of Americans on American soil. In the days and weeks that followed it became more and more clear that, for many, the strategic confusion of the 1990s had vanished along with the twin towers of the World Trade Center. In place of the previous array of competing low-level threats and challenges, there was a new stand-alone menace equal to the Red Bear. The global threat of Communism and the

Soviet Union had been replaced by what Charles Krauthammer would describe as the existential threat of Islamic Fascism, or as the neologism: Islamofascism.[3]

By the very next day the North Atlantic Council (NAC), NATO's highest decision-making body, had provisionally enacted Article Five of its founding charter, the Washington Treaty. Article Five, the very essence of NATO and the article which made the Alliance a collective defense organization, states that an attack on one NATO nation is to be considered an attack on all and that all parties to the treaty should take necessary steps in response. The enactment was provisional, since there was a requirement that the attack originate from outside the United States, i.e. not be the result of domestic actors. However, this requirement was satisfied a few weeks later when Deputy Secretary of State Dick Armitage provided his NATO colleagues with classified National Security Agency (NSA) communication intercepts that linked the hijackers with al Qaeda elements in Afghanistan. Then the invocation became a permanent and historic act. The only strange thing was the scenario in which the article had been invoked.

More than fifty years earlier, when the drafters of the Washington Treaty were preparing the text of this most important and unusually succinct document, they did so with a very clear vision of the future contingency. Drafting the 14 articles in the middle of Stalin's attempt to strangle the Western sectors of Berlin and incorporate them into his own East German empire, the requirement was clear. Western intelligence estimates incorrectly reported that the military assets of the Soviet Union were far stronger than they actually were, and that should the opportunity present itself, Stalin would instruct the Soviet units spread all over Central Europe and the East German zone of occupation to launch a blitzkrieg across a weakened West Europe (much in the fashion that Hitler's Wehrmacht had just a few years previously). As a result, the new Western military–political alliance had to incorporate a guarantee that the United States would come to the military (and even nuclear) aid of the continent in the event of such an attack.

[213]

This promise – which the former British Air Marshal Lord Timothy Garden called one of the greatest bluffs in modern military history – would become the foundation of the strategic balance between East and West. Western Europe was outnumbered and outgunned by the forces of the future Warsaw Pact (WP), yet the Kremlin was clearly informed via the text of the Washington Treaty that should it act against the free nations to the west of the Iron curtain, the United States would respond, and with nuclear weapons if necessary. Luckily for the West – and the world – the North Atlantic Council never had to invoke Article Five against the USSR and the United States never had to follow through on its political and military promise.

Yet the peculiar reality is that the first time the article was enacted was under conditions completely at odds with those envisaged by NATO's founders. Originally the scenario had been one in which the United States brings vast military aid to the nations of Western Europe because they have been attacked by the conventional (military) forces of an enemy nation (the USSR) and its satellite states (the WP countries). On September 12, 2001, the North Atlantic Council invoked Article Five after a non-state actor (al Qaeda) had executed an unconventional (terrorist) attack against the United States. Every element of the new scenario was the obverse of that for which NATO had been created. Al Qaeda was not a member of the Warsaw Pact (which was long dead) and it was not even a nation-state. Its tools were not infantry regiments or SS-20 ballistic missiles, but box-cutters, teargas and civilian jumbo jets. It was not confronting European armed forces in the Fulda Gap of Central Germany, but murdering unarmed civilians in New York, Washington and in the skies above Pennsylvania. Furthermore, it transpired not to be a case of the European nations of NATO rushing to the military aid of the United States, as the post 9/11 military operations in Afghanistan (and two years later in Iraq) would not be executed under a NATO flag, but under the exclusive control of the Pentagon and the US President.

A New Enemy?

Much incorrect information has been published about America's new enemy. Even if one ignores for a moment the myriad absurd and even at times obscene conspiracy theories alleging US Central Intelligence Agency (CIA) or Mossad involvement in the 9/11 attacks, or that al Qaeda is in fact a figment of the neoconservative imagination, the fact is that very soon after those heinous events, and still today, the internet was saturated with both willful and unwitting disinformation and the airwaves and television screens filled with the opinions of so-called "terrorism experts" who had never, for example, heard of Khalid Sheikh Mohammed or Sayyid Q'utb before 2001. Barring a few exceptions over the last six years, the fact remains that the true authorities on "political violence" – as science likes to describe terrorism – remain that handful of experts that existed before 9/11 and who had been ploughing the field for decades before; people such as Professor Stephen Sloan of Temple University, the grandfather of terrorism studies and the inventor of terrorist attack simulations, or Brian Jenkins of the RAND Corporation, an ex-special forces officer and probably the best public speaker in the field, who coined the now immortal observation that terrorists are less interested in having a lot of people die, but rather in having "a lot of people watching,"[4] or the idea of terrorism as a form of theater.

The challenge that these experts faced and continue to face today, is the question of how different the new enemy is. While politicians on both sides of the Atlantic may still differ on the issue of how one defines terrorism and argue over what the best tools to use against political violence may be, or how the balance is met between the use of force, law enforcement tools and diplomacy, there remains the burning question: how different is Osama bin Laden and his al Qaeda network to the dozens of terrorist organizations we have fought in the past and can we use the same counter-terrorism tools and strategies that previously proved successful? Although the Cold War may have been defined around the East–West nuclear standoff and the political division of the world into

Communism versus democracy, we were also threatened by numerous non-state actors that saw the killing of civilians or unarmed officials as a viable political tool.

The first characteristic of al Qaeda that was noted as being novel, or rather renewed, was the religious element. If we look far enough back in time – for terrorism is perhaps the third oldest profession after prostitution and espionage – we will find more than enough examples of religiously motivated violence by non-state actors. From the Zealots of Biblical Palestine, to the Man of the Mountain and his Cult of the Assassin, and through to the Thuggee cult of the Indian sub-continent, there are a multitude of examples of groups that killed for religious motives. Nevertheless, these foes are not understood as the targets of modern counter-terrorism policies. Such tools were formed and influenced exclusively by Western experience with twentieth century groups such as the Provisional Irish Republican Army (IRA), the Basque separatist group ETA, or the Revolutionary Armed Forces of Columbia (FARC).

Although there are a few exceptions, the vast majority of the terrorist groups which shaped modern Western counter-terrorism policies can be described as political or pragmatic actors. The end-states that these organizations wished to achieve were linked by their political and territorial nature. For every Baader Meinhof gang with vague, universal anti-Western goals, there were a dozen or more other terrorist groups which had a very clear end-state in mind, one that was linked to a specific territory and to the realization of self-determination or greater autonomy (be it in Northern Spain for ETA, Northern Ireland's annexation by Eire for the Provisional IRA, or the creation of an independent Jewish state in the case of Haganah and Irgun). Even the most famous Arab terror group of the late twentieth century, the Palestine Liberation Organization (PLO), was originally defined not on a religious world view, but instead the desire for Palestinian self-determination—as well as the destruction of Israel.

It is important to note, however, that the political nature of these end-states and the fact that often such goals are in fact realistic and realizable – such as with the creation of Israel and the greater autonomy afforded to Northern Ireland in the Belfast (Good Friday) Agreement – cannot morally justify the use of terrorist tactics. However, this is precisely the message Yasser Arafat tried to convey during his infamous armed address to the UN General Assembly in November 1974, that if the cause is just then all measures are permissible—killing children is fine as long as your goal is to create your own state.

Despite the conventional wisdom regarding freedom-fighters and terrorists, as I have noted, any definition of political violence must provide demarcation between the two groups. A terrorist is a terrorist because in trying to reach a goal, no target is off-limits. Those that cannot defend themselves are the highest-value targets to the terrorist because it is through them that fear (terror) is best spread to the broader community. A freedom-fighter or a guerilla is a quasi-soldier that attacks only those that can defend themselves, be it soldiers, the police or paramilitary forces. That is the difference between a suicide bomber killing customers in a Tel Aviv pizzeria and a militia unit attacking a heavily fortified Israeli Defense Force (IDF) check point in the Gaza Strip. Both actors may be fighting for the same cause – a free and independent Palestine – but the first is doing so with the tools of a terrorist, the latter with that of the freedom-fighter.

Al Qaeda is therefore clearly a terrorist group, but not a classically pragmatic, or political one. Or is it? To answer this question one must have a clear understanding of what bin Laden and his followers wish to achieve. Professor Sloan, observing well before 9/11 the quiet and unannounced rebirth of religiously motivated terrorism, coined the term "non-territorial terrorism."[5] With this he wished to illustrate the growth in numbers of groups that were not defined by an issue which was geographically delimited (such as independence or autonomy for a specific region).

[217]

So what does, or did, al Qaeda wish to achieve through its string of murderous attacks against civilians, from the first World Trade Center attack in 1993, through to the East African embassy bombings in 1998, 9/11 and subsequent atrocities? Is this group defined more by religion than politics? Is it geographically defined? The label Islamofascism seems to imply a welding of both, combined with a global perspective, but is this accurate?

Here the researcher is well served by bin Laden's own ego. Unlike the relatively scarce and vague ramblings of terrorists such as Ulrike Meinhof, bin Laden's statements are numerous and detailed. One doesn't even have to be an Arabist, or linguist to determine the terror leader's inner thoughts. Thanks to a surviving remnant of the Foreign Broadcast Information Service (FBIS) of the US government, anyone (with official business to do so) can read in English the vast number of bin Laden statements made since al Qaeda became an international player. This self-appointed leader is not a shy man; the first decade of material (1994–2004) compiled by the FBIS runs to almost 300 pages in translation. After reading the ninety-plus statements and interview transcripts one should be able to piece together a picture of what end-state al Qaeda wishes to achieve. The only problem is that this picture is a mosaic. Yes, it is religiously-informed throughout, but at the same time it is flavored with the clearly political, or pragmatic. The best example of this mixture of the two worldviews is the prerecorded video statement that bin Laden gave to the Al Jazeera TV station that was to be broadcast only once large-scale military operations were launched against Afghanistan (October 7, 2001). For the majority of the statement, bin Laden talks of religious motivation and the global and absolutist aim of recreating a fundamentalist Caliphate, a vast theocracy that will bring the Arab and Muslim world back to the true path described by the lives of the early Salafi generations of the Mohammedan faith. A world in which the West is no longer the dominant culture, in which politics, the law and faith are no longer separated, a world in which the religious leader is also the political leader.

It is exactly these types of pronouncements that have led many to place bin Laden and his followers in a category separate from the classic terrorists of the second half of the twentieth century. Although the IRA may have said it represented the Catholics of Northern Ireland, the annexation of the north by Eire was a purely political end-state. As such it was, importantly, an end-state open to negotiations between the IRA (Sinn Féin) and the British government. However, it is nigh impossible to envisage any political negotiations between al Qaeda and its enemy, the West, on its desired end-state. The destruction of our civilization in favor of the creation of a fundamentalist Muslim empire that includes territory that now belongs to the West (such as Andalusia) is obviously not a subject for the G-8 or NATO to discuss behind closed doors at a table with Osama bin Laden and Ayman al-Zawahiri. It is clearly a 'them and us' situation, as was the Cold War.

Yet unfortunately the picture is not so clear-cut, for in the last few seconds of the broadcast (as in many others) bin Laden changes tack. When at the end of his statement he promises that there will never be peace in the United States unless "all the infidel armies leave the land of Mohammed"[6] and until there is a free and independent Palestine, bin Laden temporarily transmogrifies himself from the transcendentally-informed terrorist to the politician, or pragmatist. Nevertheless, the overarching aim of the creation of a fundamentalist global Caliphate after the destruction of Western civilization, firmly places bin laden in the camp of the transcendentally-informed terrorist. The question now is, more than five years later, where do we stand?

The Current Campaign against Terrorism: Are we Winning?

With recent mid-term elections in the United States decidedly favoring the Democratic Party, US casualties in Iraq exceeding the number of those killed on September 11, 2001, and the release of the Iraqi Study Group's report, there is a great expectation in Washington and among allied capitals that the last two years of the Bush presidency will see significant changes in how the "Global War on Terror" is waged. Based upon an examination of developments in the counter-terrorism campaign since 2004, and recent discussions with those in the US administration who have operational responsibility for specific elements of the War on Terror, one can provide a report on the strategic balance sheet to date, as well as a prognosis for the next few months. In brief, it is clear that the administration has decided to recognize the failure of current doctrines and strategy and has given the Pentagon and combat commanders great leeway to reinvent the fundamental approach to the War on Terror

Just 48 hours before his resignation after the mid-term elections, a memo from Donald Rumsfeld was leaked to the *New York Times*. As a significant classified document leaked at a very turbulent time in American politics, it does not provide a reassuring depiction of certainty in strategic thinking amongst the highest levels of Washington's decision-makers. The brief document is little more than a shopping list of 21 various alternatives or options, some of which the former Secretary of Defense was strongly against – such as "surging" troop numbers in Iraq – and others that seem to lack any obvious benefits to the overall aims of the previously declared US policy of Iraqi democratization—for example the suggestion that US support and troops be removed from the more "uncooperative" regions of Iraq.

Given the lack of clarity regarding which of the options should be followed, much was therefore expected of the report and recommendations released by the bipartisan Iraqi Study Group (ISG). The ISG report makes stark reading, however, even the figures alone: 3,000 US dead, over 21,000 wounded, 3,000 Iraqis killed per month on average and corruption costs estimated at $5–7 billion per year, with 150,000 barrels of oil stolen per day. The total intervention bill to date is estimated at $400 billion, or $8 billion per month. The report's main suggestions are: a withdrawal of all combat brigades within 15 months, leaving only force protection, training and support units; the concurrent takeover of internal security functions by Iraqi forces; the strengthening of the central government in Baghdad, with a heavy bias toward the federal center and a weakening of autonomy for Iraq's regions; and the inclusion of Syria and Iran within the stabilization process.

Yet, as a whole, the Baker–Hamilton report proposes ideas that have already been debated for several months (such as the partition of Iraq) and which cannot be said to represent a novel contribution to the debate on rethinking US counter-terrorism policy On the other hand, some of the recommendations betray a scant disregard for the declarative 'grand strategy' of the Global War on Terror. For example the idea of opening negotiations with Iran and Syria, countries previously labeled as members of the "Axis of Evil," or as "rogue states," flatly runs against the neocon policy of reshaping the whole region, a policy which is being fronted by Secretary of State Condoleeza Rice under the title of Transformational Diplomacy, a policy which emphasizes the active undermining of states which are not liberal democracies, not their recognition as negotiating partners.

Thus some commentators have deemed the ISG report an "unusable recipe book" which demonstrates an overconfidence in the reliability of negotiations in the (post-invasion) international environment, and in the power of the State Department or the National Security Council (NSC) to stabilize the region through diplomacy, given that Iran is clearly uninterested in peace and Syria is abetting the movement of insurgents in and out of Iraq. Little mention is made of the potential need for internal reconciliation, or the desires of the Council of Representatives. The most difficult question remains: can one envisage one strong Iraqi nation-state encompassing three diverse populations, each of which wishes to dominate the other, or at best to be totally separate (such as the Kurds)?

As a result one can justifiably ask: what are the aims of the US strategy against terrorism? Or the more difficult question of whether in fact there is a doctrine at all that is driving the War on Terror. One of the first problems in answering either question relates to terminology, or labeling. Although the Bush administration has taken pains to repeatedly assert the connection between Iraq and global terrorism and persists in stating that its policies are driven by the simple logic that it is better to fight the terrorists in the Middle East than at home, the fact is that one can and should separate Salafist Jihadism with global capability from the theatre of operations that is Iraq, if only for operational and strategic reasons. In the latter case we can reasonably talk of a religiously, politically and economically fuelled internal war for national dominance by distinct ethnic and religious groupings – at times supported by exogenous forces. The other adversary – typified by the original al Qaeda – represents an enemy that may at times be similar to those forces the United States faces in Iraq (in terms of religious motive or ideology) but which, by dint of its global aims and dispersed nature, poses an altogether different challenge that will not be met primarily by military force or even nation-building exercises and which targets other nations, not just US or Iraqi government forces (*viz*. the Madrid and London attacks).

Despite the less than convincing strategic perspectives afforded by either the ISG or the leaked Rumsfeld memo, at least with regard to the global threat of Salafi extremism, the picture is not so bleak. Quietly over the last 18–24 months, various groups have been using iconoclastic approaches to tackle the question of current strategy and the issue of counter-insurgency. It was recently reported that General David Petraeus, the new commander for Iraq, had assembled a very unusual and high-powered "red team" of warrior intellectuals, dubbed "Petraeus' Guys." Methodologically, the approach is built upon a recent push by the US Army and specifically a new project of the University of Foreign Military and Cultural Studies at Fort Leavenworth. The new program aims to institutionalize permanent so-called "devil's advocate units," or "red teams" within the structure of the armed forces.[7] Unlike valiant efforts to inform policy or modify strategy from outside the administration – the most significant to date being the American Enterprise Institute (AEI) effort to strategically reinvigorate the War on Terror, led by military historian Frederick Kagan and christened "Choosing Victory" – this is not a temporary solution, or a product-based one-off. Instead Petraeus has collected a standing cadre of recognized soldier-Ph.Ds, including Col. Peter Mansoor, Col. H.R. McMaster, as well as Princeton economist Michael Meese (son of the former Attorney General) and unlike earlier ad-hoc efforts, this team will not only advise but be part of the planning process and its operational implementation. Already the group's recommendations are being aired, with the first move being one away from the so-called "fortress mentality" exhibited so far by US forces in Iraq, to the creation of numerous patrol bases in which US and coalition forces will serve alongside Iraqi military and police units.

These 'warrior scholars,' along with a handful of strategically minded diplomats beneath the cabinet and Assistant Secretary level have spent the last year and a half searching for a fresh doctrine and strategy befitting the new enemy. Events such as the first Strategic Symposium at the US Army War College in 2006, the international counter-terrorism programs launched by the George C. Marshall Center and now the latest program from the Joint Special Operations University in Florida have proposed a revisiting of older strategies and doctrines which, if duly modified, will help minimize the risk to US and allied interests. Given the fact that the United States has avoided mainland terrorist attack since 2001, there is hope that some of these are already working.

The first realization is that previous models of insurgency and counterinsurgency bear a distinct similarity to the current situation, or at least can help point the way to avoiding the mistakes made by other nations in the past. Subsequently, while the Global War on Terror may have been internally rechristened last year by the military and the Department of State as the "Long War," the number of those who now see the campaign as being one of global counterinsurgency is growing. Secondly, given the historic role of Marxist and Communist concepts within the evolution of Salafi extremism and that this form of terrorism has its origins in the religious ideologies of writers such as Q'utb, who combined Marxist ideas with post-1979 theocratic fundamentalism, there is a small group in Washington and elsewhere who are quietly arguing that the relevance of Cold War tools and concepts is greater than President Bush's political detractors would have one believe. The fact that in purely military, Clausewitzian terms, al Qaeda no longer has any obvious strategic center of gravity, except its extremist ideology, would seem to make comparisons to the last great ideological conflict an obvious choice.

Following this realization, in groundbreaking academic work that one hopes will have its just influence on the policy process, individuals such as David Kilcullen, Chief Strategist to the State Department's Office for the Coordinator for Counterterrorism, and a member of the Petraeus Red Cell, are revitalizing and modifying the tools of a previous era, especially those which we used to classify under the heading of "political warfare." In Kilcullen's most recent, soon to be published work, this Australian former military counter-insurgency expert places emphasis upon al Qaeda's techniques of penetration and subversion and how counter-subversion techniques from the Cold War must be revisited. He has also argued that terrorism can be understood as a subset of classic insurgency. In the study that brought him to the attention of the US government – *Countering Global Insurgency* – he points out that there is a greater than 85 percent correlation between Islamist insurgency and terrorist activity (or al Qaeda presence) in a given theater, i.e. "most al Qaeda activity occurs in areas of Islamist insurgency."[8] Al Qaeda should no longer be seen as providing central command and control to its numerous cells but as a sponsorship system of planning and operational tasking. "Within each country in a *jihad* theater there are local actors, issues and grievances. Many of these have little to do with the objectives of the global *jihad*, and often pre-date the *jihad* by decades or hundreds of years,"[9] in other words, a confederation of loosely linked networks, not unlike the Comintern of old. These ideas echo those that have been floated by the Advanced Research and Assessment Group (ARAG) of the UK Ministry of Defence (MoD), where former Sovietologist Chris Donnelly has been comparing original Communist ideas of revolution, to the rhetoric and propaganda used by al Qaeda.[10] The ARAG has, along with strategists such as Kilcullen, led the way in revisiting the relevance of concepts such as "resistance" in shaping terrorist behavior and the applicability once more of the tools of political warfare. (For example in the clichéd campaign for hearts and minds, it may be far easier to make the enemy look "bad" than to try and make the West look "good" in the eyes of the uncommitted members of the Muslim community.)

Nevertheless, unless both the US political will to surmount troop shortfalls in Iraq and to identify common interests amongst warring factions within the country can be found in short order, it is unlikely that even initiatives such as the new Petraeus team will be able to make a lasting contribution to the stabilization process within and around Iraq. Subsequently the vision portrayed in the US National Intelligence Estimate for Iraq, which was released recently by the National Intelligence Council, will most likely come true: in "the coming 12 to 18 months, we assess that the overall security situation will continue to deteriorate at rates comparable to the latter part of 2006."[11] Or to quote the Director of the George C. Marshall Center's Program for Terrorism and Security Studies, Professor Nick Pratt: "It is not for want of brain power that we are having the troubles that we are having in Iraq. The question is political will; domestically amongst the warring factions of Iraq and in the US with regards to the question of the size of troop surge. Warring parties can be forced into coexistence with adequate boots on the ground."[12] Only time will tell.

In the meantime we must understand two simple truths: firstly that fundamentalism itself is not the problem and secondly, that terrorism cannot be eradicated. It must be managed and the terrorists pursued and weakened until the threat they pose becomes minimal.

10

Pathways to Proliferation and Containing the Spread of WMD

Mohamed Kadry Said

Official details of the United States' Manhattan Project to develop the first atomic bomb were first released to the public on August 12, 1945 in the "Smyth Report"[1] after the bombing of Hiroshima and Nagasaki on August 6 and 9 respectively. The report was written by physicist Henry DeWolf Smyth, chairman of the department of physics at Princeton University and a consultant to the Manhattan project. Its content was personally reviewed by Project Director General Leslie Groves and others to insure that the report contained no information that would be of assistance to anyone who might try to build a nuclear weapon. The information from the Smyth Report and other contemporary published releases has been supplemented in subsequent years by numerous other histories of the Manhattan Project. The intent of all these publications has been to inform the public – according to the public's right to know – by revealing what could be revealed and to keep secret what needed to be kept secret. For this reason, the Smyth Report did not contain any details that might assist the creation of a functional weapon.

Nonetheless, despite undergoing extensive security review before release, the Smyth Report was criticized by some politicians for having given away the secret of the A-Bomb (the Hiroshima Bomb). Some still believe that the Smyth Report was used extensively in the Soviet Union to guide their own bomb project by providing details concerning what kinds

[227]

of laboratories and factories were needed, and allowing the Soviets to compare their progress with the scale of the US project.

When the existence of the atom bomb became public knowledge in August 1945, a logical question immediately arose about how long it would take before the Soviet Union developed such a weapon. The majority of the public and politicians believed that the intricacies of the atom bomb unlocked by the US scientists could remain secret for decades. However, scientists involved in atomic energy guessed that it would only take the Soviets five more years to catch up; in actual fact, it only took them four. To date, eight nations have openly conducted nuclear tests: the United States (1945); the Soviet Union (1949); Great Britain (1952); France (1960); China (1964); India (1974); Pakistan (1998); and North Korea (2006). Israel is widely believed to possess the bomb and it may have tested a nuclear device together with South Africa in 1979.

Since the Manhattan Project, the majority of scientists have argued that any modern, industrialized state could eventually build its own bomb if it chose to do so. They believe that there is no *secret* scientific theory or principle concerning the bomb. The primary difficulties relate to engineering, such as the separation of uranium-235, the production of plutonium, and the designing and construction of an actual weapon. The proliferation threat comes most often from a second tier of countries with limited indigenous scientific and technical resources; countries which would need to import much of the technology, materials and components needed. Countries in this group, like India, Pakistan, Israel, Iraq, Libya, Iran, and North Korea, have attempted to develop nuclear weapons, with differing degrees of success.

On July 1, 1968, the Nuclear Non-Proliferation Treaty (NPT) was signed by the United States, Great Britain, the Soviet Union and 59 other nations. The purpose of the treaty was to prevent the acquisition of nuclear weapons by any nation that did not already possess them. The treaty took effect in March 1970, and in 1992 was signed by China and France. As of 2000, only Cuba, Israel, India and Pakistan had not signed the NPT.

It is interesting to note that the Cold War competition between the two superpowers – the United States and the Soviet Union – ultimately had a very paradoxical effect; on the one hand, production and deployment of weapons of ever greater destructive potential increased as a result of the arms race; and on the other hand, so did the demand for controls on design and deployment of nuclear weapons so as to reduce the danger of their unintended or uncontrolled use. Such controls were manifested in the Anti-Ballistic Missile (ABM) Treaty, as well as the various agreements resulting from the Strategic Arms Limitation Talks (SALT) and the Strategic Arms Reduction Talks (START). So, while bipolarity was at times a driver of the arms race, it also provided a framework for imposing significant restrictions on nuclear weapons.

Today, the non-proliferation regime is under heavy pressure as a result of the emergence of further declared and potential nuclear powers such as North Korea and Iran. North Korea withdrew from the NPT on January 10, 2003 and continued to develop its nuclear and missile programs. In the case of Iran, many observers believe that the Iranian regime is seeking to acquire nuclear weapons—raising the specter of proliferation in the Middle East. The behavior of these two countries will have profound and direct implications on global security and on the state of proliferation across their respective regions.

Other underlying trends also threaten the non-proliferation regime, such as the spread of global terrorism and the desire of some terrorist groups to procure the materials, technology and know-how necessary to develop weapons of mass destruction (WMD). Furthermore, the anticipated drive towards civil nuclear power as a potential solution for future energy and climate security brings with it the dilemma of how to prevent this experience from being diverted to military use and falling into the hands of terrorists. On the international level, the START treaty will expire in 2009 and the world will need to begin adjusting from a bilateral disarmament framework built by the United States and the Soviet Union during the Cold War to one more suited to a potential future multi-polar,

[229]

globalized world. Furthermore, in 2010, the international community will need to review the NPT and to consider a more global and effective non-proliferation regime. Other non-proliferation issues also remain unresolved, such as the stalemate on the Comprehensive Test Ban Treaty (CTBT) and the Fissile Material Cut-off Treaty (FMCT).

The purpose of this paper is to explore the global dynamics of WMD proliferation and the impact of globalization on the future of this process, taking into consideration the changes in the global security environment since the end of the Cold War and especially in the post-9/11 era. The paper ends with a list of recommendations for measures to stem future proliferation.

Pathways to WMD Proliferation – Threats and Responses

The United Nations defines weapons of mass destruction (WMD) as "atomic explosive weapons, radioactive material weapons, lethal chemical or biological weapons, and any weapons developed in the future which have characteristics comparable in destructive effect to those weapons mentioned above."[2] Another definition provided by the US Code Title 50 describes WMD as "any weapon or device that is intended, or has the capability, to cause death or serious bodily injury to a significant number of people through the release, dissemination, or impact of toxic or poisonous chemicals or their precursors; a disease organism; radiation or radioactivity." A further, more practical definition refers to WMD as "weapons that can inflict mass casualties on combatants using nuclear and radiological devices, long-range missiles, and lethal chemical and biological agents."[3]

In the majority of cases, states pursue WMD to offset international and/or regional threats. However, this motivation cannot alone explain the timing of proliferation decisions that are more dependent on national, cultural or individual leaders' attributes. Understanding the psychology and mindset of such leaders is crucial to non-proliferation efforts. Some analysts argue that apart from national leaders, influential figures both within states and at the international level can have a profound influence on states' decisions to pursue WMD acquisition. Understanding these figures, the substance of their beliefs and claims, and the influence they have within a country at any given time can enable outside analysts and decision-makers to predict more accurately the direction and speed of that country's nuclear development.[4] The self-perpetuating technological momentum of a WMD program can sometimes propel the program faster than the development of a country's political decision-making processes and strategic judgment regarding the future use of such weapons.

Some argue that there is little to prevent a determined country from developing a WMD capability. This argument is based on the steady declassification of WMD technologies, and on the worldwide spread of technical training in the physical sciences and technology. However, others point out that nuclear weapons in particular are complicated devices, the construction of which is particularly technologically demanding. The pursuit of a "technological readiness" strategy by some countries will allow them to shorten the development time needed to produce operational weapons in emergency situations. Technologies that are no longer "state of the art" are often routinely declassified, yet they can be useful in crossing a technical barrier during the development process. The programs of Iraq, Libya, Iran and North Korea illustrate the importance of foreign training, technology and unclassified documents to WMD development. In the case of Iraq, most of the technical expertise required was obtained by sending Iraqis abroad for advanced degrees.

The amalgamation of interests and the exchange of services between countries can also sometimes fuel proliferation. Prior to the Gulf War of 1991, pathogenic, toxigenic and other biological research materials were exported to Iraq pursuant to application and licensing by the US Department of Commerce. Also, by the 1990s, Pakistani scientist A.Q. Khan and his network were providing weapons information to North Korea in exchange for information about their long-range missiles. Khan

[231]

also gave the North Koreans plans for the production of centrifuges for uranium enrichment, and is thought to have provided them with sample centrifuges.[5] For some countries the barriers to proliferation of WMD technologies are more political than technical.[6]

From the early days of the Cold War, the nature of the bipolar international order made proliferation easy and inevitable among allies and friends. It naturally created a state of nuclear balance and mutual deterrence between two rival alliances led by the United States and the Soviet Union. Each side in this power equation sought to acquire superior military might, leading to an arms race in which both superpowers sought weapons of ever-greater lethality; a process that inevitably encouraged the development of nuclear, chemical and biological weapons. With the process of decolonization, third world countries became independent and entered into regional power struggles, leading in many cases to the spread of WMD technology. The fear of the two superpowers – that a local conflict would trigger a global nuclear exchange – combined with their desire for greater freedom of action in some regions, were the incentives behind their mission to curb WMD proliferation. To this end, they imposed control mechanisms such as the Nuclear Non-Proliferation Treaty (NPT), the Biological Weapons Convention (BWC) and the Chemical Weapons Convention (CWC).[7]

Despite the value of these control mechanisms and multilateral nonproliferation regimes, they currently face a crisis in two distinct dimensions. The first is the "proliferation threat dimension"—a result of high rates of technological development and broad diffusion of existing technology in the fields of biotechnology, uranium enrichment and spent fuel reprocessing. The second is the "international response dimension" to the proliferation threat, characterized by a number of international initiatives launched to bolster the multilateral non-proliferation framework. This has been associated with a vivid debate on the legitimacy and effectiveness of "unilateral" versus "multilateral" responses to proliferation. The debate is largely driven by disagreements on whether the weapons/technologies themselves or the possession of them by specific states poses the greater proliferation threat. Those promoting the latter viewpoint criticize the principles of "nondiscrimination" and "peaceful use" enshrined in treaty regimes such as the NPT. They call for unilateral ad hoc approaches that can be tailored to each specific case. Disagreements on the appropriate means to address proliferation have produced a stalemate in collective action against WMD proliferation.[8]

The "proliferation shocks" after the Gulf War of 1991 – mainly in Iraq and the former Soviet states – triggered a number of institutional responses. Among these responses were the Cooperative Threat Reduction (CTR) initiative in 1991; the indefinite extension of the NPT in 1995; the CTBT in 1996; the establishment of the International Atomic Energy Agency's Additional Protocol for safeguards agreements in 1997; the G8 Global Partnership in 2002; the Proliferation Security Initiative (PSI, or "Cracow Initiative") in 2003; as well as measures to strengthen the Nuclear Suppliers Group (NSG) and the Australia Group (AG).[9]

In terms of proliferation threats, the number of states currently seeking WMD – and nuclear weapons in particular – is less than was predicted during the Cold War. Argentina, Brazil and South Africa have renounced nuclear weapons and placed their nuclear programs and materials under IAEA safeguards. The Independent States of the former Soviet Union have agreed to transfer inherited arsenals to Russia and signed the NPT as non-nuclear states. Libya's decision in December 2003 to dismantle its WMD programs under the IAEA and the Organization for the Prohibition of Chemical Weapons (OPCW) represented a significant victory for the nonproliferation regimes. During the same period a series of negative revelations overshadowed these positive trends, such as the unexpected scope of Iraq's WMD programs revealed through the work of the UN Special Commission (UNSCOM) after the 1991 Gulf War; the withdrawal of North Korea from the IAEA in 1994 and from the NPT in 2003; and the discovery of Iran's undeclared uranium enrichment program in 2003. Each of these revelations has sparked debate on the effectiveness of current regimes to prevent or even detect proliferation. Technological advances have also made WMD more accessible to more actors. The dilemmas of dual-use technology also include the possibility of non-state actors gaining access to WMD materials and equipment.

The Indo-US nuclear deal signed during President George W. Bush's visit to India in February 2006 has caused a stir among the nonproliferation lobby. The deal enables the United States to provide civilian nuclear technology to India—which is not a member of the NPT. According to the deal, India agrees to a number of stipulations designed to ensure that the technology or nuclear material is not diverted for use in India's weapons program. The principle opposition to the deal came from the non-proliferation community. Indeed, an analysis of the technical aspects of the deal suggests that the non-proliferation concerns were deliberately sidelined in an attempt to cement the alliance between the two countries.[10]

Impact of Unilateral US Policies on WMD Proliferation

The end of the Cold War left the former Soviet Union with a vast accumulation of WMD materials and expertise which, it was feared, could easily fall into the hands of black-market dealers. Another feature of the post-Cold War era was the emergence of the United States as the world's sole superpower. This situation has had important ramifications for US counter-proliferation policy and the future dynamics of WMD proliferation. To defend against the use of such weapons, US policy has focused on developing the National Missile Defense (NMD) program to increase US invulnerability to any future missile attack by an adversary. The American NMD program is a long-term project to deploy an effective missile shield to guard against Chinese and Russian missiles, as well as those operated by rogue states. In terms of its offensive strategy, the US administration has adopted the use of preemptive military force, i.e., it aims to destroy an enemy's WMD capabilities before they are used in combat. The *National Security Strategy of the United States of America*, released in mid-September 2002, emphasizes 'pre-emption' as a long-term military option for the United States.[11] The military interventions in Iraq and Afghanistan were clear demonstrations of how the terrorist attacks of September 11, 2001 had transformed the norms and justifications of military intervention to include the threat of WMD acquisition and global terrorism. Indeed, from the US and Israeli perspectives, military intervention has again surfaced as an option in dealing with a potential Iranian nuclear threat.

The launch of the NMD program after 9/11 resulted in the withdrawal of the United States from the ABM treaty in December 2001. This was followed by the US administration's rejection of the SALT and START agreements' design, based on Cold War nuclear parity between the United States and the Soviet Union. The Russians have responded by threatening to withdraw from the Conventional Armed Forces in Europe (CFE) treaty if the United States insists to deploying components of the NMD system in the Czech Republic and Poland. In the absence of a multilateral control regime to govern such situations, Russia and China will seek to overcome the US advantage in missile defense by expanding their nuclear arsenals and developing countermeasures against its NMD system, such as multiple warheads, decoys, anti-satellite missiles, etc.[12] Other states might respond by concentrating on the development of chemical and biological weapons. Thus, some experts view US efforts to preserve its supremacy as an important driver for WMD proliferation, rather than the opposite.[13]

Proliferation and the Threat of Nuclear Terrorism

The horrifying attacks of September 11, 2001 that took the lives of more than 3,000 people, have greatly increased the concern within the international community regarding the risks of a nuclear terrorist attack. There is a growing belief among specialists that it would be relatively easy for a terrorist group to assemble a nuclear explosive device in the heart of a major city and then detonate it with horrifying consequences.

Such a capability is likely to grant any terrorist group that possesses it an immeasurable feeling of power in addition to its value as an effective instrument for blackmail or retaliation. However, it is unlikely that a major terrorist group will be able to obtain an actual nuclear warhead. It might be much easier for such a group to obtain the key material necessary to manufacture, on site, a nuclear explosive device. If a sufficient quantity of highly enriched uranium (HEU) is procured, a small group of terrorists with sufficient knowledge of physics, explosives, electronics and machining might be able to manufacture an explosive nuclear device comparable to that which destroyed Hiroshima.

The biggest obstacle to the manufacture and detonation of such a device is the difficulty of acquiring the weapons-grade HEU. One hundred kilograms of this material is more than enough to manufacture a nuclear explosive device with a similar yield to the Hiroshima bomb.[14] Enriching uranium for nuclear weapons is a difficult and expensive technological process. It is important to note that, in addition to being used for nuclear weapons, HEU is also used as the fuel in the reactors of nuclear-propelled submarines and some Russian ice-breakers, as well as for various small scientific research reactors around the world. The quantity of HEU that exists in the world is large due to the excessive accumulation of this strategic material during the Cold War, especially in the United States and the former Soviet Union; hence, there is a high risk that some of it might be stolen or sold illegally on the black market.

The very large quantity of HEU in the former Soviet Union (now mostly in Russia), which amounts to 1,000 tons – enough for more than 10,000 nuclear explosive devices – has been a source of great concern since the end of the Cold War. In particular, legitimate fears are raised over the security of this material and the possibility of its theft or diversion to third parties. Early in the 1990s, substantial efforts were initiated to improve the safeguards of this fissile material, via the US–Russian Cooperative Threat Reduction Program (CTR). The G8 countries have proposed additional contributions under a new program entitled

"10+10 over 10" which means $10 billion from the United States plus $10 billion from the remaining G8 countries over 10 years as a time scale. The focus of the above programs is on strengthening Material Protection Control and Accounting (MPC&A) procedures at dozens of nuclear facilities throughout the former Soviet Union. Quantities of HEU also exist in other countries such as the United Kingdom (6–10 tons), France (20–30 tons), China (15–25 tons), Pakistan (0.6–0.8 tons), India, Israel, South Africa (0.4 tons) and Iran. Although most of these stockpiles are small compared to those of Russia, they would still be sufficient to manufacture a large number of nuclear explosive devices.[15]

Plutonium is the only other raw material from which nuclear bombs are now made. More demanding technological expertise is required to manufacture a nuclear explosive device based on plutonium, including experimentation with very sophisticated conventional explosives and electronic equipment. Moreover, handling plutonium entails much greater health hazards than does HEU, and transporting it clandestinely is more difficult because of its high radiation signature. Hence, plutonium nuclear explosive devices are much less likely to fall within the competence of any sub-national terrorist group. It is the HEU that presents the far greater nuclear threat. Thus, it is imperative that the world community devote immediate and substantial resources to consolidating its control over HEU, with the goal of eliminating as much of this dangerous material as quickly as possible. Further attention should also be paid to the brain drain of experts on nuclear weapons technology to states of concern (or terrorist groups) suspected of seeking to acquire nuclear weapons.

Any effective strategy for lowering the risk of nuclear terrorism must be based on the total elimination of the basic raw material, HEU, needed for the manufacture of nuclear explosive devices. From a practical point of view, it is enough to de-enrich HEU to less than 20 percent U-235 (low enriched uranium, LEU), so it cannot be used to produce a nuclear explosion. To re-enrich such a substance would be almost impossible for a terrorist group to achieve. The 1993 deal regarding HEU between the

United States and Russia called for Russia to de-enrich a substantial quantity of its HEU – 500 metric tons – and sell the resulting LEU to the United States to be used in its electricity-producing reactors under the title "From Megatons to Megawatts."[16] Unfortunately, this important achievement has been degraded by commercial considerations that stretched out its implementation to 20 years in order not to deflate the market price of LEU. In addition, attention should also be given to the risk associated with the existence of such enormous stocks of excess weapons-grade uranium in Russia and United States, the size of which is increasing because of additional reductions in US and Russian nuclear forces.

Other strategies have also been suggested, such as: eliminating as much HEU as possible through subsidizing HEU de-enrichment in Russia at a price of about US$10 for each gram of HEU eliminated (about $10 billion would be needed for the elimination of the approximately 1,000 tons of HEU remaining in Russia); transforming Russian's debts to non-interest-paying loans; and raising the awareness of policy makers in the United States and the public regarding the very real dangers posed by the large quantities of HEU that might become available to terrorist organizations or others.

Based on the *Global Fissile Material Report 2006*, issued by the International Panel on Fissile Materials (IPFM), there are at present around 1,700 tons of HEU and 500 tons of separated plutonium in the world, enough for more than 100,000 nuclear weapons. The report noted three obstacles to greatly reducing these fissile material stocks: 1) the large uncertainties regarding the size of the stockpiles held by various countries; 2) the large stockpile of weapons-grade HEU set aside by the United States, Russia and UK for their naval reactors; and 3) the growing global stockpile of civilian plutonium separated from power reactor spent fuel.[17]

India is estimated to be currently producing about 30 kilograms of weapons-grade plutonium per year. Japan currently has more than 40 tons of separated plutonium (enough for more than 5,000 nuclear weapons). In its report of 2006, the IPFM recommended that: 1) all nuclear-armed states declare publicly their stockpiles and agree on greater transparency measures with regard to the history of their production and disposition; and 2) countries employing HEU in naval reactors should move to other types of reactors, fueled with LEU. An international effort is already underway to convert civilian research reactors from HEU to LEU; 3) proposals should be made to limit further production of fissile materials, including the UN-sponsored effort to negotiate a Fissile Material Cutoff Treaty (FMCT).

Containing Chemical, Biological and Radiological Terrorism

During the 1990s, there were considerable proliferation concerns raised by linkages between corrupt state actors, organized crime and non-state terrorist groups. Theft from the former Soviet Union was one of many methods to secure WMD materials and technology. For example, the leadership of the Japanese cult Aum Shinrikyo made dozens of trips from 1991–1995 to Russia. They cultivated 35,000 members in Russia, 5,000 of them lived in Aum facilities. Aum personnel worked in Russian nuclear facilities and paid bribes to high-level Russian executive and legislative officials. In Japan, the Aum Shinrikyo cult targeted personnel with science and technical backgrounds. Those who carried out the Tokyo subway sarin gas attack in 1995 included a cardiovascular surgeon, a graduate student in particle physics, two applied physics graduates and one electrical engineer. Technological and organizational constrains imposed on non-state terrorist groups limit their freedom of action and their ability to establish ambitious scientific programs. Despite over one billion dollars in assets, extensive laboratories, and access to lab expertise, the Aum Shinrikyo failed to effectively weaponize anthrax and botulinum toxin and achieved limited results with sarin gas. The diffusion of terrorist organizations such as al Qaeda into cells might also inhibit their ability to make breakthroughs in this regard.[18]

Attempts have been made in Iraq to utilize chemical terrorism by exploding cars carrying chlorine gas. At least nine of the large-scale attacks in Iraq since the beginning of 2007 have involved the use of chlorine. These bombs cultivate a particular fear among the population because people who are not killed by the blast can die when the chlorine is dispersed and inhaled. Chlorine reacts with the water in moist human tissue, such as the eyes, nose, throat and lungs, and forms an acid which burns the tissue. Large quantities of Chlorine commonly used in water treatment plants were stolen in the Anbar province of Iraq where al Qaeda had a strong presence.[19]

Waging a terrorist attack with "dirty bombs" using radioactive material has also become a possibility. Every year thousands of commercial devices containing radioactive material are lost, abandoned or stolen. From measuring gauges to industrial food sterilizers, there are many sources of material that could be used to construct a dirty bomb which, when detonated, would spread dangerous radioactive material over a wide area. From 1996 to 2001, an average of 168 radiological sources were lost every year and never recovered in the United States alone. Of those, 20 percent were classified as risky, meaning the radioisotope was of a type that could be used to make a dirty bomb.

To reduce the chances of a nuclear or radiological dirty bomb attack, the United States is currently leading a colossal effort to install a network of preventive defenses at home and abroad. In the near future, every person and vehicle entering the United States, European Union and many other countries will be required to pass through a portal that scans them for radioactive materials. The United States is leading a global procurement drive for better detection equipment. Yet, experts say even the new generation of sensors will find it hard to detect the material used in a portable nuclear bomb since uranium-235 doesn't give off much radiation. The IAEA reports that sixteen confirmed cases of illegal trafficking of HEU had taken place over the past decade. Cases involving material that could be used to build a dirty bomb run into hundreds. In 2004, former US Defense Secretary William Perry said there was a 50–50 chance of a terrorist nuclear detonation occurring before 2010. However, Peter Zimmerman, a former chief scientist at the US Arms Control

Agency, responded: "That is unlikely, I would estimate only a 1 percent chance per year," but on the possibility of a dirty bomb being detonated, he says: "I am surprised it hasn't happened already. We've been lucky."[20]

The United States has recently launched a government effort to build a comprehensive database of nuclear and radiological materials from all over the world to help US officials quickly identify and act against those who help build "dirty bombs." The ability to determine who supplied the nuclear materials used in a bomb is critical to US efforts to shape a new policy aimed at deterring such proliferation.[21]

The Middle East: Past and Present Proliferation Dynamics

The Middle East has been a conflict-ridden region for a long time; it has become a region of concern not only as a potential developer of nuclear, chemical and biological weapons and their delivery systems, but also as the world's largest recipient of conventional weaponry. In the past two decades, the region has witnessed two major wars – the Iran–Iraq War (1980–1988) and the Gulf War of 1991 – where a considerable proliferation level of WMD and ballistic missiles have been revealed. States of the Middle East seek to acquire WMD for a variety of different reasons including to develop a nuclear deterrent, to compete in an arms race with neighbors, to defend against outside power projection, or to compensate for conventional weakness and the cost of conventional weapons acquisition—particularly those with a high technological value.

Israel was the first state in the region to pursue an independent nuclear and missile capability. In the fall of 1956, France agreed to provide Israel with a 24 mega-watt reactor and to build a chemical processing plant at Dimona, which became the foundation of the Israeli nuclear program. Intelligence and expert reports estimate that Israel has produced 100 to 200 nuclear devices, including warheads for its mobile Jericho-1 and Jericho-2 ballistic missiles and for delivery by aircraft, in addition to other tactical applications.[22] Israel has been considered for a long time the only nuclear-weapons-capable state in the Middle East, yet it has not overtly demonstrated a nuclear capability, preferring instead a policy of "nuclear ambiguity." Beside its sophisticated nuclear military capability, Israel has an active chemical weapons program and has reportedly conducted biological warfare activities at the Biological Research Institute in Ness Ziona.[23]

Within the context of its strategic ties with the United States, Israel has succeeded in removing many of the restrictions associated with this relationship. In March 2000, Israel and the United States signed an energy cooperation accord that gives Israeli scientists access to US Department of Energy laboratories. The accord will increase cooperation between the two countries in 25 "civilian" nuclear and non-nuclear areas, including in stemming the flow of WMD technology and expertise from the countries of the former Soviet Union.[24]

The threat perceived by the Arab and non-Arab countries as a result of Israel's build-up of conventional and non-conventional arms, has prompted the initiation of counter-armament programs. However, the scope of such programs is limited in size and capability compared to the Israeli systems already deployed. Owing to the fact that many Middle Eastern states face difficulties in financing their conventional arms buildup, some have pursued WMD to compensate for the unfavorable balance in conventional weapons and to deter outside intervention. Iran is suspected of having chemical and biological weapons and of conducting nuclear research efforts. Through three decades (1970s–1990s) Iraq sponsored sophisticated missile and WMD development programs. Syria, Libya and Egypt have also been assumed by Western sources to possess chemical warfare capabilities.[25]

The multiple nuclear tests of both India and Pakistan in May 1998, coupled with their advanced missile and space programs have echoed in the nearby Gulf countries and elsewhere in the Middle East. The Gulf is a sensitive area of confrontation, not far from the Indian and Pakistani nuclear missile threats. In March 1999, India sent for the first time its aircraft carrier INS Viraat to the Gulf as part of its continuing "military diplomacy" to increase New Delhi's influence in the region. The Indian

Navy held its first naval exercises with Kuwait and Iran and conducted one-day maneuvers with the navies of Saudi Arabia and Oman as part of its strategic thrust in the area.[26]

The recent Iranian drive to acquire a nuclear capability has sparked greater concerns in the Gulf and the Middle East, compelling other countries to consider the development of their own indigenous programs. In February 2007, Gulf Cooperation Council (GCC) representatives met with International Atomic Energy Agency (IAEA) officials in Vienna to consider a feasibility study for a nuclear program. Egypt also declared that it would consider renewing its interest in a peaceful nuclear program for power generation. Some experts suggest that Saudi Arabia and Egypt are the most likely candidates to go nuclear in response to an Iranian bomb.[27]

The Middle East entered a new period of uncertainty after 9/11. The suspects were from the region, and the "root causes" were clearly linked to the region's security dilemmas. The Middle East entered a new phase of transformation with the US war on Iraq, which has among its causes the perceived Iraqi acquisition of WMD. The nuclear threat in the Middle East is also linked to other dangers associated with WMD, their delivery systems, and the conventional military balance. The conflict pattern in the Middle East, while attracting the involvement of major powers, stayed "regional" for a long time. However, the US-led war on Iraq in 2003 has changed many regional strategic realities. The suspected ambitions of countries such as Iran to acquire a nuclear capability aim to deter not only regional threats but also interventions by outside powers. Only by providing vision and hope for the Middle East peace process between Israel and the Arab countries, together with the establishment of a wider security and cooperation regime in the region, can the dangers of WMD proliferation be brought under control. Thus, a politically and legally binding WMD-free zone will become the central objective of any potential regional security regime in the Middle East.

Impact of Globalization on WMD Proliferation

Policy makers combating proliferation must take into account the fact that the process of technological diffusion in a globalized world is irreversible. While fissile material production remains challenging, between fourteen and eighteen states are either already enriching uranium or are conducting enrichment-related research; a number that is likely to continue to grow. About fifteen countries can produce ballistic missiles and enhance their characteristics for longer range, better accuracy, and the introduction of solid-fuel propellants. Hundreds of countries have infrastructure that could be used for chemical weapons production, while only a dozen countries are believed to be engaged in biological weapons development. In the world of chemical and biological weapons, much of the expertise and equipment is readily available in the private sector.

Some analysts dispute the relationship between globalization and proliferation. They argue that globalization is a very broad, sweeping and evolved process, while proliferation is a narrow, secretive process that is only exercised by countries outside world system regulations choosing not to be part of the ever-expanding process of globalization. This explains, from their point of view, why proliferation is so limited compared to the huge spread of the global economy.[28]

The increasing ease of air travel, financial transactions, and trade may play a key role in enabling the emergence of complicated, global, proliferation networks. Increased privatization of trade, financial and information flows have widened the "non-governed" spaces in the international system. This has provided space and resources for non-state actors to exploit, leaving states devoid of control over such activities.

Globalization also serves as an important backdrop to the emergence of proliferation networks. Combating networks is different to combating separate entities. The study of complex proliferation networks reveals some common characteristics. For example: the whole of the network can be greater than the sum of the parts; it is difficult to ascertain a simple cause and effect logic; small changes in the context can have greater

[244]

broader effects; and problems can become dramatically better or worse at key "tipping points." Key nodes are those that affect most of the network performance; removing these key nodes – or individuals – can shatter the whole network. Also, some networks may be resistant to random attacks.[29]

In 2004 and after years of total denial, the Pakistani government admitted that a group of Pakistani scientists working in domestic nuclear institutions had been involved in the proliferation of nuclear-related technologies, equipment, and know how to Iran, North Korea and Libya. It seems that this group also approached Syria and Iraq to arrange clandestine business with them. The change in the Pakistani position from denial to admittance came after Libya formally decided to terminate its clandestine WMD program in October 2003 and after Iran agreed to cooperate with the IAEA and disclose details of its clandestine uranium enrichment program. The investigation of the Iranian and Libyan cases revealed the central role of Dr. A.Q. Khan, the former head of Pakistan's Khan Research Laboratories (KRL), in the clandestine trade. Detailed information was disclosed about middle men, companies, false end-user certificates, transfer of blueprints from one country, manufacture in another, transshipment to a third, before delivery to its final destination. Deliveries also included design drawings, components and complete assemblies of Pakistan's P-1 and P-2 centrifuge models including the blueprint of an actual nuclear warhead from KRL. There is also evidence that Pakistani scientists held briefing sessions separately for Iranian and Libyan counterparts in Karachi, locations in Casablanca and in Istanbul.

The key innovation in Khan's proliferation network was the offer of a "one-stop shop" for nuclear technologies. He integrated what was earlier a disaggregated market place into a single outlet where interested clients could find sensitive technology, designs, engineering and consultants to develop a nuclear weapons capability. The IAEA Director-General Mohamed ElBaradei described the Khan network as an underground "international Wal-Mart" for nuclear weapons technologies.

Khan's proliferation motives appear to range from profit and ideology to his own megalomania. However, the Pakistani government cannot be distanced completely from this activity because it is difficult to believe that a diversion of such massive scale and scope over period of nearly two decades could have occurred without the knowledge of authorities within the Pakistani government. Khan made nuclear transfers to Iran under the cover of a peaceful nuclear cooperation agreement signed in the mid 1980s. It seems from some historical records that the former Pakistani president, the late General Zia-ul-Haq, was aware of Iran's interest in purchasing Pakistani uranium enrichment technology.

Providing assistance for Iran might be one of Pakistani policies at certain times. In the past it also might have been in the interest of the Pakistani military to finance the military budget through nuclear technology sales. It is also possible that the Pakistani military approved limited transfers of nuclear and missile technologies and know-how to Iran and North Korea, yet, Khan and his associates abused their authority and made unauthorized sales of goods and services and reaped huge personal fortunes in the process. Most proliferation specialists and independent observers believe that Khan's clandestine trade in nuclear technologies and know-how was the greatest proliferation scandal in history.

The A.Q. Khan network introduced a new model of proliferation involving networked-types of proliferators who had exploited loose export control regulations to market sensitive nuclear technologies and applications. The ability of such a network to survive suggests that behind the façade of centralized control, Pakistan's strategic military-industrial complex is dangerously fragmented, compartmentalized, and autonomous; that government agencies lack effective oversight; and individuals act as authorities unto themselves. In light of their alleged past behavior, it is possible that such individuals, motivated by ideology or financial gain, might share secrets concerning the dark nuclear arts with other countries and terror groups. It is this combination of factors: the military's desperation for nuclear and missile deliverables; undeveloped institutions;

the personalization of power; the fragmented structure of authority; and the absence of civilian oversight that provided the opportunity for Khan and his associates to peddle their dangerous wares on the international market.

Specialists agree that proliferation networks do represent a significant phenomenon that makes WMD acquisition easier. There has not yet been a high profile chemical or biological weapons network similar to that of A.Q. Khan. However, the A.Q. Khan network indicates that there are individuals who are willing to sell dangerous technologies with very few questions asked.

Proliferation networks make WMD acquisition less detectable, and allow buyers to skip research and development stages and head towards the more immediate prospect of WMD acquisition. It would have taken Iran far longer to develop centrifuge capabilities without Khan's assistance. It is also questionable if Libya would have been able to make any significant progress without outside aid. This means that countries and their intelligence agencies that are fighting proliferation have less time to detect the threat and to react. When networks replace states as proliferation actors it means that there is no "return address" to respond to. Non-state actors are likely to be less deterred than states. Despite the fact that A.Q. Khan would have been unable to set up his procurement network without the assistance of the Pakistani state, the Pakistani government ultimately put the responsibility on his shoulders and his group. Proliferation networks are simply the most recent innovation in this offense–defense proliferation struggle.

Globalization could also turn out to be a true deterrent to proliferators through containment and sanctions—rather than bombing. The capacity of globalization to launch collective punishment on proliferators is becoming more and more effective. The selective UN Security Council sanctions against Libya were the trigger both for the resolution of the Lockerbie terrorist bombing case and the process of normalizing US–Libyan relations, culminating in Libyan abandonment of their nuclear program. The sanctions the Security Council imposed – with support from Russia and China – against the North Korean and Iranian nuclear programs in

2006 constituted the first enforcement measures the council has ever taken against weapons technology acquisition by a country that is not attacking or occupying any of its neighbors. Global acceptance of the notion that sovereign countries are not free to acquire whatever technology (or weapons) they deem necessary for their own defense is on the rise, and shows how important globalization is in containing proliferation.[30]

Conclusions

With ongoing events in Iraq and Afghanistan, and the rising dangers of nuclear proliferation and global terrorism, the world in 2006 and 2007 has witnessed a growing global appreciation of the seriousness of the threat of WMD and in particular nuclear weapons. This appreciation has been expressed on numerous different occasions by high-level officials, politicians, intellectuals and Scientists. In the January 4 issue of the *Wall Street Journal* an important commentary appeared by George Shultz, William Perry, Henry Kissinger and Sam Nunn calling for "A World Free of Nuclear Weapons."[31] In a response to this op-ed, on January 31, Mikhail Gorbachev called for the goal of eliminating nuclear weapons to be put back on the agenda, not in the distant future but as soon as possible. And in a speech by Margaret Beckett, the Foreign Secretary of the United Kingdom, delivered to the Carnegie Endowment Conference in Washington, DC she asked for a vision for a world free of nuclear weapons and action for progressive steps to reduce warhead numbers and to limit the role of nuclear weapons in security policy.

Considering the rise in global awareness of the seriousness of the WMD threat and the need to contain/eliminate it, the future global agenda should include the following:

- A substantial reduction in the stockpile size of all nuclear states' arsenals and reaffirmation of the commitment to pursue nuclear disarmament.
- The complete elimination of short-range nuclear weapons designed for forward deployment.

- Advancement of a global agenda to achieve the goal of WMD-free world.
- Reinforcement of the NPT regime by preventing the development of nuclear weapons capabilities under the guise of civilian nuclear programs.
- Involving Israel, Pakistan and India in the NPT.
- Securing existing WMD stockpiles through multilateral cooperative threat reduction programs and by using the Proliferation Security Initiative (PSI) to interdict illegal trade of WMD technology and materials.
- The launch of a cooperative initiative to disrupt proliferation networks through increased law enforcement, intelligence and military cooperation.
- Negotiation of the first global Fissile Material Cut-off Treaty.
- Guarantees of full funding and implementation of the International Monitoring System of the Comprehensive Test Ban Treaty (CTBT) to ensure a continued moratorium on nuclear testing.
- A reduction in the demand for WMD through resolution of ongoing regional disputes.
- Strengthening the role of the UN Security Council by enhancing the effectiveness of the treaty regimes and their verification mechanisms in order to face the dilemmas of nuclear civil programs and dual-use technologies and their negative impacts on non-proliferation efforts.
- "Containing" not "bombing" in the fight against proliferation. Globalization of trade, financial markets, transportation and communication networks could be used to produce deterrents and to inflict serious punishment on WMD proliferators.
- Raising the bar of responsibility of civil society and the business community in fighting WMD proliferation.
- Accommodating unilateral and multilateral initiatives to develop a coherent multi-layered system to combat WMD proliferation.

Finally, evidence shows that in the short term the world might face a new proliferation outbreak point if the international community of states fails to pursue urgent measures vigorously, collectively and without delay.

WILLIAM S. COHEN is the Chairman and CEO of the Cohen Group, a Washington, DC-based firm providing international business consulting services. In 1996, Secretary Cohen was nominated by President Clinton to serve as Secretary of Defense (1997–2001). It was the first time in modern US history that a president had named an elected official from the opposition party to a cabinet position.

As a three-term United States Senator from Maine (1979–1997), Secretary Cohen chaired the Armed Services Committee's Seapower and Force Projection Subcommittee and the Government Affairs Committee's Government Oversight Subcommittee.

As Chairman of the Committee on Aging, Secretary Cohen led efforts to reform Medicare and was a central player in the health care reform debates of the 1990s. For ten years, Secretary Cohen was also a member and Vice Chairman of the Select Committee on Intelligence.

As a freshman member of the US Congress, Secretary Cohen was given the task by the House Judiciary Committee of developing on national television the evidentiary base for the impeachment of President Nixon. He then cast critical votes on three counts to impeach a president of his own party. In later years he was also involved in another historic congressional inquiry—this time into the Iran-Contra Affair.

Secretary Cohen has served on several national boards and study committees including the Council on Foreign Relations, the Center for Strategic and International Studies, the School for Advanced International Studies, the Brookings Institute, Empower America and the CBS Corporation. He donated his papers from his three decades of public service to the University of Maine. The University is also home to the William S. Cohen Center for International Policy and Commerce.

DUANE WINDSOR is the Lynette S. Autrey Professor of Management in the Jesse H. Jones Graduate School of Management, Rice University (Houston, Texas) and has been a member of the university faculty since 1977. He received a Bachelor of Arts degree in Political Science from Rice University; and a Doctor of Philosophy (Ph.D) degree in Political Economy and Government from Harvard University.

Professor Windsor's current research interests emphasize global corporate social responsibility, stakeholder theory and corporate political strategy. Another important concern is the relationship among markets, laws and ethics, and the resulting implications for businesses and societies.

In January 2007, Dr. Windsor was appointed editor of the quarterly journal *Business and Society*, sponsored by the International Association for Business and Society (IABS) and published by Sage Publications. He has served as president of the IABS and was the 2006–2007 Division Chair of Social Issues in Management (SIM)—a division of the Academy of Management. For three years, he edited the printed proceedings of the annual IABS conference. He is among several associate editors of the *Encyclopedia of Business Ethics and Society* (edited by Dr. Robert W. Kolb for Sage Publications and published in 2007), to which he has also contributed a number of entries.

Dr. Windsor has published articles in various journals including *Business and Society*, *Business Ethics Quarterly*, *Cornell International Law Journal*, *Interfaces*, *Journal of Corporate Citizenship*, *Journal of Management Studies*, *Journal of Public Affairs* and *Public Administration Review*. He has published a number of monographs including *The Rules of the Game in the Global Economy: Policy Regimes for International Business* (with Lee E. Preston, first edition 1992 and revised edition 1997) and *The Foreign Corrupt Practices Act: Anatomy of a Statute* (with George C. Greanias, 1982).

JEFFREY H. BERGSTRAND is Professor of Finance in the Mendoza College of Business at the University of Notre Dame, a Fellow of the Kellogg Institute for International Studies at the same university, and a Research Associate of CESifo Group (an international network of researchers based in Munich). He has taught economics and finance in the undergraduate, MBA and Executive MBA programs in the Mendoza College of Business for over 20 years. In 2004, 2005 and 2006, he was a Visiting Scholar at the European Commission in Brussels, Belgium, at the IFO Institute/University of Munich in Germany, and at the Leverhulme Centre for Research on Globalization and Economic Policy at the University of Nottingham in England, respectively. His research on international trade flows, free trade agreements, foreign direct investment and multinational firms has been published in over 30 articles in journals such as the *American Economic Review, Economic Journal, Review of Economics and Statistics, Journal of International Economics, Journal of International Money and Finance* and as chapters in various books.

From 1996 to 2003, he was a co-editor of the *Review of International Economics* and remains currently on its Editorial Board. In 2001, he co-authored the lead article in the *Journal of International Economics*, "The Growth of World Trade: Tariffs, Transport Costs and Income Similarity," (with Scott L. Baier) which won the Jagdish Bhagwati Award of 2003 for the Best Paper in the *Journal of International Economics* for the period 2001–2002. His current research focuses on economic determinants of multinational firm behavior and foreign direct investment (with Peter Egger) and under a grant from the US National Science Foundation, on the "Causes and Consequences of the Growth of Regionalism" (with Scott Baier). His most recent published article, "Do Free Trade Agreements Actually Increase Members' International Trade?" (with Scott Baier) appeared in the *Journal of International Economics* (March 2007). His paper entitled "Do Economic Integration Agreements Actually Work? Issues in Understanding the Causes and Consequences of the Growth of Regionalism," is due to be published in *The World Economy*. His most

[253]

recent co-edited volume with Antoni Estevadeordal and Simon Evenett, "The Sequencing of Regional Economic Integration," was published in the January 2008 issue of *The World Economy.*

SCOTT L. BAIER is Associate, Professor of Economics at Clemson University and a Visiting Scholar at the Federal Reserve Bank of Atlanta. He received a Ph.D from Michigan State University in 1996 and previously worked at the University of Notre Dame. His research focuses on international trade, economic growth, and development. His project, "The Causes and Consequences of the Growth of Regionalism" was supported by a grant from the National Science Foundation. Two of Baier's articles have been recognized with "Best Paper" awards. His recent paper, "How Important are Capital and Total Factor Productivity for Economic Growth?" (with Robert Tamura and Gerald Dwyer), won the 2007 Best Article Award in *Economic Inquiry.* His paper on "The Growth of World Trade" (with Jeffrey Bergstrand) won the Bhagwati Award for the best paper in the *Journal of International Economics* for the period 2001–2002.

JOHN F. MAHON is the first John M. Murphy Chair of International Business Policy and Strategy, Professor of Management at the Maine Business School and the Founding Director of the School of Policy and International Affairs (SPIA), University of Maine. Previously, John Mahon was Professor of Strategy and Policy and Chair of that Department at the School of Management, Boston University. He received his DBA from Boston University, his MBA from Bryant College (with honors), and his BSc in Economics from the Wharton School at the University of Pennsylvania. He has authored or co-authored over 120 articles, monographs and book chapters, two books, and over 90 cases or teaching notes in strategy, general management, and public policy and public affairs. He has recently served as Provost, *ad interim* at the University of Maine (2004–2006). Prof. Mahon was awarded the Intellectual Leadership Award of the Issue Management Council (a national organization in

Washington, DC) and has won recognition for teaching, research and service at local and national levels.

Prof. Mahon has taught in a variety of executive education programs in universities and has served as an executive educator or consultant for various Fortune 500 firms. In addition, he has served in a similar capacity with a number of organizations in the public sector, trade associations and government agencies at the local, state and federal levels. Prof. Mahon is a former Editor of *Business and Society*, and serves on editorial boards at *Alliance, Case Research Journal*, and the *International Journal of Public Affairs*. He is also the first academic to serve as Vice-President of the Issue Management Council. He also serves on the Board of Trustees of the Public Affairs Foundation in Washington, DC, holds the position of Research Fellow at the Centre for Public Affairs (Australia) and is affiliated with the European Centre for Public Affairs (Belgium).

PATRICK A. MCLAUGHLIN is a Ph.D student in the John E. Walker Department of Economics at Clemson University, where he received his Master's degree in 2004. He was the recipient of the John E. Walker Fellowship in 2007 and was also a Graduate Research Fellow at the Property and Environment Research Center (PERC) in 2007. His research on international trade flows and free trade agreements, written with Jeffrey Bergstrand, Scott Baier and Peter Egger, entitled "Do Economic Integration Agreements Actually Work? Issues in Understanding the Causes and Consequences of the Growth of Regionalism," will be published in *The World Economy*. Some of his recent research focuses on the consequences of European Union environmental regulations on international trade flows, while other work investigates the impact of antitrust regimes on foreign direct investment.

STEVEN L. WARTICK is Professor of Management at the College of Business Administration at the University of Northern Iowa (UNI), where he teaches courses in Strategic Management and International Business. He earned his Ph.D in Business Administration from the University of

Washington; he also holds BBA and MPA degrees, both from the University of Missouri, Kansas City.

Professor Wartick has published numerous articles and presented dozens of papers relating to corporate social performance, issues management and business–government relations. He has presented his research at conferences in North America, Europe and Asia. Professor Wartick is co-author of two books: *Business–Government Relations and Interdependence: A Managerial and Analytic Perspective* (1988) and *International Business and Society* (1999). His research has been supported by grants from several sources including the Financial Executives Research Foundation and the Harry J. Loman Research Foundation.

Professor Wartick has been especially active in the Social Issues in Management (SIM) Division of the Academy of Management and in the International Association for Business and Society (IABS). He has served as both Chair of the SIM Division and as President of IABS. Professor Wartick has also served on the Editorial Board and as a Special Consulting Editor for the *Academy of Management Review*, and he is a former Editor of *Business and Society* (the Journal of the International Association for Business and Society). Professor Wartick is also an active member of the Academy of International Business.

BAHMAN BAKTIARI is Director of Research and Academic Programming at the William S. Cohen Center for International Policy and Commerce. He received his Ph.D from the Woodrow Wilson Department of Government and Foreign Affairs at the University of Virginia. He was a Visiting Professor of Political Science at the American University in Cairo (1999–2001).

Professor Baktiari's most recent work, "Iran's Conservative Revival," appeared in *Current History* (January 2007). His other publications include "Reform and Democracy in Islam," in Robert Hefner, *Remaking Muslim Politics* (Princeton University Press, 2005) and "Doubting Iran's Reforms," which appeared in *Current History* (January 2003). His book chapter (co-authored with Asef Bayat, American University, Cairo) entitled "Revolutionary Iran and Egypt: Exporting Inspirations and Anxiety," was published in *Iran and the Surrounding World: Interactions in Culture and Cultural Politics*, edited by Nikke Keddie and R. Mathee (University of Washington Press, 2002). He also co-edited a series of articles entitled "Social and Political Developments in Iran," published in the *Journal of South Asian and Middle Eastern Studies* (Fall 2001). His book, *Parliamentary Politics in Revolutionary Iran: Institutionalization of Factional Politics,* was published by the University Press of Florida in 1997. Some of his opinion pieces on the Middle East have been published in the *Christian Science Monitor*, the Council on Foreign Relations' *Muslim Politics Report*, *Maine Sunday Telegram*, and *Al-Ahram* weekly.

HASSAN ABU NIMAH is a former Jordanian diplomat, writer and lecturer. He was appointed Director of the Royal Institute for Inter-Faith Studies (RIIFS) in April 2004. Most recently Mr. Abu Nimah served as the Hashemite Kingdom of Jordan's Ambassador and Permanent Representative to the United Nations (1995–2000). He began his diplomatic career in 1965 as Third Secretary to the Jordanian Embassy in Kuwait. During the next 13 years, he undertook various diplomatic assignments in Baghdad, Washington, DC and London, interspersed with periods spent as the Head of the Research Department at the Foreign Ministry in Amman. Promoted to Ambassador in 1978, he served as Jordan's envoy to the Benelux countries (Belgium, the Netherlands and Luxembourg) and to the European Community, the European Parliament and the Council of Europe.

In 1990 Mr. Abu Nimah was named Jordan's Permanent Representative to the UN Food and Agricultural Organization, the World Food Program and the UN Fund for Agricultural Development. During the same period, he also served as Jordan's Ambassador to Italy and as non-resident Ambassador to Portugal and San Marino. From 1993–1994, Mr. Abu Nimah was a member of the Jordanian delegation to the peace talks between Jordan and Israel, which took place in Washington, DC. Since the 1970s, he has regularly contributed articles and commentary (in English and Arabic) to several newspapers, including *Al-Rai*, *Al-Dustour*, *Sawt al-Jeel* and the *Jordan Times* (based in Amman), *Al-Quds al-Arabi*, *Al-Sharq al-Awsat*, the *Financial Times* (London), and the *Daily Star* (Beirut). He currently writes on a weekly basis for *Al-Rai* and the *Jordan Times*. Mr. Abu Nimah lectures on international relations, diplomatic practice and international law at the Jordan Institute of Diplomacy in Amman.

SEBESTYÉN L. V. GORKA was born to Hungarian parents living in forced exile in the United Kingdom. After the fall of Communism, Sebestyén moved to Hungary, where he became an internationally recognized expert on defense reform and international terrorism. Since then he has been a Kokkalis Fellow at the John F. Kennedy School of Government, Harvard; a consultant to the RAND Corporation in Washington and Adjunct Professor for Terrorism and Security Studies at the George C. Marshall Center, Germany. In 2003 Sebestyén and his wife founded the Institute for Transitional Democracy and International Security (ITDIS). As Founding Director of ITDIS, Sebestyén Gorka appears frequently in the international media, promoting views on democracy and how to cope with international terrorism, including the BBC, the *Financial Times*, Reuters, *The Times*, *Jane's Terrorism Monitor*, *Newsweek*, *Business Week* and *Human Events*.

Sebestyén Gorka has been a Fellow of the Terrorism Research Center in Virginia and a Founding Member of the US Council for Emerging National Security Affairs. He was an ambassadorial briefer for the US Department of State and a featured speaker for *The Economist*, London, the US Army War College and the Joint Special Operations University, Florida. He has also advised the international oil company Shell on minimizing vulnerability to terrorist attack. Sebestyén Gorka is a four-time holder of State Secretary and Deputy State Secretary awards for work executed in the field of defense diplomacy, and is an alumnus of the

Salzburg Seminar and the US Atlantic Council. He has published over 100 articles, book chapters and monographs internationally on the topics of terrorism, Russia and the Newly Independent States (NIS), biological terrorism and organized crime in publications such as the *NATO Review*, the *Harvard International Review*, the *World Policy Journal*, *Nature* and *Defense News*. He is a lead analytical contributor to the UK-based Jane's Information Group publications and has also written for *Pinkerton's Global Intelligence Report*.

MOHAMED KADRY SAID, MAJOR GENERAL (RETD.) is Military and Technology Advisor at the Al-Ahram Center for Political and Strategic Studies. He serves on the Committee for Strategic Planning at the Egyptian Council for Space Research, Science and Technology, and is a member of the Egyptian Council for Foreign Affairs and the Council of the Pugwash Organization for Science and World Affairs. Dr. Said has participated in several Arab–Israeli "Track Two" activities and has lectured on Middle East security at the Center for Security Policy in Geneva; the Center for Defense Studies in Brussels; and the Institute of National Defense in Lisbon. Dr. Said holds a BSc in Military Science and Aerospace Engineering from the Military Technical College (MTC), Cairo (1970), and a Ph.D in Aerospace Engineering from the École Nationale Supérieure de l'Aéronautique et de l'Espace (ENSAE) in Toulouse, France (1981). He served in the Egyptian Armed Forces as an Air Defense Officer and as a Staff Member in the Military Technical College. After his retirement, he joined the Al-Ahram Center in July 1998. He is a frequent writer for *Al-Ahram* newspaper, *Al-Siyassa Al-Dawliya* (International Politics) journal, and *Weghat Nazar* (Points of View) magazine. His areas of interest are military strategy, arms control, proliferation, and issues relating to the Arab–Israeli conflict.

Dr. Said is a Member of the Euro-Mediterranean Security and Cooperation (EuroMeSCo) Working Group on the Euro-Med Security Charter and contributor to its final reports on "Building Blocks for the

Euro-Med Charter on Peace and Stability"(January 2000) and "Barcelona Plus: Towards a Euro-Mediterranean Community of Democratic States" (April 2005). He has been the organizer, agenda-setter and editor of the final reports of many events such as the "Inside the Middle East" annual seminar with the Brookings Institution's Center for Executive Education (Cairo, March 2006 and March 2007); the UN High-Level Panel Cairo Conference with the UN University (September 2004); Conferences of the Consortium of Research Institutes Project on Mideast Regional Cooperation and Security (2004–2006); and the Arab Perspectives and Formulations on Humanitarian Intervention project with the Gulf Research Center (GRC) and the International Institute for Strategic Studies (IISS) of London (Dubai, February–May 2003). He was also head of the Organizing Committee of the Pugwash Annual Conference in Cairo, November 2006.

ROBERT K. SCHAEFFER is a Professor of Global Sociology at Kansas State University. He received a BA and graduated with honors in Sociology from the University of California at Santa Cruz in 1975. He received an MA in Sociology from the State University of New York (SUNY) at Binghamton in 1977 and a Ph.D in the same field in 1985. Dr. Schaeffer worked as a journalist for the *Maine Times*, Friends of the Earth and Greenpeace (1982–1990). Thereafter, he accepted a position as an Assistant Professor at San Jose State University in 1990 and was promoted to Associate Professor in 1995. In 2000, he accepted a position at Kansas State University, being promoted two years later to Professor. Dr. Schaeffer teaches global sociology and conducts research on partition and divided states, ethnic conflict and war, democratization and globalization, social movements and environmental change.

In 1992, Dr. Schaeffer was invited to join the Pugwash Conferences on Science and World Affairs. The Pugwash Conferences, founded by Albert Einstein and Bertrand Russell in 1957, won the Nobel Peace Prize in 1995. Dr. Schaeffer is the author of *Warpaths: The Politics of Partition*

(1990); *War in the World-System* (1990); *Power to the People: Democratization Around the World* (1997); *Understanding Globalization: The Social Consequences of Economic, Political and Environmental Change* (1997, 2002, 2005); and *Severed States: Dilemmas of Democracy in a Divided World* (1999). He is the co-author, with Dr. Torry Dickinson, of *Fast Forward: Work, Gender and Protest in a Changing World* (2001) and *Transformations: Feminist Pathways to Global Change* (2007).

JOHN RAPLEY is the author of *Globalization and Inequality: Neoliberalism's Downward Spiral* (Lynne Rienner Publishers, 2004). He received his BA (Hons) from Carleton University, and his MA and Ph.D degrees from Queen's University with a postdoctoral fellowship at Oxford University. He currently serves as President of the Caribbean Policy Research Institute, an independent think tank affiliated to the University of the West Indies, Mona. During 2000–2001, he was a Visiting Fellow at Georgetown University. He is also a member of the Institut d'Etudes Politiques at Aix-en-Provence, France.

Among Dr. Rapley's other publications are *Ivoirien Capitalism: African Entrepreneurs in Cote d'Ivoire* (Boulder: Lynne Rienner, 1993), *Understanding Development: Theory and Practice in the Third World* (London: UCL Press and Boulder, CO: Lynne Rienner, 1996) and *Globalization and Inequality* (Boulder and London: Lynne Rienner, 2004). His current research interests are globalization and neoliberalism. He also writes a weekly column on foreign affairs for *The Gleaner* (one of Jamaica's daily newspapers).

Keynote Address

1. OECD, "China could become world's largest exporter by 2010," September 16, 2005 (www.oecd.org/document/15/0,3343,en_2649_34571 _35363023_1_1_1_1,00.html).

2. CNN, "China to overtake US with world's highest CO_2 emissions this year – IEA," (http://money.cnn.com/news/newsfeeds/articles/newstex/ AFX-0013-20857754.htm).

3. Thomas Friedman, *The World is Flat: A Brief History of the Twenty-First Century* (New York, NY: Farrar, Straus and Giroux, 2005).

4. Ibid.

5. Ibid.

6. Secretary William Cohen and Admiral James Loy, "Fact, not Fear," *Wall Street Journal*, February 28, 2006.

Chapter 1

1. Emma Aisbett, "Why are the Critics so Convinced that Globalization is Bad for the Poor?" NBER Globalization and Poverty Conference (September 10–12), October 3, 2004 draft. Bruno S. Frey et al., "Consensus and dissension among economists: An empirical inquiry," *American Economic Review* vol. 79, no. 5 (December 1984): 986–994, cited by Douglas A. Irwin, *Against the Tide: An Intellectual History of Free Trade* (Princeton, NJ: Princeton University Press, 1996), 3, n. 1, reported survey results estimating that about 95 percent of economists in the United States (Table 2, Proposition 1, p. 991) and

88 percent of economists in the United States, Austria, France, Germany and Switzerland as a five-country set (Table 1, Proposition 1, p. 988) support fully or with qualification the statement that "tariffs and import quotas reduce general economic welfare."

2. See Branko Milanovic, "The two faces of globalization: Against globalization as we know it," *World Development* vol. 31, no. 4 (April 2003): 667–683.

3. Alan S. Blinder, "Free trade's great, but offshoring rattles me," *Washington Post*, May 6, 2007, B04; Ralph E. Gamory and William J. Baumol, *Global Trade and Conflicting National Interest* (Cambridge, MA: MIT Press, 2000); Paul A. Samuelson, "Where Ricardo and Mill rebut and confirm arguments of mainstream economists supporting globalization," *The Journal of Economic Perspectives* vol. 18, no. 3 (Summer 2004): 135–146.

4. There are significant differences among economic welfare, economic wealth, and personal happiness. Irwin discusses the problem (Douglas Irwin, *Against the Tide*, op. cit., chapter 12). To avoid technical digression, this paper assumes simply that these dimensions move together sufficiently to ignore the differences for purposes of general exposition. Figure 1.1 defines a vertical axis in terms of per capita real well-being and then "measures" that notion over time in terms of gross domestic product (GDP).

5. Alan S. Blinder, "Offshoring: The next industrial revolution?" *Foreign Affairs* vol. 85, no. 2 (March–April 2006): 113–128, at 114.

6. Michael C. Jensen, "Value maximization and the corporate objective function," in Michael Beer and Nitin Nohria (eds) *Breaking the Code of Change* (Boston, MA: Harvard Business School Press, 2000), 37–57. Economic development involves structural changes in an economy over time. Economic growth is increasing wealth, measured in some consistent manner, over time.

7. Douglas Irwin, *Against the Tide*, op. cit., cites Harry G. Johnson, *Aspects of the Theory of Tariffs* (Cambridge, MA: Harvard University Press, 1971).

8. The Group of Eight (G8) comprises Canada, France, Germany, Italy, Japan, Russia, the UK and the United States. The European Commission (EC) also attends.

9. Paul H. Rubin, "Folk economics," *Southern Economic Journal* vol. 70. no. 1 (July 2003): 157–171.

10. Alan S. Blinder defines "offshoring" or "offshore outsourcing" as "the migration of jobs, but not the people who perform them, from rich countries to poor ones." Alan S. Blinder, "Offshoring," op. cit., 113.

11. Paul A. Samuelson, "Where Ricardo and Mill rebut," op. cit., 135.

12. Paul Krugman, "Trade has problems, but answer isn't shutting it down," *Houston Chronicle*, January 4, 2007 (City & State).

13. Carol Graham, "Stemming the Backlash Against Globalisation," Brookings Policy Brief No. 78, 2001.

14. Associated Press (AP), "Bush Economist: Outsourcing Remark Misunderstood," February 19, 2004 (http//:www.foxnews.com/story/0,2933,111715,00.html), accessed June 8, 2007.

15. Ibid.

16. Douglas A. Irwin, "'Outsourcing' is good for America," *New York Times*, January 28, 2004.

17. Harold D. Lasswell, *Politics: Who Gets What, When, How—With Postscript* (New York, NY: Meridian Books, 1958).

18. C. K. Prahalad, *The Fortune at the Bottom of the Pyramid: Eradicating Poverty Through Profits* (Upper Saddle River, NJ: Wharton School Publishing, 2005).

19. Geoffrey Garrett, "Globalization's Missing Middle," *Foreign Affairs* vol. 83, no. 6 (November–December 2004): 72–83.

20. "Long run is a misleading guide to current affairs. In the long run we are all dead." John Maynard Keynes, *A Tract on Monetary Reform* (London: Macmillan, 1923), chapter 3.

21. Nicholas Kaldor introduced and John R. Hicks refined, in the late 1930s, the principle of hypothetical compensation in connection with evaluating the effects of international trade. Unlike the case of Pareto improvements in which one party is better off without another party being worse off, in hypothetical compensation one party can be worse off; Murray C. Kemp and Paul Pezanis-Christou, "Pareto's compensation principle," *Social Choice and Welfare* vol. 16, no. 3 (May 1999): 441–444.

22. Carol Graham, "Stemming the Backlash Against Globalisation," op. cit.

23. Douglas Irwin, *Against the Tide*, op. cit., cites John Stuart Mill, *Principles of Political Economy* (London: Longmans, Green, 1848, 1909), 920.

24. The first industrial revolution, beginning in Britain, focused on the rise of manufacturing in the 18th century coinciding with publication of Adam Smith's *An Inquiry into the Nature and Causes of the Wealth of Nations* (1776). The second industrial revolution in the 20th century featured a shift in jobs from manufacturing to services. The third industrial revolution now beginning is the information age. Each of these industrial revolutions caused massive economic and social adjustments (Alan S. Blinder, "Offshoring," op. cit., 116–117).

25. Lee E. Preston and Duane Windsor, *The Rules of the Game in the Global Economy: Policy Regimes for International Business* (Dordrecht, The Netherlands: Kluwer Academic Publishers, 2nd ed., 1997). In 2001, Argentina defaulted on international debt and stopped payments on its bonds. In 2005, it restructured about US$104 billion

in foreign debt, offering about 30 cents on the dollar. About 25 percent of bondholders (holding roughly US$20 billion in debt obligations) refused the offer. About 100 lawsuits have been filed against Argentina; see Bill Faries, "Holders of Argentine debt are going on the offensive: Group intensifies efforts as nation tries to restructure Paris Club loans," *Houston Chronicle*, April 12, 2007 (Business).

26. Duane Windsor and Kathleen A. Getz, "Regional market integration and the development of global norms for enterprise conduct: The case of international bribery," *Business & Society* vol. 38, no. 4 (December 1999): 415–449.

27. In early June 2007, an attempted Senate effort to pass a bipartisan immigration bill supported by both President Bush and the Senate majority leader (Harry Reid, D-Nev.) foundered. The bill had "tepid support from the public, business and immigrant-rights interests" (Michelle Mittelstadt, "Deadlock in the Senate: Immigration bill fails crucial vote—This summer could be last chance for Bush's top domestic initiative," *Houston Chronicle*, June 8, 2007. A key stumbling block is the question of "amnesty" for illegal aliens with respect to future citizenship status. There are an estimated 12 million illegal aliens in the US, many of whom are Hispanic. There are important reservations about the effects of immigration, of both skilled and unskilled labor, on US economic conditions; Pamela Constable, "Skilled foreign workers add fuel to immigration debate: Companies say more of them are needed, but critics say they harm US professionals," *Houston Chronicle*, May 26, 2007; Froma Harrop, "The working class is not stupid about immigration: Froma Harrop criticizes the motives behind a union's proposal to expand the supply of low-cost labor pouring into the United States," *Houston Chronicle*, May 22, 2007(City & State); George F. Will, "Importing underclass that will bankrupt the country: George F. Will says proposed immigration reforms ensure the growth of a permanent poverty class

and guarantee huge entitlement costs," *Houston Chronicle*, May 24, 2007 (City & State).

28. See Ronald Findlay, "Comparative advantage," *The New Palgrave: A Dictionary of Economics* (London & New York, NY: Macmillan & Stockton 1987), 514–517.

29. One study reported that ethanol might increase ozone levels even more than gasoline does; Seth Borenstein, "Ethanol may raise ozone levels more than gasoline, study says," *Houston Chronicle*, April 18, 2007 (Business). Agriculture may have significant greenhouse gas emission effects; Bruce A. McCarl and Uwe A. Schneider, 2000, "U.S. agriculture's role in a greenhouse gas emission mitigation world: An economic perspective," *Review of Agricultural Economics* vol. 22, no. 1 (Spring 2000): 134–159.

30. The mutually beneficial effect of trade is better than simple Pareto improvement, which requires only that one party gain without harming any other party.

31. Opportunity cost is the worth of one use of some resource relative to the next best alternative use of that resource. For example, if one can earn a 4 percent return on a risk-free bond and 6 percent on a low-risk equity, then the true "profit" on the equity is only 2 percent (ignoring the risk premium) because one can always earn 4 percent on the bond.

32. Robert Torrens, *Essay on the External Corn Trade* (London: J. Hatchard, 1815).

33. David Ricardo, *On the Principles of Political Economy and Taxation* (1817; London: John Murray, 1821, third edition); 1821 edition available in P. Sraffa (ed.) with the assistance of M. H. Dobb, *The Works and Correspondence of David Ricardo Vol. 1* (Cambridge, UK: University of Cambridge Press, 1951).

34. Douglas A. Irwin, *Against the Tide*, op. cit., 90

35. Paul A. Samuelson, "The way of an economist," in Paul A. Samuelson (ed.), *International Economic Relations: Proceedings of the Third Congress of the International Economic Association* (London: Macmillan, 1969), 1–11.

36. Paul A. Samuelson, "Where Ricardo and Mill rebut," op. cit.

37. Jagdish Bhagwati, "Coping with antiglobalization: A trilogy of discontents," *Foreign Affairs* vol. 81, no. 1 (January–February 2002): 2–5; and "Why Your Job isn't Moving to Bangalore," *New York Times*, January 22, 2004 (Editorial).

38. Friedrich Hayek, "The use of knowledge in society," *American Economic Review* vol. 35, no. 4 (September 1945): 519–530.

39. See also Ralph E. Gamory and William J. Baumol, *Global Trade and Conflicting National Interest*, op. cit.

40. Paul H. Rubin, "Folk economics," op. cit.

41. Alan S. Blinder, "Offshoring," op. cit., 114.

42. Ibid.

43. Alan S. Blinder, "Let's save free trade from its own deficits: It's imperative to turn back the tide of high-paying US jobs moving offshore," *Houston Chronicle*, May 13, 2007 (Outlook).

44. Joseph A. Schumpeter, *The Theory of Economic Development* (Cambridge, MA: Harvard University Press, 1934); and *Capitalism, Socialism and Democracy* (New York, NY: Harper, 1942, 1947, 1950; 1975).

45. See William J. Baumol, "Entrepreneurship in Economic Theory," *American Economic Review: Papers and Proceedings* vol. 58, no. 2 (May 1968): 64–71.

46. Michael E. Porter, *The Competitive Advantage of Nations* (New York, NY: Free Press, 1990).

47. See Donella H. Meadows, Dennis L. Meadows, Jørgen Randers and William W. Behrens, *The Limits to Growth: A Report for The Club of Rome's Project on the Predicament of Mankind* (New York, NY: Universe Books, 1972); and Donella Meadows, Jørgen Randers and Dennis Meadows, *Limits to Growth: The 30-Year Update* (White River Junction, VT: Chelsea Green Publishing Co., 2004).

48. Thomas Malthus, *An Essay on the Principle of Population* (London: Printed for J. Johnson in St. Paul's Church-Yard, 1798). For example, it is known that, in an isolated area (such as an island), a deer population may first expand beyond available resources and then collapse below a stable level.

49. Joseph A. Schumpeter, *Capitalism, Socialism and Democracy*, op. cit., 82–85.

50. Geoffrey Garrett, "Globalization's missing middle," op. cit.

51. A. T. Kearney, "Measuring globalization," *Foreign Policy* no. 148 (March–April 2004): 52–60; Fifth Annual A. T. Kearney / Foreign Policy Globalization Index (Carnegie Endowment for International Peace). Gross domestic product (GDP) is domestic production before exports and not including imports, which are counted in gross national product (GNP). GDP thus excludes international trade activities.

52. In this vein, CNN on-air personality Lou Dobbs keeps reporting on a theme he characterizes as war on the middle class in the United States.

53. Alan S. Blinder provides a classification of types of jobs in the United States and an estimate of their degree of exposure to offshoring. The difficulty in forecasting effects of globalization on advanced country employment is the extreme heterogeneity of the labor force. Personal services are likely to remain in a particular country. Impersonal services can be offshored. The dividing line between these types of

services can move over time due to improvements in information technology. At the end of 2004, there were 14.3 million manufacturing jobs in the United States; virtually all such jobs might be offshored. In contrast, about 7.6 million jobs in construction and mining would not move (although such jobs could disappear due to reductions in such activities or substitution of capital for labor). About 22 million government jobs would likely remain at home. Some proportion of 15.6 million retail trade jobs might move offshore due to online retailing. There were another 73.6 million jobs at the end of 2004. Blinder estimates that overall the number of service jobs vulnerable to offshoring might be two to three times the total number of manufacturing jobs, so something like 28 to 42 million jobs. Specific remedies are likely to prove very difficult (Alan S. Blinder, "Offshoring," op. cit., 119–122, 124).

54. Alan S. Blinder, "Offshoring," op. cit., 126.

55. Ibid, 118.

56. David C. Johnston, "US income gap growing wider: The rich are getting richer while the poor have lost some ground, recent tax data show," *Houston Chronicle*, March 29, 2007; "Americans' average income falls again: 2005 is fifth consecutive year of decline," *Houston Chronicle*, August 21, 2007 (Business).

57. Alan S. Blinder, "Offshoring," op. cit., 127; Thomas Friedman reports that call center activities may expand in Kenya (Thomas L. Friedman, "Phone lines provide Kenya with new economic lifeline," *Houston Chronicle*, April 4, 2007, B1.

58. Molly Selvin, "Men in their 30s making less than dads did: Generation gap raises doubts about American dream," *Houston Chronicle*, May 26, 2007, A6.

59. Mortimer B. Zuckerman, "Uneasy in the middle," *U.S. News & World Report*, June 11, 2007, 72.

60. Paul Krugman, "What's good for corporations is good for executives," *Houston Chronicle*, June 7, 2007, B7 (City & State).

61. Isaac Ehrlich, "The Mystery of Human Capital as Engine of Growth, or Why the US Became the Economic Superpower in the 20th Century," NBER Working Paper No. W12868, 2007 (http://ssrn.com/abstract=960443).

62. Brett Clanton, "Why Halliburton chose Dubai: growth—But oil-services firm will continue to add Houston jobs, its CEO says," *Houston Chronicle*, May 6, 2007, A1, A15.

63. Halliburton also announced that it will cease business in Iran. It also ceased operations in Iraq through its April 2007 sell of the KBR construction and services unit; Jim Krane (AP), "Halliburton's relocated CEO outlines major shift in focus: A big focus," *Houston Chronicle*, May 23, 2007, D3 (Business).

64. Ibid.

65. Ibid.

66. Ibid.

67. Ibid. Such shifts in global orientation of established European, as well as American, firms generate issues as illustrated by recent controversies concerning the German company SAP and the move of the production of century-old HP brown sauce from central England to the Netherlands by the US owner H. J. Heinz Co. (Phred Dvorak and Leila Abboud, "Difficult upgrade: SAP's plan to globalize hits cultural barriers—Software giant's shift irks German engineers," *Wall Street Journal* CCXLIX (110), May 11, 2007, A1, A8; Jane Wardell, "Loss of sauce production puts Britons in a big snit," *Houston Chronicle*, March 18, 2007, D5.

68. Lisa Margonelli, "All pumped up: Five myths that fuel $3 gas stories—Fill-up prices are high for many reasons but these," *Houston Chronicle*, June 10, 2007, E1, E5 (Outlook).

69. Shannon Kathleen O'Byrne, "Economic justice and global trade: An analysis of the libertarian foundations of the free trade paradigm," *American Journal of Economics and Sociology* vol. 55, no. 1 (January 1996): 11–15.

70. James Mann, "A brand new model—made in China: Country proves it doesn't need democracy or free market to succeed," *Houston Chronicle*, May 27, 2007, E4 (Outlook).

71. John Otis, "Venezuelan chief leads drive to expanded socialism," *Houston Chronicle*, May 25, 2007, A28.

72. Gavin Rabinowitz, "Mangoes from India, motorcycles from US," *Houston Chronicle*, April 14, 2007, D6 (Business).

73. "China: US pistachio shipment rejected," *Houston Chronicle*, June 10, 2007, A25.

74. Pierre-Richard Agénor, "Does Globalization Hurt the Poor?" World Bank Development Research Group Working Paper 2922, 2002.

75. C. K. Prahalad, *The Fortune at the Bottom of the Pyramid*, op. cit.

76. Irma Adelman, "Fallacies in Development Theory and Their Implications for Policy," California Agricultural Experiment Station, Giannini Foundation of Agricultural Economics, Department of Agricultural and Resource Economics and Policy, University of California at Berkeley, Working Paper no. 887, May 1999.

77. Bob Sutcliffe, "World inequality and globalization," *Oxford Review of Economic Policy* vol. 20, no. 1 (Spring 2004): 15–37.

78. See A. T. Kearney, "Measuring globalization," op. cit.; Francois Bourguignon and Christian Morrison, "Inequality among world

citizens, 1820–1992," *American Economic Review* vol. 92, no. 4 (September 2002): 727–744; Alan V. Deardorff, "Rich and poor countries in neoclassical trade and growth," *The Economic Journal* vol. 111, issue 470 (April 2001): 277–294; George E. Johnson and Frank P. Stafford, "International competition and real wages," *American Economic Review: Papers and Proceedings* vol. 82, no. 2 (May 1993): 127–130; Ronald W. Jones, "Globalization and the distribution of income: The economic arguments," Proceedings of the National Academy of Sciences of the United States of America vol. 100, no. 19 (September 2003): 11158–11162; Francisco Rodriguez and Dani Rodrik, "Trade policy and economic growth: A skeptic's guide to the cross-national evidence," *NBER Macroeconomics Annual* 15, 2000, 261–325; L. Alan Winters, Neil McCulloch and Andrew McKay, "Trade liberalization and poverty: The evidence so far," *Journal of Economic Literature* vol. 42, no. 1 (March 2004): 72–115.

79. See Martin Ravallion, "The Debate on Globalization, Poverty and Inequality: Why Measurement Matters," World Bank Development Research Group Working Paper 3038, 2003. Bob Sutcliffe (accessed June 10, 2007) updated his 2004 findings cited in note 76 above at: (http://siteresources.worldbank.org/INTDECINEQ/Resources/PSBSut cliffe.pdf).

80. L. Alan Winters, et al., "Trade liberalization and poverty," op. cit.

81. Ibid.

82. Werner Antweiler, Brian R. Copeland and M. Scott Taylor, "Is free trade good for the environment?" *American Economic Review* vol. 91, no. 4 (September 2001): 877–908.

83. These estimates come from the US Census Bureau (accessed June 9, 2007) at http://www.census.gov/ipc/www/world.html).

84. Michael T. Klare cautions that resource shortages could lead in some circumstances to local or regional resource wars over water, for

example. Conflict diamonds are another related illustration; Michael T. Klare, Resource Wars: *The New Landscape of Global Conflict* (New York, NY: Metropolitan Books, Henry Holt & Co., 2001).

85. Alan Zarembo and Thomas H. Maugh, "Warming report paints a grim picture: Scientists say the poor likely will be the hardest hit, as water and food will become scarce," *Houston Chronicle*, April 7, 2007, A20.

86. Susmit Dasgupta, Benoit Laplante, Craig Meisner, David Wheeler and David J. Yan, "The Impact of Sea Level Rise on Developing Countries: A Comparative Analysis," World Bank Policy Research, WP No. 4136, 2007 (http://ssrn.com/abstract=962790).

87. These estimates use Geographic Information System (GIS) software and "best available" data.

88. Sandra Rollings-Magnusson and Robert C. Magnusson, "The Kyoto Protocol: Implications of a flawed but important environmental policy," *Canadian Public Policy / Analyse de Politiques* vol. 26, no. 3 (September 2000): 347–359.

89. "China unseats U.S. as top CO2 emitter," *Houston Chronicle*, June 21, 2007, D1 (Business).

90. Thomas C. Schelling, "What makes greenhouse sense?" *Foreign Affairs* vol. 81, no. 3 (May–June 2002): 2–9.

91. Clive Crook, "Bush may be on to something ..." *Financial Times*, June 7, 2007, 15; Jo Johnson, "Worlds collide in India over global warming," *Financial Times*, June 7, 2007, 15; and Mark Landler and Judy Dempsey, "US mulls global plan to halve emissions: But the G8 deal does not commit nation to specific greenhouse gas cuts by 2050," *Houston Chronicle*, June 8, 2007, A1, A13.

92. Clive Crook, "Bush may be on to something ..." op. cit.

93. Geoffrey Garrett, "Globalization's missing middle," op. cit.

94. Alan S. Blinder, "Offshoring," op. cit.

Chapter 2

1. Robert Lawrence, *A US–Middle East Trade Agreement: A Circle of Opportunity* (Washington, DC: Peterson Institute for International Economics), Table 2.9, 45.

2. Ibid., 46.

3. Ibid.

4. Nicolas Peridy, "Trade Prospects of the New EU Neighborhood Policy," *Global Economy Journal*, vol. 5, no. 1 (January 2005).

5. Ibid.

6. Thomas Freidman, *The World is Flat* (New York, NY: Farrar, Strauss and Giroux, 2005).

7. Ibid.

8. Scott L. Baier and Jeffrey H. Bergstrand, "The Growth of World Trade: Tariffs, Transport Costs, and Income Similarity," *Journal of International Economics*, vol. 53, no. 1 (February 2001): 1–27.

9. Anderson, James E., and Eric van Wincoop, "Trade Costs," *Journal of Economic Literature* vol. 62, no. 3 (September 2004): 691–751.

10. Steven Brakman and Charles van Marrewijk, "It's A Big World After All," CESifo Working Paper No. 1964, April 2007.

11. Jonathan Eaton and Samuel Kortum, "Technology, Geography, and Trade," *Econometrica* vol. 70. no. 5 (September 2002): 1741–1779.

12. Dean A. DeRosa and John P. Gilbert, "Predicting Trade Expansion under FTAs and Multilateral Agreements," Peterson Institute for International Economics, Working Paper, October 2005, 5–13.

13. Elhanan Helpman and Paul Krugman, *Market Structure and Foreign Trade* (Cambridge, MA: MIT Press, 1985).

14. Ibid. It can be readily shown that $GDPi\ GDPj = (GDPi + GDPj)\ si\ sj$, where $si = GDPi\ /\ (GDPi + GDPj)$ and the trade flow will be maximized – for given $(GDPi + GDPj)$ – when $si = sj$.

15. James E. Anderson and Eric van Wincoop, "Gravity with Gravitas: A Solution to the Border Puzzle," *American Economic Review* vol. 93, no. 1 (March 2003); James E. Anderson and Eric van Wincoop, "Trade costs," *Journal of Economic Literature* vol. 62, no. 3 (September 2004); and Scott L. Baier and Jeffrey H. Bergstrand, "*Bonus Vetus* OLS: A Simple Approach for Approximating International Trade-Cost Effects using the Gravity Equation," working paper, 2007.

16. We use the term "partial" to recognize that this is the direct effect on trade of a FTA, and does not account for "general-equilibrium" offsetting effects, such as that the FTA may reduce both countries overall multilateral price resistance terms, which can then tend to offset the partial effect, cf., Anderson and van Wincoop, "Gravity with Gravitas ..." op. cit. However, in recent other work by the authors, we argue that these potentially-offsetting effects may be quite small, cf., Baier and Bergstrand, "*Bonus Vetus* OLS ..." op. cit.

17. Scott L. Baier and Jeffrey H. Bergstrand, "Do Free Trade Agreements Actually Increase Members' International Trade?" *Journal of International Economics* vol. 71, no. 1 (March 2007).

18. Robert Z. Lawrence, *Regionalism, Multilateralism and Deeper Integration* (Washington, DC: The Brookings Institution, 1996), 17.

19. Ibid., 7.

20. Ibid.

21. Robert Gilpin, *The Challenge of Global Capitalism* (Princeton, NJ: Princeton University Press, 2000), 108; italics added.

22. Ernest H. Preeg, *From Here to Free Trade* (Chicago, IL: The University of Chicago Press, 1998), 50.

23. "A Domino Theory of Regionalism," in Richard Baldwin, Pentti Haaparanta and Jaakko Klander (eds), *Expanding Membership of the European Union* (New York, NY: Cambridge University Press, 1995).

24. C. Fred Bergsten, "Competitive Liberalization and Global Free Trade: A Vision for the Early 21st Century," Working Paper 96–15 (Washington, DC: Institute for International Economics, 1996).

25. Scott L. Baier and Jeffrey H. Bergstrand, "Economic Determinants of Free Trade Agreements," *Journal of International Economics* vol. 64, no. 1 (October 2004): 29–63.

26. Ibid.

27. Dean A. DeRosa and John P. Gilbert, "Predicting trade expansion under FTAs and multilateral agreements," Peterson Institute for International Economics Working Paper 05–13, October 2005.

28. Sucharita Ghosh and Steven Yamarik, "Are Regional Trading Arrangements Trade Creating? An Application of Extreme Bounds Analysis" *Journal of Internationl Economics* vol. 63, no. 2 (July 2004): 369–395.

29. Baier and Bergstrand, March 2007, op. cit.

30. Ibid.

31. DeRosa and Gilbert, 2005, op. cit.

32. Scott L. Baier, Jeffrey H. Bergstrand and Erika Vidal, "Free Trade Agreements in the Americas: Are the Trade Effects Larger than

Anticipated?" *The World Economy* vol. 30, no. 9 (September 2007): 1347–1377.

33. For data reasons, we could not include the benefits for a FTA of differences in relative factor endowments, which would have raised the probability marginally.

Chapter 3

1. Maria Beatriz Rocha Trinidade, "Portugal," in Ronald E. Krane (ed.), *International Labor Migration in Europe* (New York, NY: Praeger, 1979), 171; David D. Gregory and J. Cazorla Perez, "Intra-European Migration and Regional Development: Spain and Portugal," in Rosmarie Rogers (ed.), *Guests Come to Stay: The effects of European Labor Migration on Sending and Receiving Countries* (Boulder, CO: Westview Press, 1985), 237. See also Robert K. Schaeffer, *Power to the People: Democratization Around the World* (Boulder, CO: Westview Press, 1997), 66–7.

2. Schaeffer, *Power to the People*, op. cit., 67.

3. Caglar Keyder, "The American Recovery of Southern Europe: Aid and Hegemony," in Giovanni Arrighi (ed.), *Semiperipheral Development: The Politics of Southern Europe in the Twentieth Century* (Beverly Hills, CA: Sage, 1985), 141–42.

4. Schaeffer, *Power to the People*, op. cit., 67–9; Giovanni Arrighi, "Fascism to Democratic Socialism: Logic and Limits of a Transition," in Arrighi, *Semiperipheral Development*, op. cit., 265, 268.

5. Schaeffer, *Power to the People*, op. cit., 69–71.

6. Schaeffer, *Power to the People*, op. cit., 182–83.

7. Konrad H. Jarausch, *The Rush to German Unity* (Oxford: Oxford University Press, 1994), 15, 17; J.F. Brown, *Surge to Freedom: The End of Communist Rule in Eastern Europe* (Durham, NC: Duke University

Press, 1991), 136; Melvin Croan, "Germany and Eastern Europe," in Joseph Held (ed.), *The Columbia History of Eastern Europe in the Twentieth Century* (Columbia University Press, 1992), 24.

8. Schaeffer, *Power to the People*, op. cit., 183–84.

9. Schaeffer, *Power to the People*, op. cit., 131.

10. Robert Schaeffer, *Warpaths: The Politics of Partition* (New York, NY: Hill and Wang, 1990), 155.

11. Schaeffer, *Warpaths*, op. cit., 156.

12. See "Partition in Palestine: 1948," in Robert Schaeffer, *Understanding Globalization: The Social Consequences of Political, Economic and Environmental Change,* 3rd Ed. (Lanham, MD: Rowman and Littlefield, 2005), 235–254.

13. United Nations, "International Migration 2006" (http://www.un.org/esa/population/publications/2006Migration_Chart/2006IttMig_chart.htm).

14. Dan Bilefsky, "Latvia Fears New 'Occupation' by Russians but Needs the Labor," *New York Times*, November 16, 2006, A17.

15. "In Singapore in 1994, 95 percent of Filipino overseas contract workers lacked work permits from the Philippines government. The official figures based on legal migration therefore severely underestimate the number of migrants." Janet Henshall Momsen (ed.), *Gender, Migration and Domestic Service* (London: Routledge, 1999), 7

16. United Nations, "International Migration 2002" (United Nations: St/ESA/Ser.A/219, 2003).

17. Matthew Brunwasser, "Romania, a Poor Land, Imports Poorer Workers: Replacements for Dwindling Labor Pool," *New York Times*, April 11, 2007; John Tagliabue, "The Gauls at Home in Erin:

Opportunity Knocks in Ireland, and the French Answer," *New York Times*, June 2, 2006; Judy Demsey, "Polish Labor Crunch as Workers Go West," *New York Times,* November 19, 2006.

18. Brunwasser, "Romania," op. cit.; Dempsey, "Polish Labor Crunch," op. cit.

19. Brunwasser, "Romania," op. cit.

20. "Free Trade Agreements" in Robert K. Schaeffer, *Understanding Globalization: The Social Consequences of Political, Economic, and Environmental Change*, 2nd Ed. (Lanham, MD: Rowman and Littlefield, 2003), 242–43.

21. United Nations, "International Migration 2006," op. cit.

22. United Nations, "International Migration 2002," op. cit.

23. Robert K. Schaeffer, "The Rise of China," in *Understanding Globalization*, 3rd Ed., 199–200.

24. Ibid.

25. Ibid., 201–206.

26. Robert K. Schaeffer, "Dilemmas of Sovereignty and Citizenship in the Republican Interstate System," in Mitja Zagar, Boris Jesih and Romana Bester (eds), *The Constitutional and Political Regulation of Ethnic Relations and Conflicts* (Ljubljana: Institute for Ethnic Studies, 1999), 11. See also James Kettner, *The Development of the Concept of American Citizenship, 1608-1870* (Chapel Hill, NC: University of North Carolina Press, 1978).

Chapter 4

1. J. Bhagwati, "Borders Beyond Control," in Anthony M. Messina and Gallya Lahava (eds.), *The Migration Reader* (Boulder, CO: Lynne Rienner, 2003), 552–568.

2. Nermin Abad-Unat, "Turkish migration to Europe," in Robin Cohen (ed.), *The Cambridge Survey of World Migration* (Cambridge: Cambridge University Press, 1995), 274–278; Manolo Abella, "Asian Migrant and Contract Workers in the Middle East," in Robin Cohen (ed.), *The Cambridge Survey of World Migration* (Cambridge: Cambridge University Press, 1995), 418–423; J. Bahgwati, op. cit.; J.S. Birks and A. Sinclair, *International Migration and Development in the Arab Region* (Geneva: International Labour Office, 1980); Stephen Castles and Mark J. Miller, *The Age of Migration: International Population Movements in the Modern World* (New York, NY: The Guilford Press, 1993); Imre Ferenczi, *International Migrations, Volume I: Statistics* (New York, NY: National Bureau of Economic Research, 1929); Timothy J. Hatton and Jeffrey G. Williamson, *The Age of Mass Migration: Causes and Impact* (New York, NY: Oxford University Press, 1998); Douglas S. Massey, "International Migration and Economic Development in Comparative Perspective," *Population and Development Review* 14 (1988), 383–414; Douglas S. Massey et al., *Worlds in Motion: Understanding International Migration at the End of the Millennium* (Oxford: Oxford University Press, 1998); and Hania Zlotnik, "International Migration: Causes and Effects," in Laurie Ann Mazur (ed.), *Beyond the Numbers: A Reader on Population, Consumption, and the Environment* (Washington, DC: Island Press, 1994), 359–377.

3. The European Union is concerned with large surges in migration in the future as a result of climate change. See S. Castle, "Migration to Surge, EU Leaders are Told: Warned of Fallout on Climate Change," *International Herald Tribune,* March 8–9, 2008, 3.

4. There are several definitions of outsourcing in both the literature and in practice. In this analysis outsourcing is the contracting of services that are normally provided by a company's own employees to another firm. Usually this firm is in another country, and the firms that provide these services usually specialize in certain areas—for example, a call center, payroll and accounting services or email services.

5. G. Wan, "WIDER Seminar on International Migration and Development: Patterns, Problems and Policies," address at UN Headquarters, New York, September 12, 2006.

6. James Martin 21st Century School, University of Oxford (http://www.21school.ox.ac.uk/institutes/migration.cfm), accessed 13 March 2008.

7. Philip L. Martin and Mark J. Miller, "Guestworkers: Lessons from Western Europe," *Industrial and Labor Relations Review* vol. 33, no. 3 (1980): 315–330.

8. Wayne A. Cornelius, et al., "Introduction: The Ambivalent Quest for Immigration Control" in Wayne A. Cornelius, Philip L. Martin and James F. Hollifield (eds.), *Controlling Immigration: A Global Perspective* (Stanford, CA: Stanford University Press, 1994), 3–42; and George Dib, "Laws Governing Migration in Some Arab Countries," in Reginald T. Appleyard (ed.), *International Migration Today, Volume I: Trends and Prospects* (Perth: University of Western Australia for the United Nations Educational, Scientific, and Cultural Organization [UNESCO], 1988), 168–179.

9. J. Slocum, "International Migration Trends," a presentation at the Chicago Matters event, Chicago, November 29, 2006.

10. Sudarsan Raghavan, "War in Iraq Propelling a Massive Migration: Wave Creates Tension Across the Middle East," *Washington Post*, February 4, 2007, A01.

11. The *Forced Migration Review* estimates that 1 in 6 Iraqis is displaced and over two million are in exile and another two million are displaced internally.

12. J. Fallows, "Declaring Victory," *Atlantic Monthly*, September 2006.

Chapter 5

1. The conference was held on April 23–25, 2007 at the Emirates Center for Strategic Studies and Research (ECSSR) in Abu Dhabi, UAE. The author would like to thank the co-sponsors (ECSSR and the William S. Cohen Center for International Policy and Commerce) for the invitation to present an abbreviated version of this paper at the conference.

2. See Gerald F. Cavanagh, *American Business Values in Transition*, 2nd Ed. (Englewood Cliffs, NJ: Prentice-Hall, 1984). See especially Chapter 2 which describes and explains the historical roots of Western business systems and the evolution of business toward societal legitimacy.

3. Howard H. Bowen, *Social Responsibilities of the Businessman* (New York, NY: Harper, 1953).

4. Theodore Levitt, "The Dangers of Social Responsibility," *Harvard Business Review* vol. 36, no. 3 (September–October, 1958).

5. Milton Friedman, *Capitalism and Freedom* (Chicago, IL: University of Chicago Press, 1962).

6. J. J. Servan-Schreiber, *The American Challenge* (New York, NY: Avon Books, 1967).

7. Richard J. Barnet and Ronald E. Muller, *Global Reach: The Power of the Multinational Corporation* (New York, NY: Simon and Schuster, 1974).

8. Kenule "Ken" Saro-Wiwa, who led a campaign in Nigeria against environmental damage associated with the operations of oil companies such as Shell, was killed in 1995. For more details about the death of Mr. Saro-Wiwa see Anne T. Lawrence, "Stakeholder Management: Shell Oil in Nigeria," *Case Research Journal* (Fall–Winter, 1997): 1–21.

9. See Richard Wokutch, "Corporate Social Responsibility Japanese Style," *Academy of Management Executive* vol. 4, no. 2 (1990): 56–74; or more recently see Ariane Berthoin Antal and Andre Sobczak, "Corporate Social Responsibility in France: A Mix of National Traditions and International Influences," *Business & Society* vol. 46, no. 1 (March, 2007): 9–32.

10. David Welch, "Why Toyota is Afraid of being Number One," *Business Week*, March 5, 2007, 42–50.

11. "Brazilian Firm to Buy Sought-After US Meatpacker Swift," *Des Moines Register*, May 30, 2007, 8C.

12. Miguel Heft, "Google's Chief Gets $1 in Pay; His Security Costs $532,755," *New York Times*, April 5, 2007, C3.

13. "Many Hurt by Watch List, Group Says," *Des Moines Register*, March 28, 2007, A4.

14. Ibid.

15. Elizabeth Kelleher, "Congress Moves to Change Foreign Investment Review Process," *International Information Programs*, July 27, 2006 (www.usinfo.state.gov).

16. Jerry Perkins, "Farm Chief Wants Ban on Foreign Ownership," *Des Moines Register*, February 24, 2006, A1.

17. William Petroski, "A Road of Apprehension Swerves Superhighway Idea," *Des Moines Register*, September 24, 2006, D1–D2.

18. Eamon Javers, "The Divided States of America," *Business Week*, April 16, 2007, 67.

19. "US Free-Trade Pact with South Korea Would Enhance Partnership," *International Information Programs*, June 13, 2007 (www.usinfo.state.gov).

20. PricewaterhouseCoopers, *The Last Ten Years: A Review, 2007* (www.pwc.com/extweb/insights.nsf/docid/9FB653B2B4C3A5778525726D00645353).

21. Thomas Friedman, *The World Is Flat: A Brief History of the 21st Century* (New York, NY: Farrar, Straus and Giroux, 2005).

22. Ibid., 297

23. See Duane Windsor, "Toward A Global Theory of Cross-Border and Multilevel Corporate Political Theory," *Business & Society* vol. 46, no. 2 (June 2007): 253–278; and Ruth V. Aguilera, Deborah E. Rupp, Cynthia A. Williams and Jyoti Ganapathi, "Putting The S Back in Corporate Social Responsibility: A Multilevel Theory Of Social Change in Organizations," *Academy of Management Review* vol. 32, no. 3 (2007): 836–863.

24. Pete Engardio, "The Future of Outsourcing." *Business Week*, January 30, 2006, 50–58.

25. Peter Engardio, "Let's Offshore the Lawyers," *Business Week*, September, 18, 2006, 42–43.

26. John Carey, "Lighting a Fire under Global Warming," *Business Week*, April 16, 2007.

27. Sarah Stromberg, "Decorah Joins Fight against Global Warning," *Cedar Falls-Waterloo Courier*, April 6, 2007, A1 & A8.

28. Jennifer Jacobs, "Plan Would Wean Iowa Off Foreign Oil By 2025," *Des Moines Register*, March 7, 2007 (www.desmoinesregister.com)

29. Alan Clendenning, "Bush Trip to Brazil to Back Ethanol," *Des Moines Register*, March 5, 2007, A2.

30. Richard Siklos, "Discovery to Start Channel Focusing on Green Movement," *New York Times*, April 5, 2007, C3.

31. PricewaterhouseCoopers, op. cit.

32. Alan Reder, *75 Best Business Practices for Socially Responsible Companies* (New York, NY: G.P. Putnam's Sons, 1995).

33. For a good discussion of this background see Donna J. Wood, "Corporate Social Performance Revisited," *Academy of Management Review* vol. 16, no. 4 (October 1991): 691–718.

34. Archie B. Carroll, "A Three-Dimensional Conceptual Model of Corporate Social Performance," *Academy of Management Review* vol. 4, no. 4 (October 1979): 497–505.

35. For background see "Bush, Congress Clash over Ports Sale," *CNN* (www.cnn.com/2006/POLITICS/02/21/port.security) and Nina Easton, "After Dubai Ports, US Courts Foreign Investment," Fortune, March 5, 2007 (www.money.cnn.com/2007/03/05/magazines/fortune/pluggedin_eas).

36. Ronald K. Mitchell, Bradley R. Agle and Donna J. Wood, "Toward A Theory Of Stakeholder Identification And Salience: Defining The Principle Of What Really Counts," *Academy of Management Review* vol. 22, no. 4 (October 1997): 853–866.

[287]

37. To understand the type of argument and backlash about which Toyota is concerned, consider the following "Letter to the Editor" from the April 28, 2007, *Louisville, Kentucky, Courier-Journal* (page A10): "I just read the news about Toyota surpassing General Motors in global sales of automobiles. I wonder if all the people in the United Stated who buy these foreign products realize what that means? Let me give you a little clue. Let's say Toyota keeps climbing and the big three (GM, Ford and Chrysler) keep faltering and eventually go out of business. You will have no US companies producing automobiles. The public will be in the hands of foreign auto producers, who send their profits back to their home base. The middle class will erode here, and if you don't think that will have an effect on the job you currently hold, then you are living in a dream world. You think the oil companies have a cartel on the price of gasoline now? Just wait till the automakers have the same power in the auto sector. You will pay through the nose for your next foreign import."

38. Pete Engardio and Michael Arndt, "What Price Reputation?" *Business Week*, July 9 & 16, 70–79.

39. David Welch, op. cit., 44.

40. Ibid.

41. Ibid.

42. Anne Fisher, "America's Most Admired Companies," *Fortune*, March 19, 2007, 88–130.

43. Jeffrey Sonnenfeld, "The Real Scandal at BP," *Business Week*, May 14, 2007, 98.

44. Kinder, Lydenburg, Domini & Co., *KLD Database* (Boston, MA: Social Investment Fund, KLD & Co., 1992–present).

45. SAM Indexes Gmbh, *Dow Jones Sustainability Indexes*, September 30, 2006 (www.sustainability-index.com/06_htmle/indexes/overview/html).

46. David Welch, "Why Hybrids are such a Hard Sell," *Business Week*, March 19, 2007, 45.

47. Jon Birger, "The Great Corn Gold Rush," *Fortune*, April 16, 2007, 75–79.

48. PricewaterhouseCoopers (PwC) has described the implementation of CSR as "trickier than it looks" (http://www.pwc.com/extweb/ service.nsf/docid/E2BD269E623824C). To successfully implement CSR, PWC offers the following six step process: (1) agreeing what CSR means; (2) deciding who "owns" CSR; (3) getting executive buy-in; (4) making it happen; (5) sustaining the momentum; and (6) getting the credit.

49. World Bank, Simeon Djankov, Caralee McLiesh, International Finance Corporation and Michael U. Klein, *Doing Business In 2004: Understanding Regulation* (London: Oxford University Press and World Bank Publications, October 2003).

50. PricewaterhouseCoopers, *Ten Year Review*, op. cit.

51. PricewaterhouseCoopers, *Tenth Annual Global CEO Survey, 2007* (www.pwc.com/extweb/home.nsf/docid/2AE969AC42DD721A85257 25E007D7CF).

52. Environics International, *The Corporate Social Responsibility Index*, July 2001 (www.globescan.com/csrm_research_findings.htm).

53. PricewaterhouseCoopers, *Fifth Annual Global CEO Survey, 2002* (www.pwc.com/gx/eng/eng/pubs/ceosurvey/2007/5th_ceo_survey.pdf.)

54. Business in the Community, *Corporate Responsibility Index, 2005: Executive Summary* (www.bitc.org.uk/crindex).

55. International Institute for Sustainable Development, "Corporate Social Responsibility (CSR)," *Business and Sustainable Development: A Global Guide* (www.bsdglobal.com/ issues/sr_sr.asp)

56. Ibid.

57. PricewaterhouseCoopers, *Tenth Annual*, op. cit.

58. Ibid.

59. International Institute for Sustainable Development, op. cit.

60. Petra Christmann and Glen Taylor, "Firm Self-Regulation through International Certifiable Standards: Determinants of Symbolic Versus Substantive Implementation," *Journal of International Business Studies* vol. 37, no. 6 (November 2006): 863–878.

61. Environics International, op. cit.

62. Pete Engardio and Michael Arndt, op. cit.

63. International Institute for Sustainable Development, "Corporate Social Responsibility Monitor," *Business and Sustainable Development: A Global Guide* (www.bsdglobal.com/ issues/sr_csrm.asp).

64. See Peter Coy and Jack Ewing, "Where Are All the Workers?" *Business Week*, April 9, 2007, 28–31; and Geri Smith, "Factories Go South. So Does Pay," *Business Week*, April 9, 2007, 76.

65. Thomas Friedman, op. cit.

66. Pete Engardio, "Global Compact, Little Impact," *Business Week*, July 12, 2004, 86.

67. C. Schmidt, "The ISO Global Social Responsibility Standard, 2005–2008," *ECOLOGIA* (www.ecologia.org/isosr).

68. United Nations UN), "What is the Global Compact?" (www.unglobalcompact.org/AboutTheGC/html).

69. Environics International, op. cit.

70. Ibid.

71. Financial Times Stock Exchange (FTSE), *Semi Annual Review of the FTSE4GOOD Indices*, March 2007 (www.ftse.com/Indices/FTSE4GOOD _Index_Series/Downloads/FTSE4GOOD_March_2007_ Review. pdf).

72. PricewaterhouseCoopers, *Tenth Annual ...*, op. cit.

Chapter 6

1. Two exceptions to this are the recently published book by John Esposito, *Religion and Globalization: World Religions in Historical Perspectives* (Oxford: Oxford University Press, 2007); and Peter Beyer's *Religion and Globalization* (Thousand Oaks, CA: Sage Press, 1994).

2. Manfred B. Steger, *Globalization: A very Short Introduction* (Oxford, Oxford University Press, 2003); Masao Miyoshi, *The Cultures of Globalization* (Durham, NC: Duke University Press, 1998); John Tomlinson, *Globalization and Culture* (Chicago, IL: University of Chicago Press, 1999).

3. B. Barber, *Jihad vs. McWorld: How Globalism and Tribalism are Reshaping the World* (New York, NY: Ballantine Books, 1996).

4. Ilan Pappé, *Modern Middle East* (New York, NY: Routledge, 2005).

5. C.A. Cerami, "The US Eyes Greater Europe," *The Spectator*, October 5, 1962, quoted in Martha Van Der Bly, "Globalization: A Triumph of Ambiguity," *Current Sociology* vol. 53, no. 6 (November 2005): 877.

6. Joseph Prabhu, "Globalization and the Emerging World Order," *ReVision* vol. 22, no. 2 (1999): 2–7.

7. Martin Wolf, *Why Globalization Works* (New Haven, CT: Yale University Press, 2004).

8. Ibid., 141

9. Ibid., 45; it is ironic that the dominant role Wolf gives to market forces in shaping virtually all aspects of society is a view associated with his nemesis, the German socialist Karl Marx, who also made the same argument.

10. Jan Aart Scholte, *Globalization: A Critical Introduction* (New York, NY: Palgrave, 2005), 81.

11. Roland Robertson, *Globalization: Social Theory and Global Culture* (London: Sage press, 1992), 102.

12. Scholte, op. cit., 424.

13. Andre. G. Frank and Barry K. Gills (eds), *The World System: Five Hundred Years or Five Thousand?* (New York, NY: Routledge. 1993), 3.

14. Amartya Sen, "Globalization: Past and Present," Ishizaka Lectures (1), 2002 (http://www.ksg.harvard.edu/gei/Text/Sen-Pubs/Sen_Globalization_ past_present.pdf).

15. Göran Therborn, "Globalizations: Dimensions, Historical Waves, Regional Effects, Normative Governance," *International Sociology* vol. 15, no. 2 (June 2000): 151–79.

16. Peter Beyer, op. cit.

17. Anthony Giddens, *Runaway World* (New York, NY: Routledge, 2001), 22–23.

18. Renato Ortiz, "Notes on Religion and Globalization," *Nepantla: Views from South* vol. 4, no. 3 (2003): 423–448.

19. World Council of Churches (WCC), *Together on the Way*, 50th Anniversary Meeting report, 1998 (www.wcc-coe.org/wcc/assembly/or-01.html).

20. Ibid.

21. Robertson, op. cit., 1992.

22. Jeffrey Haynes, "Religion and International Relations after 9/11," *Democratization* vol. 12, no. 3 (June 2005): 398–413.

23. Peter Beyer, "Secularization from the Perspective of Globalization: A Response to Karel Dobbelaere," *Sociology of Religion* (Fall 1999)**:** 229.

24. Samuel P. Huntington, *The Clash of Civilizations and the Remaking of World Order* (New York, NY: Simon & Schuster, 1996).

25. "Islam and International Politics: Examining Huntington's 'Civilizational Clash' Thesis," *Totalitarian Movements & Political Religions* vol. 2, no. 1 (Summer 2001).

26. Sean L. Yom, "Islam and Globalization: Secularism, Religion, and Radicalism," *International Politics and Society* vol. 4 (2002).

27. See "Responses to Huntington," *Foreign Affairs* vol. 72, no. 4 (July–August 1993).

28. For an excellent discussion of globalization's impact in the Middle East see Toby Dodge and Richard Higgott (eds), *Globalization and the Middle East: Islam, Economy, Society, and Politics* (London: Royal Institute of International Affairs, 2002).

29. Thomas Friedman, *The World is Flat: A Brief History of the Twenty-First Century* (New York, NY: Farrar, Strauss and Giroux, 2005).

30. Ibid., 459.

31. Ibid., 328.

32. Jonathan Sacks, *The Dignity of Difference: How to Avoid the Clash of Civilizations* (London: Continuum Publishing Group, 2002).

33. Ibid., 46.

Chapter 7

1. The question is, in fact, drawn from Cullen Murphy, *Are We Rome?* (Boston and New York: Houghton Mifflin, 2007).

2. See John Rapley, "The New Middle Ages," *Foreign Affairs* vol. 85, no. 3 (May–June 2006).

3. For an overview of this argument, see John Rapley, *Globalization and Inequality* (Boulder, CO: Lynne Rienner, 2004).

4. See, for example, David Dollar and Art Kraay, "Trade, Growth, and Poverty," *Finance and Development* vol. 38, no. 3 (September 2001); see also David Dollar, *Globalization, Poverty and Inequality since 1980* (Washington, DC: World Bank Policy Research Working Paper 3333, June 2004); but cf. Nancy Birdsall, *Asymmetric Globalization: Global Markets Require Global Politics* (Washington, DC: Center for Global Development Paper 12, October 2002). Even if the Dollar–Kraay thesis were vindicated, though, it would only acquit trade liberalization policies, not the other elements of free-market policy reforms.

5. Nita Rudra, "Are Workers in the Developing World Winners or Losers in the Current Era of Globalization?" *Studies in Comparative International Development*, vol. 40, no. 3 (September 2005): 29–64; Branko Milanovic, "Can We Discern the Effect of Globalization on Income Distribution? Evidence from Household Surveys," *World Bank Economic Review* vol. 19, no. 1 (2005): 21–

44; L. Alan Winters, et al., "Trade Liberalization and Poverty: The Evidence So Far," *Journal of Economic Literature* vol. 42, no. 1 (March 2004): 72–115; for cases, see Daniel Fernandez Kranz, "Why Has Wage Inequality Increased More in the USA than in Europe? An Empirical Investigation of the Demand and Supply of Skill," *Applied Economics* vol. 38, no. 7 (April 2006): 771–788; Anirudh Krishna, et al., "Why Growth is not Enough: Household Poverty Dynamics in Northeast Gujarat, India," *Journal of Development Studies* vol. 41, no. 7 (July 2005): 1163–1192; Vamsi Vakulabharanam, "Growth and Distress in a South Indian Peasant Economy during the Era of Economic Liberalisation," *Journal of Development Studies* vol. 41, no. 6 (June 2005): 971–997; Yoko Kijima, "Why Did Wage Inequality Increase? Evidence from Urban India 1983–99," *Journal of Development Economics* vol. 81, no. 1 (2006): 97–117; Sebastian Galiani and Pablo Sanguinetti, "The Impact of Trade Liberalization on Wage Inequality: Evidence from Argentina," *Journal of Development Economics* vol. 72, no. 2 (2003): 497–513.

6. The Gini coefficient measures inequality of income distribution, with a high Gini coefficient value indicating greater inequality.

7. Frances Stewart, *Horizontal Inequalities: A Neglected Dimension of Development* (WIDER Annual Lecture no. 5. Helsinki: United Nations World Institute for Development Economics Research, 2001); cf. Amy Chua, *World on Fire* (New York, NY: Random House, 2003).

8. Monty G. Marshall, "Global Trends in Violent Conflict." In Monty G. Marshall and Ted Robert Gurr (eds), *Peace and Conflict 2005* (College Park, Maryland: Department of Government and Politics, Center for International Development and Conflict Management, 2005).

9. See, for example, Paul Collier and Anke Hoeffler, "Greed and Grievance in Civil War," *Oxford Economic Papers* vol. 56, no. 4 (2004): 563–595.

10. In the 2003 revision to its report on world urbanization, the UN Population Division calculated that 3 billion of the world's people currently live in cities. Assuming an average population density in these cities of 3,000 people per km^2 (which is conservative, given the much higher population densities of many cities, especially those in developing countries), that would mean they would occupy a space of about 1 million km^2, well under 1 percent of the planet's land surface. See United Nations, *World Urbanization Prospects: The 2003 Revision* (New York, NY: Department of Economic and Social Affairs, Population Division, 2004).

11. See Nita Rudra, "Globalization and the Decline of the Welfare State in Less-Developed Countries," *International Organization* vol. 56, no. 2 (Spring 2002): 411–445.

12. Saskia Sassen, "Cities and Communities in the Global Economy," *American Behavioral Scientist* vol. 39 no. 5 (March 1996): 629–639.

13. *Financial Times* (London), March 17, 2000.

14. For a full discussion, see John Rapley, "Convergence: Myths and Realities," *Progress in Development Studies* vol. 1, no. 4 (October 2001): 295–308.

15. See David Dollar, *Globalization, Poverty and Inequality since 1980* (Washington, DC: World Bank Policy Research Working Paper 3333, June 2004).

16. For examples of "conditional" convergence thought, see Robert J. Barro and Xavier Sala-i-Martin, *Economic Growth* (Cambridge, MA: MIT Press, 1995) and Gregory N. Mankiw, et al., "A Contribution to

the Empirics of Economic Growth," *Quarterly Journal of Economics* vol. 107, no. 2 (May 1992): 407–437.

17. For this discussion, see the conclusion of John Rapley, *Understanding Development*, 3rd Ed. (Boulder, CO: Lynne Rienner, 2007).

18. This paragraph drew upon conversations with Peter Heather and Chris Wickham (Oxford, England; June 2007).

19. Chris Wickham, *Framing the Early Middle Ages* (Oxford: Oxford University Press, 2005), 88, 210; Peter Heather, *The Fall of the Roman Empire* (New York, NY: Oxford University Pres, 2005).

20. Wickham, *Framing...* chapter 3, op. cit.

21. Chris Wickham, "The Other Transition: From the Ancient World to Feudalism," *Past & Present* no. 103 (May 1984), 3–36.

22. See note 15.

23. Wickham, "The Other Transition ..." op. cit.; Fredric Cheyette, "The Origin of European Villages and the First European Expansion," *Journal of Economic History* vol. 37, no. 1 (March 1977): 182–206.

24. Heather, *The Fall of the Roman Empire*, op. cit.

25. Georges Duby, *The Chivalrous Society*, translated by Cynthia Postan (Berkeley and Los Angeles, CA: University of California Press, 1977).

26. See, for example, Niall Ferguson, *Colossus: The Rise and Fall of the American Empire* (New York, NY: Penguin, 2005).

27. See, for example, Paul Kennedy, *The Rise and Fall of the Great Powers* (New York, NY: Random House, 1987).

28. Samuel J. Palmisano, "The Globally Integrated Enterprise," *Foreign Affairs* vol. 85, no. 3 (May–June 2003): 127–136.

29. See Rapley, *Globalization and Inequality*, chapter 5, op. cit.

30. Rosemary Sayigh, *Too Many Enemies: The Palestinian Experience in Lebanon* (London: Zed Books, 1994), 183.

31. Ahmed Rashid, "Pakistan: Trouble Ahead, Trouble Behind," *Current History* vol. 95, no. 600 (April 1996): 160.

32. Dipankar Gupta, *Nativism in a Metropolis: The Shiv Sena in Bombay* (New Delhi: Manohar, 1982).

33. For more details see Rapley, *Globalization and Inequality*, op. cit.

34. John Rapley, "Jamaica: Negotiating Law and Order with the Dons," *NACLA Report on the Americas* vol. 37, no. 2 (September–October 2003): 25–29.

35. Desmond Enrique Arias, "The Dynamics of Criminal Governance: Networks and Social Order in Rio de Janeiro," *Journal of Latin American Studies* vol. 38, no. 2 (May 2006): 293–325.

36. Robert I. Rotberg, "Failed States, Collapsed States, Weak States: Causes and Indicators," in Robert Rotberg (ed.), *State Failure and State Weakness in a Time of Terror* (Washington, DC: Brookings Institution, 2003).

37. Wickham, "The Other Transition …" op. cit.

38. See his 1918 speech "Politics as Vocation."

39. For examples, see Morris Berman, *Dark Ages America* (New York and London: Norton, 2006) and Jane Jacobs, *Dark Age Ahead* (New York, NY: Random House, 2004).

40. For an example of this sort of reasoning, see Julian Simon (ed.), *The State of Humanity* (Oxford: Blackwell, 1995).

41. Arjun Appadurai, *Modernity at Large: Cultural Dimensions of Globalization* (Minneapolis, MN: University of Minnesota Press, 1996).

Chapter 8

1. "Globalization," Wikipedia (http://en.wikipedia.org/wiki/Globalization).

2. Ibid.

3. Ibid.

4. Laila Sharaf, "Globalization and Governance in the Arab World," a lecture delivered at the conference on *Globalization: Misery or Chance for Arab Societies?* organized by the French Institute for the Middle East in Amman on 7–8 December 2005. The lecture appeared in the *Al Nashra* periodical (Issue no. 36, January 2006, 18–22), published by the Royal Institute for Inter-Faith Studies, Amman.

5. Ibid.

6. Charter of the United Nations, Chapter I, Article 2, Principle 1 emphasizing the principle of equality of all member states.

7. Gordon Prather, "Enabling Bush's Wars of Aggression," April 28, 2007 (www. antiwar.com/prather/?articleid=10890).

8. Cristovam Buarque, *Gold Curtain: The Shocks of the End of the Twentieth Century and a Dream for the Twenty-First*, translated by Linda Jerome (São Paulo, Brazil: Paz e Terra, 1995), 35.

Chapter 9

1. Philip H. Gordon, "Recasting the Atlantic Alliance," *Survival* vol. 38, no. 1 (Spring 1996).

2. "The Sources of Soviet Conduct," *Foreign Affairs* vol. 25, no. 4 (July 1947).

3. For a detailed discussion of the origins of the term see (http://en.wikipedia.org/wiki/Islamofascism), and for Krauthammer's discussion of the existential threat. posed by it see "The Unipolar Moment Revisted," Charles Krauthammer, *The National Interest* no. 70 (Winter 2002/2003).

4. Brian Jenkins, "International Terrorism: A New Mode of Conflict," in David Carlton and Carlo Schaerf (eds), *International Terrorism and World Security* (London: Croom Helm, 1975).

5. Stephen Sloan, *The Anatomy of Non-Territorial Terrorism: An Analytical Essay*, Clandestine Tactics and Technology Series, Bureau of Operations and Research, Gaithersburg, 1978.

6. "Compilation of Usama Bin Ladin Statements 1994–January 2004," Foreign Broadcast Information Service (FBIS) report, GMP20040209000243, February 9, 2004.

7. "Red Team U. creates critical thinkers," Associated Press, (http://archives.neohapsis.com/archives/isn/2007-q2/0217.html); also see (http://www.leavenworth.army.mil).

8. Lt. Col. David Kilcullen, "Countering Global Insurgency," *Small Wars Journal* (November 2004) (www.smallwarsjournal.com/documents/kilcullen1.pdf).

9. Ibid.

10. Discussion with the author, Budapest, March 2005.

11. *Prospects for Iraq's Stability: A Challenging Road Ahead*, US National Intelligence Council (Washington, DC: US Government Printing Office, January 2007).

12. Discussion with the author, George C. Marshall Center, Garmisch-Partenkirchen, March 2006.

Chapter 10

1. Henry DeWolf Smyth, "Atomic Energy for Military Purposes," *The Official Report on the Development of the Atomic Bomb under the Auspices of the United States Government, 1940–1945*; released to the public on August 12, 1945.

2. Steve Tulliu and Thomas Schmalberger, "Coming to terms with security: A lexicon for Arms Control, Disarmament and Confidence-Building," the United Nation Institute for Disarmament Research (UNIDIR), UNIDIR/2003/33, 9.

3. James A. Russell, "WMD Proliferation, Globalization, and International Security: Whither the Nexus and National Security?" *Strategic Insights* vol. 5, no. 6 (July 2006): 1.

4. Peter R. Lavoy and Robin Walker, "Nuclear Weapons Proliferation: 2016" Conference Report, Monterey, California, July 28–29, 2006.

5. Jeremy Bernstein, "Where those reactors and centrifuges came from," *New York Times*, March 10, 2007.

6. Jonathan L. Katz, "Limiting the Nuclear Club – Iraq, North Korea et al.," *Strategic Review* no. XXII (Winter 1994): 74.

7. Michael T. Klare, "US Supremacism and Weapons of Mass Destruction in the 21st Century," the Foreign Policy in Focus Project, Weapons of Mass Destruction Conference (http://www.fpif.org/presentations/wmd01/klare.html).

8. Natasha Bajema, "Weapons of Mass Destruction and the United Nations: Diverse Threats andCollective Responses," International Peace Academy (IPA) Report, June 2004, 4.

9. Ibid., 7.

10. Moeed Yusuf, "The Indo-US Nuclear Deal: An Impact Analysis," 56th Pugwash Conference, Cairo, Egypt, November 11–15, 2006.

11. *The National Security Strategy of the United States of America*, The White House, September 2002.

12. See recent reports on China's Anti-Satellite Test by Phillip C. Saunders and Charles D. Lutes in "China ASAT Test: Motivations and Implications," National Defense University, June 2007; and by Ashley J. Tellis, "Punching the US Military's Soft Ribs: China's Anti-satellite Weapon Test in Strategic Perspective," Carnegie Endowment for International Peace, June 2007.

13. Michael T. Klare, op. cit., 6.

14. Francesco Calogero, "The twin risks of nuclear weapons proliferation and nuclear terrorism," the 10th PICC Seminar on International Security, Xiamen, Fujiian Province, China, September 25–28, 2006.

15. "Nuclear Terrorism: The Danger of Highly Enriched Uranium (HEU)," *Pugwash Issue Brief* vol. 2, no. 1 (September 2002): 8.

16. See: "Megaton to Megawatts: The US-Russia Highly Enriched Uranium Agreement," Center for Defense Information (CDI); (http://www.cdi.org/friendlyversion/printversion.cfm?documentID=2210).

17. See: (www.fissilematerials.org/ipfm/site_down/ipfmreport06.pdf).

18. Michael T. Klare, op. cit., 6.

19. Henry Porter, "When Will Islam Damn the Chlorine Bombers?" *The Observer* (London), April 22, 2007.

20. James Bloom, "Waging war with the dirty bombers," *The Guardian* (London), April 26, 2007.

21. Gopal Ratnam, "US Creates Nuclear Forensics Center," *Defense News* vol. 21, no. 41 (October 23, 2006): 1.

22. See: "Israel's Nuclear Weapons" at Federation of American Scientists (http://www.fas.org/nuke/guide/israel/nuke/), October 23, 2002, 3.

23. Barry R. Schneider (ed.), *Middle East Security Issues: In the shadow of Weapons of Mass Destruction Proliferation*, USAF Counter-Proliferation Center (AU Press, Dec. 1999), 25.

24. "Israel granted access to US DoE nuclear projects," *Jane's Defense Weekly*, March 1, 2000.

25. See: Anthony H. Cordesman, "The Military Balance in the Middle East: an Executive Summary," IGCC Policy Paper 49, March 1999, 88.

26. Rahul Bedi, "India dispatches aircraft carrier to the Gulf," *Jane's Defense Weekly*, March 10, 1999.

27. Dalia Dassa Kaye and Frederic M. Wehrey, "A Nuclear Iran: The Reactions of Neighbors," *Survival* vol. 49, no. 2 (Summer 2007): 111–128.

28. H.H. Gaffney, "Globalization and Nuclear Proliferation," *Strategic Insights* vol. 5, no. 6 (July 2006): 2.

29. James A. Russell and Christopher Clary, "Globalization and WMD Proliferation Networks: Challenges to US Security," Conference Report, Naval Postgraduate School, Monterey, California, June 29–July 1, 2005.

30. Jeffrey Laurenti, "Contain Iran, Not Bomb it," The Century Foundation, Taking Note, May 2, 2007.

31. George Schultz, "A World Free of Nuclear Weapons," *Wall Street Journal*, January 4, 2007, A15.

BIBLIOGRAPHY

"Brazilian Firm to buy Sought-After US Meatpacker Swift." *Des Moines Register*, May 30, 2007.

"Bush, Congress Clash Over Ports Sale." *CNN* (www.cnn.com/2006/POLITICS/02/21/port.security).

"China to overtake US with world's highest CO_2 emissions this year— IEA." CNN, November 9, 2007 (http://money.cnn.com/news/news feeds/articles/newstex/AFX-0013-20857754.htm).

"China unseats US as top CO_2 emitter." *Houston Chronicle* 106 (251), June 21, 2007.

"China: US pistachio shipment rejected." *Houston Chronicle* 106 (240), June 10, 2007.

"Islam and International Politics: Examining Huntington's 'Civilizational Clash' Thesis." *Totalitarian Movements & Political Religions* vol. 2, no. 1 (Summer 2001).

"Israel granted access to US DoE nuclear projects." *Jane's Defence Weekly*, March 1, 2000.

"Many Hurt by Watch List, Group Says." *Des Moines Register*, March 28, 2007.

"Nuclear Terrorism: The Danger of Highly Enriched Uranium (HEU)." *Pugwash Issue Brief* vol. 2, no. 1 (September 2002).

"Responses to Huntington." *Foreign Affairs* vol. 72, no. 4 (July–August 1993).

"The Sources of Soviet Conduct." *Foreign Affairs* vol. 25, no. 4 (July 1947).

"US Free-Trade Pact With South Korea Would Enhance Partnership." *International Information Programs*, June 13, 2007 (www.usinfo. state.gov).

A.T. Kearney. "Measuring globalization." *Foreign Policy* no. 148 (March–April 2004).

Adelman, Irma. "Fallacies in Development Theory and Their Implications for Policy." California Agricultural Experiment Station, Giannini Foundation of Agricultural Economics, Department of Agricultural and Resource Economics and Policy, University of California at Berkeley, Working Paper No. 887, May 1999.

Agénor, Pierre-Richard. "Does Globalization Hurt the Poor?" World Bank Development Research Group Working Paper 2922, 2002.

Aguilera, Ruth V., Deborah E. Rupp, Cynthia A. Williams and Jyoti Ganapathi. "Putting the S Back in Corporate Social Responsibility: A Multilevel Theory of Social Change In Organizations." *Academy of Management Review*, vol. 32, no. 3 (2007).

Aisbett, Emma. "Why are the Critics so Convinced that Globalization is Bad for the Poor?" NBER Globalization and Poverty Conference (September 10–12, 2004).

Anderson, James E. and Eric van Wincoop. "Gravity with Gravitas: A Solution to the Border Puzzle." *American Economic Review* vol. 93, no. 1 (March 2003).

Anderson, James E. and Eric van Wincoop. "Trade Costs." *Journal of Economic Literature* vol. 62, no. 3 (September 2004).

Andreas, Peter. *Border Games: Policing the U.S.–Mexico Divide* (Ithaca, NY: Cornell University Press, 2000).

Antal, Ariane Berthoin and Andre Sobczak. "Corporate Social Responsibility in France: A Mix of National Traditions and International Influences." *Business & Society* vol. 46, no. 1 (March, 2007).

Antweiler, Werner, Brian R. Copeland and M. Scott Taylor. "Is free trade good for the environment?" *American Economic Review* vol. 91, no. 4 (September 2001).

Appadurai, Arjun. *Modernity at Large: Cultural Dimensions of Globalization* (Minneapolis, MN: University of Minnesota Press, 1996).

Appleyard, Reginald T. (ed.) *International Migration Today, Volume I: Trends and Prospects* (Perth: University of Western Australia for the United Nations Educational, Scientific and Cultural Organization, 1988).

Arias, Desmond Enrique. "The Dynamics of Criminal Governance: Networks and Social Order in Rio de Janeiro." *Journal of Latin American Studies*, vol. 38, no. 2 (May 2006).

Arrighi, Giovanni (ed.) *Semiperipheral Development: The Politics of Southern Europe in the Twentieth Century* (Beverly Hills, CA: Sage, 1985).

Associated Press (AP). "Red Team U. creates critical thinkers" (http://archives.neohapsis.com/archives/isn/2007-q2/0217.html).

Associated Press (AP). "Bush Economist: Outsourcing Remark Misunderstood," February 19, 2004 (http//:www.foxnews.com/story/0,2933,111715,00.html), accessed June 8, 2007.

Baier, Scott L. and Jeffrey H. Bergstrand. "*Bonus Vetus* OLS: A Simple Approach for Approximating International Trade-Cost Effects using the Gravity Equation." Working paper, 2007.

Baier, Scott L. and Jeffrey H. Bergstrand. "Do Free Trade Agreements Actually Increase Members' International Trade?" *Journal of International Economics* vol. 71, no. 1 (March 2007).

Baier, Scott L. and Jeffrey H. Bergstrand. "Economic Determinants of Free Trade Agreements." *Journal of International Economics* vol. 64, no. 1 (October 2004).

Baier, Scott L. and Jeffrey H. Bergstrand. "The Growth of World Trade: Tariffs, Transport Costs, and Income Similarity." *Journal of International Economics* vol. 53, no. 1 (February 2001).

Baier, Scott L., Jeffrey H. Bergstrand and Erika Vidal. "Free Trade Agreements in the Americas: Are the Trade Effects Larger than Anticipated?" *The World Economy* vol. 30, no. 9 (September 2007).

Bajema, Natasha. "Weapons of Mass Destruction and the United Nations: Diverse Threats and Collective Responses." International Peace Academy (IPA) Report, June 2004.

Baldwin, Richard, Pentti Haaparanta and Jaakko Klander (eds). *Expanding Membership of the European Union* (New York, NY: Cambridge University Press, 1995).

Barber, B. *Jihad vs. McWorld: How Globalism and Tribalism are Reshaping the World* (New York, NY: Ballantine Books, 1996).

Barnet, Richard J. and Ronald E. Muller. *Global Reach: The Power of the Multinational Corporation* (New York, NY: Simon and Schuster, 1974).

Barro, Robert J. and Xavier Sala-i-Martin. *Economic Growth* (Cambridge, MA: MIT Press, 1995).

Baumol, William J. "Entrepreneurship in economic theory." *American Economic Review: Papers and Proceedings* vol. 58, no. 2 (May 1968).

Bedi, Rahul. "India dispatches aircraft carrier to the Gulf." *Jane's Defence Weekly*, March 10, 1999.

Beer, Michael and Nitin Nohria (eds.) *Breaking the Code of Change* (Boston, MA: Harvard Business School Press, 2000).

Bergsten, Fred C. "Competitive Liberalization and Global Free Trade: A Vision for the Early 21st Century." Working Paper (Washington, DC: Institute for International Economics, 1996).

Berman, Morris. *Dark Ages America* (New York and London: Norton, 2006).

Bernstein, Jeremy. "Where those reactors and centrifuges came from?" *New York Times*, March 10, 2007.

Beyer, Peter. "Secularization from the Perspective of Globalization: A Response to Karel Dobbelaere." *Sociology of Religion* (Fall 1999).

Bhagwati, Jagdish. "Coping with antiglobalization: A trilogy of discontents." *Foreign Affairs* vol. 81, no. 1 (January–February 2002).

Bhagwati, Jagdish. "Why your Job isn't moving to Bangalore." *New York Times*, January 22, 2004.

Bilefsky, Dan. "Latvia Fears New 'Occupation' by Russians but Needs the Labor." *New York Times*, November 16, 2006.

Birdsall, Nancy. *Asymmetric Globalization: Global Markets Require Global Politics*, Paper 12 (Washington, DC: Center for Global Development, October 2002).

Birger, Jon. "The Great Corn Gold Rush." *Fortune*, April 16, 2007.

Birks, J.S. and A. Sinclair. *International Migration and Development in the Arab Region* (Geneva: International Labor Office, 1980).

Blinder, Alan S. "Free trade's great, but offshoring rattles me." *Washington Post*, May 6, 2007.

Blinder, Alan S. "Let's save free trade from its own deficits: It's imperative to turn back the tide of high-paying US jobs moving offshore." *Houston Chronicle* 106 (212), May 13, 2007.

Blinder, Alan S. "Offshoring: The next industrial revolution?" *Foreign Affairs* vol. 85, no. 2 (March–April 2006).

Bloom, James. "Waging war with the dirty bombers." *The Guardian* (London), April 26, 2007.

Borenstein, Seth (Associated Press). "Ethanol may raise ozone levels more than gasoline, study says." *Houston Chronicle* 106 (187), April 18, 2007.

Bourguignon, Francois and Christian Morrison. "Inequality among world citizens, 1820–1992." *American Economic Review* vol. 92, no. 4 (September 2002).

Bowen, Howard R. *Social Responsibilities of the Businessman* (New York, NY: Harper, 1953).

Brakman, Steven and Charles van Marrewijk. "It's a Big World After All." CESifo Working Paper no. 1964, April 2007.

Brown, J.F. *Surge to Freedom: The End of Communist Rule in Eastern Europe* (Durham, NC: Duke University Press, 1991).

Brunwasser, Matthew. "Romania, a Poor Land, Imports Poorer Workers: Replacements for Dwindling Labor Pool." *New York Times*, April 11, 2007.

Buarque, Cristovam. *Gold Curtain: The Shocks of the End of the Twentieth Century and a Dream for the Twenty-First*. Translated by Linda Jerome (São Paulo, Brazil: Paz e Terra, 1995).

Business in the Community. *Corporate Responsibility Index, 2005*: *Executive Summary* (www.bitc.org.uk/crindex).

Calavita, Kitty. *Inside the State: The Bracero Program, Immigration and the INS* (New York, NY: Routledge, 1992).

Calogero, Francesco. "The twin risks of nuclear weapons proliferation and nuclear terrorism." 10th PICC Seminar on International Security, Xiamen, Fujiian Province, China, September 25–28, 2006.

Carey, John. "Lighting a Fire under Global Warming." *Business Week*, April 16, 2007.

Carlton, David and Carlo Schaerf (eds). *International Terrorism and World Security* (London: Croom Helm, 1975).

Carroll, Archie B. "A Three-Dimensional Conceptual Model of Corporate Social Performance." *Academy of Management Review* vol. 4, no. 4 (October 1979).

Castle, S. "Migration to Surge, EU Leaders are told: Warned of Fallout on Climate Change." *International Herald Tribune*, March 8–9, 2008

Castles, Stephen, and Godula Kosack. *Immigrant Workers and Class Structure in Western Europe* (London: Oxford University Press, 1973).

Castles, Stephen, and Mark J. Miller. *The Age of Migration: International Population Movements in the Modern World* (New York, NY: The Guilford Press, 1993).

Cavanagh, Gerald F. *American Business Values in Transition*, 2nd Ed. (Englewood Cliffs, NJ: Prentice-Hall, 1984).

[311]

Center for Defense Information (CDI). "Megaton to Megawatts: The US–Russia Highly Enriched Uranium Agreement" (http://www.cdi.org/friendlyversion/printversion.cfm?documentID=2210).

Cheyette, Fredric. "The Origin of European Villages and the First European Expansion." *Journal of Economic History* vol. 37, no. 1 (March 1977).

Christmann, Petra and Glen Taylor. "Firm Self-Regulation through International Certifiable Standards: Determinants of Symbolic Versus Substantive Implementation." *Journal of International Business Studies* vol. 37, no. 6 (November 2006).

Chua, Amy. *World on Fire* (New York: Random House, 2003).

Clanton, Brett. "Why Halliburton chose Dubai: Growth—but oil-services firm will continue to add Houston jobs, its CEO says." *Houston Chronicle* 106 (205), May 6, 2007.

Clendenning, Alan. "Bush Trip to Brazil to Back Ethanol." *Des Moines Register*, March 5, 2007.

Cohen, Robin (ed.) *The Cambridge Survey of World Migration* (Cambridge: Cambridge University Press, 1995).

Cohen, Secretary William and Admiral James Loy. "Fact, not Fear." *Wall Street Journal*, February 28, 2006.

Collier, Paul and Anke Hoeffler. "Greed and Grievance in Civil War." *Oxford Economic Papers* vol. 56, no. 4 (2004).

Constable, Pamela. "Skilled foreign workers add fuel to immigration debate: Companies say more of them are needed, but critics say they harm US professionals." *Houston Chronicle* 106 (225), May 26, 2007.

Cordesman, Anthony H. "The Military Balance in the Middle East: an Executive Summary." IGCC Policy Paper 49, March 1999.

Cornelius, Wayne A., Philip L. Martin and James F. Hollifield (eds). *Controlling Immigration: A Global Perspective* (Stanford, CA: Stanford University Press, 1994).

Coy, Peter and Jack Ewing. "Where are All the Workers?" *Business Week*, April 9, 2007.

Crook, Clive. "Bush may be on to something." *Financial Times*, June 7, 2007.

Curtin, Philip D. *The Atlantic Slave Trade: A Census* (Madison, WI: University of Wisconsin Press, 1969).

Dasgupta, Susmit, Benoit Laplante, Craig Meisner, David Wheeler and David J. Yan. "The Impact of Sea Level Rise on Developing Countries: A Comparative Analysis." World Bank Policy Research WP No. 4136, 2007 (http://ssrn.com/abstract=962790).

Deardorff, Alan V. "Rich and poor countries in neoclassical trade and growth." *The Economic Journal* vol. 111, no. 470 (April 2001).

Demsey, Judy. "Polish Labor Crunch as Workers Go West." *New York Times,* November 19, 2006.

DeRosa, Dean A. and John P. Gilbert. "Predicting Trade Expansion under FTAs and Multilateral Agreements." Peterson Institute for International Economics Working Paper 05-13, October 2005.

Djankov, Simeon, Caralee McLiesh, Michael U. Klein, World Bank and International Finance Corporation. *Doing Business in 2004: Understanding Regulation* (London: Oxford University Press and World Bank Publications, October 2003).

Dollar, David and Art Kraay. "Trade, Growth, and Poverty." *Finance and Development*, vol. 38, no. 3 (September 2001).

Dollar, David. *Globalization, Poverty and Inequality since 1980* (Washington, DC: World Bank Policy Research Working Paper 3333, June 2004).

Duby, Georges. *The Chivalrous Society*. Translated by Cynthia Postan (Berkeley and Los Angeles, CA: University of California Press, 1977).

Dvorak, Phred and Leila Abboud. "Difficult upgrade: SAP's plan to globalize hits cultural barriers—Software giant's shift irks German engineers." *Wall Street Journal* CCXLIX (110), May 11, 2007.

Easton, Nina. "After Dubai Ports, US Courts Foreign Investment." *Fortune*, March 5, 2007 (www.money.cnn.com/2007/03/05/magazines/fortune/pluggedin_eas).

Eaton, Jonathan and Samuel Kortum. "Technology, Geography, and Trade." *Econometrica* vol. 70, no. 5 (September 2002).

Ehrlich, Isaac. "The Mystery of Human Capital as Engine of Growth, or Why the US Became the Economic Superpower in the 20th Century." NBER Working Paper No. W12868, 2007 (http://ssrn.com/abstract=960443).

Engardio, Pete and Michael Arndt. "What Price Reputation?" *Business Week*, July 9 & 16.

Engardio, Pete. "Global Compact, Little Impact." *Business Week*, July 12, 2004.

Engardio, Pete. "Let's Offshore the Lawyers." *Business Week*, September, 18, 2006.

Engardio, Pete. "The Future of Outsourcing." *Business Week*, January 30, 2006.

Environics International. *The Corporate Social Responsibility Index*, July 2001 (www.globescan.com/csrm_research_findings.htm).

Espenshade, Thomas J. and Charles A. Calhoun. "An Analysis of Public Opinion toward Undocumented Immigration." *Population Research and Policy Review* 12, 1993.

Espenshade, Thomas J. and Katherine Hempstead. "Contemporary American Attitudes toward U.S. Immigration." *International Migration Review* 30, 1996.

Estevadeordal, Antoni, 2007. "The Rise of Regionalism." Presentation at the conference, *The New Regionalism: Progress, Setbacks, and Challenges.* Washington, DC: Inter-American Development Bank. February 9–10, 2006.

Fallows, J. "Declaring Victory." *Atlantic Monthly*, September 2006.

Faries, Bill (Bloomberg News). "Holders of Argentine debt are going on the offensive: Group intensifies efforts as nation tries to restructure Paris Club loans." *Houston Chronicle* 106 (181), April 12, 2007.

Federation of American Scientists. "Israel's Nuclear Weapons" (http://www.fas.org/nuke/guide/israel/nuke/), October 23, 2002.

Ferenczi, Imre. *International Migrations, Volume I: Statistics* (New York, NY: National Bureau of Economic Research, 1929).

Ferguson, Niall. *Colossus: The Rise and Fall of the American Empire* (New York, NY: Penguin, 2005).

Financial Times (London), March 17, 2000.

Financial Times Stock Exchange (FTSE). *Semi Annual Review of the FTSE4GOOD Indices*, March 2007 (www.ftse.com/Indices/FTSE4GOOD _Index_Series/Downloads/FTSE4GOOD _March_2007_Review.pdf).

Findlay, Ronald. "Comparative advantage." *The New Palgrave: A Dictionary of Economics* (London & New York, NY: Macmillan & Stockton 1987).

[315]

Fisher, Anne. "America's Most Admired Companies." *Fortune*, March 19, 2007.

Foreign Broadcast Information Service (FBIS). "Compilation of Usama Bin Ladin Statements 1994–January 2004." FBIS report, GMP 20040209000243, February 9, 2004.

Frank, Andre. G. and Barry K. Gills (eds). *The World System: Five Hundred Years or Five Thousand?* (New York, NY: Routledge. 1993).

Frey, Bruno S., Werner W. Pommerehne, Friedrich Schneider and Guy Gilbert. "Consensus and dissension among economists: An empirical inquiry." *American Economic Review* vol. 74, no. 4 (December 1984).

Friedman, Milton. *Capitalism and Freedom* (Chicago, IL: University of Chicago Press, 1962).

Friedman, Thomas. "Phone lines provide Kenya with new economic lifeline." *Houston Chronicle* 106 (173), April 4, 2007.

Friedman, Thomas. *The World Is Flat: A Brief History of the 21st Century* (New York, NY: Farrar, Straus, and Giroux, 2005).

Gaffney, H.H. "Globalization and Nuclear Proliferation." *Strategic Insights* vol. 5, Issue 6 (July 2006).

Galiani, Sebastian and Pablo Sanguinetti. "The Impact of Trade Liberalization on Wage Inequality: Evidence from Argentina." *Journal of Development Economics* vol. 72, no. 2 (2003).

Gamory, Ralph E. and William J. Baumol. *Global Trade and Conflicting National Interest* (Cambridge, MA: MIT Press, 2000).

Garrett, Geoffrey. "Globalization's missing middle." *Foreign Affairs* vol. 83, no. 6 (November–December 2004).

Ghosh, Sucharita and Steven Yamarik. "Are Regional Trading Arrangements Trade Creating? An Application of Extreme Bounds Analysis." *Journal of International Economics* vol. 63, no. 2 (July 2004).

Giddens, Anthony. *Runaway World* (New York, NY: Routledge, 2001).

Gilpin, Robert. *The Challenge of Global Capitalism* (Princeton, NJ: Princeton University Press, 2000).

Gordon, Philip H. "Recasting the Atlantic Alliance." *Survival* vol. 38, no. 1 (Spring 1996).

Graham, Carol. "Stemming the Backlash against Globalization." Brookings Policy Brief No. 78, 2001.

Gupta, Dipankar. *Nativism in a Metropolis: The Shiv Sena in Bombay* (New Delhi: Manohar, 1982).

Harrop, Froma. "The working class is not stupid about immigration: Froma Harrop criticizes the motives behind a union's proposal to expand the supply of low-cost labor pouring into the United States." *Houston Chronicle* 106 (221), May 22, 2007.

Hatton, Timothy J. and Jeffrey G. Williamson. *The Age of Mass Migration: Causes and Impact* (New York, NY: Oxford University Press, 1998).

Hayek, Friedrich. "The use of knowledge in society." *American Economic Review* vol. 35, no. 4 (September 1945).

Haynes, Jeffrey. "Religion and International Relations after 9/11." *Democratization* vol. 12, no. 3 (June 2005).

Heather, Peter. *The Fall of the Roman Empire* (New York: Oxford University Press, 2005).

Heft, Miguel. "Google's Chief Gets $1 in Pay; His Security Costs $532,755." *New York Times*, April 5, 2007.

Held, Joseph (ed.). *The Columbia History of Eastern Europe in the Twentieth Century* (New York, NY: Columbia University Press, 1992).

Helpman, Elhanan and Paul Krugman. *Market Structure and Foreign Trade* (Cambridge, MA: MIT Press, 1985).

Hollifield, James F. "Migration and International Relations: Cooperation and Control in the European Community." *International Migration Review* 26, 1992.

Huntington, Samuel P. *The Clash of Civilizations and the Remaking of World Order* (New York, NY: Simon & Schuster, 1996).

International Institute for Sustainable Development (IISD). "Corporate Social Responsibility (CSR)." *Business and Sustainable Development: A Global Guide.* (www.bsdglobal.com/issues/sr_sr.asp)

Irwin, Douglas A. "'Outsourcing' is Good for America." *New York Times*, January 28, 2004.

Irwin, Douglas A. *Against the Tide: An Intellectual History of Free Trade* (Princeton, NJ: Princeton University Press, 1996).

Jacobs, Jane. *Dark Age Ahead* (New York, NY: Random House, 2004).

Jacobs, Jennifer. "Plan Would Wean Iowa Off Foreign Oil By 2025." *Des Moines Register*, March 7, 2007 (www.desmoinesregister.com).

Jarausch, Konrad H. *The Rush to German Unity* (Oxford: Oxford University Press, 1994).

Javers, Eamon. "The Divided States of America." *Business Week*, April 16, 2007. Johnson, George E. and Frank P. Stafford. "International competition and real wages." *American Economic Review: Papers and Proceedings* vol. 82, no. 2 (May 1993).

Johnson, Harry G. *Aspects of the Theory of Tariffs* (Cambridge, MA: Harvard University Press, 1971).

Johnson, Jo. "Worlds collide in India over global warming." *Financial Times*, June 7, 2007.

Johnston, David C. "Americans' average income falls again: 2005 is fifth consecutive year of decline." *Houston Chronicle* 106 (312), August 21, 2007.

Johnston, David C. "US income gap growing wider: The rich are getting richer while the poor have lost some ground, recent tax data show." *Houston Chronicle* 106 (167), March 29, 2007.

Jones, Ronald W. "Globalization and the distribution of income: The economic arguments." *Proceedings of the National Academy of Sciences of the United States of America* vol. 100, no. 19 (September 2003).

Katz, Jonathan L. "Limiting the Nuclear Club—Iraq, North Korea et al." *Strategic Review* XXII (Winter 1994).

Kaye, Dalia Dassa and Frederic M. Wehrey. "A Nuclear Iran: The Reactions of Neighbors." *Survival* vol. 49, no. 2 (Summer 2007).

Kelleher, Elizabeth. "Congress Moves to Change Foreign Investment Review Process." *International Information Programs*, July 27, 2006 (www.usinfo.state.gov).

Kemp, Murray C. and Paul Pezanis-Christou. "Pareto's compensation principle." *Social Choice and Welfare* 16 (3), May 1999.

Kennedy, Paul. *The Rise and Fall of the Great Powers* (New York, NY: Random House, 1987).

Kettner, James. *The Development of the Concept of American Citizenship, 1608–1870* (Chapel Hill, NC: University of North Carolina Press, 1978).

Keynes, John Maynard. *A Tract on Monetary Reform* (London: Macmillan, 1923).

Kijima, Yoko. "Why Did Wage Inequality Increase? Evidence from Urban India 1983–99." *Journal of Development Economics* vol. 81, no. 1 (2006).

Kilcullen, Lt. Col. David. "Countering Global Insurgency." *Small Wars Journal*, November 2004 (www.smallwarsjournal.com/documents/kilcullen1.pdf).

Kinder, Lydenburg, Domini & Co. *KLD Database* (Boston, MA: Social Investment Fund, KLD & Co., 1992–present).

Klare, Michael T. "US Supremacism and Weapons of Mass Destruction in the 21st Century." Foreign Policy in Focus Project, Weapons of Mass Destruction Conference (http://www.fpif.org/presentations/wmd01/klare.html).

Klare, Michael T. *Resource Wars: The New Landscape of Global Conflict* (New York, NY: Metropolitan Books, Henry Holt & Co., 2001).

Krane, Jim. "Halliburton's relocated CEO outlines major shift in focus: A big focus." *Houston Chronicle* 106 (222), May 23, 2007.

Krane, Ronald E. (ed.) *International Labor Migration in Europe* (New York, NY: Praeger, 1979).

Kranz, Daniel Fernandez. "Why has Wage Inequality Increased More in the USA than in Europe? An Empirical Investigation of the Demand and Supply of Skill." *Applied Economics* vol. 38, no. 7 (April 2006).

Krishna, Anirudh, et al. "Why Growth is not Enough: Household Poverty Dynamics in Northeast Gujarat, India." *Journal of Development Studies*, vol. 41, no. 7 (July 2005).

Krugman, Paul. "Trade has problems, but answer isn't shutting it down," *Houston Chronicle* 106 (83), January 4, 2007.

Krugman, Paul. "What's good for corporations is good for executives." *Houston Chronicle* 106 (206), June 7, 2007.

Landler, Mark and Judy Dempsey. "US mulls global plan to halve emissions: But the G8 deal does not commit nation to specific greenhouse gas cuts by 2050." *Houston Chronicle* 106 (238), June 8, 2007.

Lasswell, Harold D. *Politics: Who Gets What, When, How—With Postscript* (New York, NY: Meridian Books, 1958).

Laurenti, Jeffrey. "Contain Iran, Not Bomb it." The Century Foundation, Taking Note, May 2, 2007.

Lavoy, Peter R. and Robin Walker. "Nuclear Weapons Proliferation: 2016." Conference Report, Monterey, California, July 28–29, 2006.

Lawrence, Anne T. "Stakeholder Management: Shell Oil in Nigeria." *Case Research Journal* (Fall/Winter 1997).

Lawrence, Robert. *A US–Middle East Trade Agreement: A Circle of Opportunity* (Washington, DC: Peterson Institute for International Economics).

Lawrence, Robert. *Regionalism, Multilateralism, and Deeper Integration* (Washington, DC: The Brookings Institution, 1996).

Letter to the Editor. *Louisville, Kentucky, Courier-Journal*, April 28, 2007.

Levitt, Theodore. "The Dangers of Social Responsibility." *Harvard Business Review* vol. 36, no. 3 (September–October 1958).

Malthus, Thomas. *An Essay on the Principle of Population* (London: Printed for J. Johnson in St. Paul's Church-Yard, 1798).

Mankiw, Gregory N. et al. "A Contribution to the Empirics of Economic Growth." *Quarterly Journal of Economics* vol. 107, no 2 (May 1992).

Mann, James. "A brand new model—made in China: Country proves it doesn't need democracy or free market to succeed." *Houston Chronicle* 106 (226), May 27, 2007.

Margonelli, Lisa. "All pumped up: Five myths that fuel $3 gas stories—Fill-up prices are high for many reasons but these." *Houston Chronicle* 106 (240), June 10, 2007.

Marshall, Monty G. and Ted Robert Gurr (eds). *Peace and Conflict 2005* (College Park, Maryland: Department of Government and Politics, Center for International Development and Conflict Management, 2005).

Martin, Philip L. and Mark J. Miller. "Guestworkers: Lessons from Western Europe." *Industrial and Labor Relations Review* vol. 33, no.3 (1980).

Massey, Douglas S. "International Migration and Economic Development in Comparative Perspective." *Population and Development Review* 14, 1988.

Massey, Douglas S. "Social Structure, Household Strategies, and the Cumulative Causation of Migration." *Population Index* 56, 1990.

Massey, Douglas S., Joaquin Arango, Ali Kouaouci, Adela Pelligrino and J. Edward Taylor. *Worlds in Motion: Understanding International Migration at the End of the Millennium* (Oxford: Oxford University Press, 1998).

Massey, Douglas S., Joaquin Arango, Graeme Hugo, Ali Kouaouci, Adela Pellegrino and J. Edward Taylor. "Theories of International

Migration: A Review and Appraisal." *Population and Development Review* 19, 1993.

Mazur, Laurie Ann. "International migration 1965–96: An Overview." *Population and Development Review* 24, 1998.

Mazur, Laurie Ann (ed.) *Beyond the Numbers: A Reader on Population, Consumption, and the Environment* (Washington, DC: Island Press, 1994).

McCarl, Bruce A. and Uwe A. Schneider. "U.S. agriculture's role in a greenhouse gas emission mitigation world: An economic perspective." *Review of Agricultural Economics* vol. 22, no. 1 (Spring 2000).

Meadows, Donella H., Dennis L. Meadows, Jørgen Randers and William W. Behrens. *The Limits to Growth: A Report for The Club of Rome's Project on the Predicament of Mankind* (New York, NY: Universe Books, 1972).

Meadows, Donella H., Jørgen Randers and Dennis Meadows. *Limits to Growth: The 30-Year Update* (White River Junction, VT: Chelsea Green Publishing Co., 2004).

Messina, Anthony M. and Gallya Lahava (eds). *The Migration Reader* (Boulder, CO: Lynne Rienner, 2003).

Meyers, Eytan. *The political economy of international migration policy: A comparative and quantitative study*. Ph.D dissertation, Department of Political Science, University of Chicago, 1995.

Milanovic, Branko. "Can We Discern the Effect of Globalization on Income Distribution? Evidence from Household Surveys." *World Bank Economic Review*, vol. 19, no. 1 (2005).

Milanovic, Branko. "The two faces of globalization: Against globalization as we know it." *World Development* vol. 31, no. 4 (April 2003).

Mill, John Stuart. *Principles of Political Economy* (London: Longmans, Green, 1848, 1909).

Mitchell, Ronald K., Bradley R. Agle and Donna J. Wood. "Toward A Theory of Stakeholder Identification and Salience: Defining The Principle Of What Really Counts." *Academy of Management Review* vol. 22, no. 4 (October 1997).

Mittelstadt, Michelle. "Deadlock in the Senate: Immigration bill fails crucial vote—This summer could be last chance for Bush's top domestic initiative." *Houston Chronicle* 106 (238), June 8, 2007.

Miyoshi, Masao. *The Cultures of Globalization* (Durham: Duke University Press, 1998).

Momsen, Janet Henshall (ed.) *Gender, Migration and Domestic Service* (London: Routledge, 1999).

Murphy, Cullen. *Are We Rome?* (Boston and New York: Houghton Mifflin, 2007).

O'Byrne, Shannon Kathleen. "Economic justice and global trade: An analysis of the libertarian foundations of the free trade paradigm." *American Journal of Economics and Sociology* vol. 55, no. 1 (January 1996).

Organization for Economic Cooperation and Development (OECD). "China could become world's largest exporter by 2010," September 16, 2005 (www.oecd.org/document/15/0,3343,en_2649_34571_35363023_1_1_1_1,00.html).

Ortiz, Renato. "Notes on Religion and Globalization." *Nepantla: Views from South* vol. 4, no. 3 (2003).

Otis, John. "Venezuelan chief leads drive to expanded socialism." *Houston Chronicle* 106 (225), May 25, 2007.

Palmisano, Samuel J. "The Globally Integrated Enterprise." *Foreign Affairs* vol. 85, no. 3 (May–June 2003).

Pappé, Ilan. *Modern Middle East* (New York, NY: Routledge, 2005).

Peridy, Nicolas. "Trade Prospects of the New EU Neighborhood Policy." *Global Economy Journal* vol. 5, no. 1 (2005).

Perkins, Jerry. "Farm Chief wants Ban on Foreign Ownership." *Des Moines Register*, February 24, 2006.

Petroski, William. "A Road of Apprehension Swerves Superhighway Idea." *Des Moines Register*, September 24, 2006.

Porter, Henry. "When Will Islam Damn the Chlorine Bombers?" *The Observer* (London), April 22, 2007.

Porter, Michael E. *The Competitive Advantage of Nations* (New York, NY: Free Press, 1990).

Prabhu, Joseph. "Globalization and the Emerging World Order." *ReVision* 22 (2), 1999.

Prahalad, C.K. *The Fortune at the Bottom of the Pyramid: Eradicating Poverty through Profits* (Upper Saddle River, NJ: Wharton School Publishing, 2005).

Prather, Gordon. "Enabling Bush's Wars of Aggression," April 28, 2007 (www.antiwar.com/prather/?articleid=10890).

Preeg, Ernest H. *From Here to Free Trade* (Chicago, IL: The University of Chicago Press, 1998).

Preston, Lee E. and Duane Windsor. *The Rules of the Game in the Global Economy: Policy Regimes for International Business* (Dordrecht, The Netherlands: Kluwer Academic Publishers, 2nd Ed., 1997).

PricewaterhouseCoopers. *Fifth Annual Global CEO Survey, 2002* (www.pwc.com/gx/eng/eng/pubs/ceosurvey/2007/5th_ceo_survey.pdf).

PricewaterhouseCoopers. *Tenth Annual Global CEO Survey, 2007* (www.pwc.com/extweb/home.nsf/docid/2AE969AC42DD721A85257 25E007D7CF).

PricewaterhouseCoopers. *The Last Ten Years: A Review, 2007* (www.pwc.com/extweb/insights.nsf/docid/9FB653B2B4C3A5778525726 D00645353).

PricewaterhouseCoopers. *Trickier Than it Looks* (http://www.pwc.com/extweb/ service.nsf/docid/E2BD269E623824C).

Prospects for Iraq's Stability: A Challenging Road Ahead. US National Intelligence Council (Washington, DC: US Government Printing Office, January 2007).

Rabinowitz, Gavin (Associated Press). "Mangoes from India, motorcycles from US." *Houston Chronicle* 106 (183), April 14, 2007.

Raghavan, Sudarsan. "War in Iraq Propelling a Massive Migration: Wave Creates Tension Across the Middle East." *Washington Post*, February 4, 2007.

Rapley, John. "Convergence: Myths and Realities." *Progress in Development Studies*, vol. 1, no. 4 (October 2001).

Rapley, John. "Jamaica: Negotiating Law and Order with the Dons." *NACLA Report on the Americas*, vol. 37, no. 2 (September–October 2003).

Rapley, John. "The New Middle Ages." *Foreign Affairs* vol. 85, no. 3 (May–June 2006).

Rapley, John. *Globalization and Inequality* (Boulder, CO: Lynne Rienner, 2004).

Rapley, John. *Understanding Development*, 3rd Ed. (Boulder, CO: Lynne Rienner, 2007).

Rashid, Ahmed. "Pakistan: Trouble Ahead, Trouble Behind." *Current History* vol. 95, no. 600 (April 1996).

Ratnam, Gopal. "US Creates Nuclear Forensics Center." *Defense News* vol. 21, no. 41 (October 23, 2006).

Ravallion, Martin. "The Debate on Globalization, Poverty and Inequality: Why Measurement Matters." World Bank Development Research Group Working Paper 3038, 2003.

Reder, Alan. *75 Best Business Practices for Socially Responsible Companies* (New York, NY: G.P. Putnam's Sons, 1995).

Ricardo, David. *The Principles of Political Economy and Taxation*, 3rd Ed. (London: John Murray, 1821).

Robertson, Roland. *Globalization: Social Theory and Global Culture* (London: Sage Press, 1992).

Rodriguez, Francisco and Dani Rodrik. "Trade policy and economic growth: A skeptic's guide to the cross-national evidence." *NBER Macroeconomics Annual* 15, 2000.

Rogers, Rosmarie (ed.) *Guests Come to Stay: The effects of European Labor Migration on Sending and Receiving Countries* (Boulder, CO: Westview Press, 1985).

Rollings-Magnusson, Sandra and Robert C. Magnusson. "The Kyoto Protocol: Implications of a flawed but important environmental policy." *Canadian Public Policy / Analyse de Politiques* vol. 26, no. 3 (September 2000).

Rose, Andrew. "Do We Really Know that the WTO Increases Trade?" *American Economic Review* vol. 94, no. 1 (March 2004).

Rotberg, Robert I. (ed.) *State Failure and State Weakness in a Time of Terror* (Washington, DC: Brookings Institution, 2003).

Rubin, Paul H. "Folk Economics." *Southern Economic Journal* vol. 70, no. 1 (July 2003).

Rudra, Nita. "Are Workers in the Developing World Winners or Losers in the Current Era of Globalization?" *Studies in Comparative International Development* vol. 40, no. 3 (September 2005).

Rudra, Nita. "Globalization and the Decline of the Welfare State in Less-Developed Countries." *International Organization* vol. 56, no. 2 (Spring 2002).

Russell, James A. "WMD Proliferation, Globalization, and International Security: Whither the Nexus and National Security?" *Strategic Insights* vol. 5, issue 6 (July 2006).

Russell, James A. and Christopher Clary. "Globalization and WMD Proliferation Networks: Challenges to US Security." Conference Report, Naval Postgraduate School, Monterey, California, June 29–July 1, 2005.

Sacks, Jonathan. *The Dignity of Difference: How to Avoid the Clash of Civilizations* (London: Continuum Publishing Group, 2002).

SAM Indexes Gmbh. *Dow Jones Sustainability Indexes*, September 30, 2006 (www.sustainability-index.com/06_htmle/indexes/overview/html).

Samuelson, Paul A. (ed.) *International Economic Relations: Proceedings of the Third Congress of the International Economic Association* (London: Macmillan, 1969).

Samuelson, Paul A. "Where Ricardo and Mill rebut and confirm arguments of mainstream economists supporting globalization." *The Journal of Economic Perspectives* vol. 18, no. 3 (Summer 2004).

Sassen, Saskia. "Cities and Communities in the Global Economy." *American Behavioral Scientist*, vol. 39, no. 5 (March 1996).

Sayigh, Rosemary. Too Many Enemies: The Palestinian Experience in Lebanon (London: Zed Books, 1994).

Schaeffer, Robert K. Power to the People: Democratization around the World (Boulder, CO: Westview Press, 1997).

Schaeffer, Robert K. Understanding Globalization: The Social Consequences of Political, Economic and Environmental Change, 3rd ed. (Lanham, MD: Rowman and Littlefield, 2005).

Schaeffer, Robert K. *Warpaths: The Politics of Partition* (New York, NY: Hill and Wang, 1990).

Schelling, Thomas C. "What makes greenhouse sense?" *Foreign Affairs* vol. 81, no. 3 (May–June 2002).

Schmidt, C. "The ISO Global Social Responsibility Standard, 2005–2008." *ECOLOGIA* (www.ecologia.org/isosr).

Schneider, Barry R. (ed.) *Middle East Security Issues: In the shadow of Weapons of Mass Destruction Proliferation*. USAF Counter-Proliferation Center (AU Press, December 1999).

Scholte, Jan Aart. *Globalization: A Critical Introduction* (New York, NY: Palgrave, 2005).

Schultz, George. "A World Free of Nuclear Weapons." *Wall Street Journal*, January 4, 2007.

Schumpeter, Joseph A. *Capitalism, Socialism and Democracy* (New York, NY: Harper, 1942, 1947, 1950, 1975).

Schumpeter, Joseph A. *The Theory of Economic Development* (Cambridge, MA: Harvard University Press, 1934).

Selvin, Molly. "Men in their 30s making less than dads did: Generation gap raises doubts about American dream." *Houston Chronicle* 106 (225), May 26, 2007.

Sen, Amartya. "Globalization: Past and Present." Lecture 1, Ishizaka Lectures, 2002 (http://www.ksg.harvard.edu/gei/Text/Sen-Pubs/Sen_Globalization_past_present.pdf).

Servan-Schreiber, J.J. *The American Challenge* (New York, NY: Avon Books, 1967).

Sharaf, Laila. "Globalization and Governance in the Arab World." *Al Nashra* no. 36 (Amman: Royal Institute for Inter-Faith Studies, January 2006).

Siklos, Richard. "Discovery to Start Channel Focusing on Green Movement." *New York Times*, April 5, 2007.

Simon, Julian (ed.) *The State of Humanity* (Oxford: Blackwell, 1995).

Sloan, Stephen. *The Anatomy of Non-Territorial Terrorism: An Analytical Essay.* Clandestine Tactics and Technology Series, Bureau of Operations and Research, Gaithersburg, 1978.

Slocum, J. "International Migration Trends." Presentation at the Chicago Matters Event, Chicago, November 29, 2006.

Smith, Adam. *An Inquiry into the Nature and Causes of the Wealth of Nations* (London: Printed for W. Strahan and T. Cadell, 1766).

Smith, Geri. "Factories Go South. So Does Pay." Business Week, April 9, 2007.

Smyth, Henry DeWolf. "Atomic Energy for Military Purposes." Official Report on the Development of the Atomic Bomb under the Auspices of the United States Government, 1940–1945, August 12, 1945.

Sonnenfeld, Jeff. "The Real Scandal at BP." *Business Week*, May 14, 2007.

Steger, Manfred B. *Globalization: A very Short Introduction* (Oxford: Oxford University Press, 2003).

Stewart, Frances. *Horizontal Inequalities: A Neglected Dimension of Development*. WIDER Annual Lecture No. 5 (Helsinki: United Nations World Institute for Development Economics Research, 2001).

Stromberg, Sarah. "Decorah Joins Fight against Global Warning." *Cedar Falls-Waterloo Courier*, April 6, 2007.

Sutcliffe, Bob. "World inequality and globalization." *Oxford Review of Economic Policy* vol. 20, no. 1 (Spring 2004).

Tagliabue, John. "The Gauls at Home in Erin: Opportunity Knocks in Ireland, and the French Answer." *New York Times*, June 2, 2006.

The National Security Strategy of the United States of America. The White House, September 2002.

Therborn, Göran. "Globalizations: Dimensions, Historical Waves, Regional Effects, Normative Governance." *International Sociology* vol. 15, no. 2 (June 2000).

Tomlinson, John. *Globalization and Culture* (Chicago, IL: University of Chicago Press, 1999).

Torrens, Robert. *Essay on the External Corn Trade* (London: J. Hatchard, 1815).

Tulliu, Steve and Thomas Schmalberger. "Coming to terms with security: A lexicon for Arms Control, Disarmament and Confidence-Building." United Nations Institute for Disarmament Research (UNIDIR), UNIDIR/2003/33.

United Nations (UN). *Charter of the United Nations*, 1945.

United Nations (UN). "International Migration 2006" (http://www.un.org/ esa/population/publications/2006Migration_Chart/2006IttMig_chart.htm).

United Nations (UN). "International Migration 2002" (United Nations: St/ESA/Ser.A/219, 2003).

United Nations (UN). "What is the Global Compact?" (www.unglobal compact.org/AboutTheGC/ html).

United Nations (UN). *World Urbanization Prospects: The 2003 Revision* (New York, NY: Department of Economic and Social Affairs, Population Division, 2004).

Vakulabharanam, Vamsi. "Growth and Distress in a South Indian Peasant Economy during the Era of Economic Liberalization." *Journal of Development Studies* vol. 41, no. 6 (June 2005).

Van Der Bly, Martha. "Globalization: A Triumph of Ambiguity." *Current Sociology* vol. 53, no. 6 (November 2005).

Wan, G. "WIDER Seminar on International Migration and Development: Patterns, Problems and Policies." Address at UN Headquarters, New York, September 12, 2006.

Wardell, Jane (Associated Press). "Loss of sauce production puts Britons in a big snit." *Houston Chronicle* 106 (156), March 18, 2007.

Welch, David. "Why Hybrids Are Such A Hard Sell." *Business Week*, March 19, 2007.

Welch, David. "Why Toyota is Afraid of Being Number One." *Business Week*, March 5, 2007.

Wickham, Chris. "The Other Transition: From the Ancient World to Feudalism." *Past & Present* no. 103 (May 1984).

Wickham, Chris. *Framing the Early Middle Ages* (Oxford: Oxford University Press, 2005).

Wikipedia. "Globalization" (http://en.wikipedia.org/wiki/Globalization).

Will, George F. "Importing underclass that will bankrupt the country: George F. Will says proposed immigration reforms ensure the growth of a permanent poverty class and guarantee huge entitlement costs." *Houston Chronicle* 106 (223), May 24, 2007.

Windsor, Duane and Kathleen A. Getz. "Regional market integration and the development of global norms for enterprise conduct: The case of international bribery." *Business & Society* vol. 38, no. 4 (December 1999).

Windsor, Duane. "Toward A Global Theory of Cross-Border and Multilevel Corporate Political Theory." *Business & Society* vol. 46, no. 2 (June 2007).

Winters, L. Alan, Neil McCulloch and Andrew McKay. "Trade liberalization and poverty: The evidence so far." *Journal of Economic Literature* vol. 42, no. 1 (March 2004).

Wokutch, Richard. "Corporate Social Responsibility Japanese Style." *Academy of Management Executive* vol. 4, no. 2 (1990).

Wolf, Martin. *Why Globalization Works* (New Haven, CT: Yale University Press, 2004).

Wood, Donna J. "Corporate Social Performance Revisited." *Academy of Management Review* vol. 16, no. 4 (October 1991).

World Council of Churches (WCC). *Together on the Way.* 50th Anniversary Meeting report, 1998 (www.wcc-coe.org/wcc/assembly/or-01.html).

Yom, Sean L. "Islam and Globalization: Secularism, Religion, and Radicalism." *International Politics and Society* vol. 4 (2002).

Yusuf, Moeed. "The Indo-US Nuclear Deal: An Impact Analysis." 56th Pugwash Conference, Cairo, November 11–15, 2006.

Zagar, Mitja, Boris Jesih and Romana Bester (eds). *The Constitutional and Political Regulation of Ethnic Relations and Conflicts* (Ljubljana: Institute for Ethnic Studies, 1999).

Zarembo, Alan and Thomas H. Maugh. "Warming report paints a grim picture: Scientists say the poor likely will be the hardest hit, as water and food will become scarce." *Houston Chronicle* 106 (176), April 7, 2007.

Zuckerman, Mortimer B. "Uneasy in the middle." *U.S. News & World Report* 142 (21), June 11, 2007.